Educational Assessment

Also Available from Bloomsbury

Knowledge, Policy and Practice in Teacher Education,
edited by Maria Teresa Tatto and Ian Menter
Policy, Belief and Practice in the Secondary English Classroom,
Bethan Marshall, Simon Gibbons, Louise Hayward and Ernest Spencer
The Promise and Practice of University Teacher Education,
Alexandra C. Gunn, Mary F. Hill, David A.G. Berg and Mavis Haigh
Developing Culturally and Historically Sensitive Teacher Education, edited by
Yolanda Gayol Ramírez, Patricia Rosas Chávez and Peter Smagorinsky
International Perspectives on Knowledge and Curriculum, edited by
Brian Hudson, Niklas Gericke, Christina Olin-Scheller and Martin Stolare
Navigating Teacher Education in Complex and Uncertain Times,
Carmen I. Mercado
Assessment for Social Justice, Jan McArthur

Educational Assessment

The Influence of Paul Black on Research, Pedagogy and Practice

Edited by
Christine Harrison, Constant Leung
and David Pepper

BLOOMSBURY ACADEMIC
LONDON • NEW YORK • OXFORD • NEW DELHI • SYDNEY

BLOOMSBURY ACADEMIC
Bloomsbury Publishing Plc, 50 Bedford Square, London, WC1B 3DP, UK
Bloomsbury Publishing Inc, 1385 Broadway, New York, NY 10018, USA
Bloomsbury Publishing Ireland, 29 Earlsfort Terrace, Dublin 2, D02 AY28, Ireland

BLOOMSBURY, BLOOMSBURY ACADEMIC and the Diana logo are
trademarks of Bloomsbury Publishing Plc

First published in Great Britain 2024
Paperback edition published 2025

Copyright © Christine Harrison, Constant Leung and David Pepper
and contributors, 2024

Christine Harrison, Constant Leung and David Pepper have
asserted their right under the Copyright, Designs and Patents Act, 1988,
to be identified as Editor of this work.

Cover designer: Grace Ridge
Cover image © ggebl / Adobe Stock

All rights reserved. No part of this publication may be: i) reproduced or transmitted
in any form, electronic or mechanical, including photocopying, recording or by
means of any information storage or retrieval system without prior permission
in writing from the publishers; or ii) used or reproduced in any way for the training,
development or operation of artificial intelligence (AI) technologies, including
generative AI technologies. The rights holders expressly reserve this publication
from the text and data mining exception as per Article 4(3) of the
Digital Single Market Directive (EU) 2019/790.

Bloomsbury Publishing Plc does not have any control over, or responsibility for,
any third-party websites referred to or in this book. All internet addresses given
in this book were correct at the time of going to press. The author and publisher
regret any inconvenience caused if addresses have changed or sites have ceased
to exist, but can accept no responsibility for any such changes.

A catalogue record for this book is available from the British Library.

A catalog record for this book is available from the Library of Congress.

ISBN: HB: 978-1-3502-8849-2
PB: 978-1-3502-8853-9
ePDF: 978-1-3502-8850-8
eBook: 978-1-3502-8851-5

Typeset by Integra Software Services Pvt. Ltd.

For product safety related questions contact productsafety@bloomsbury.com.

To find out more about our authors and books visit www.bloomsbury.com
and sign up for our newsletters.

Contents

List of Figures   vii
List of Tables   viii
List of Contributors   ix

Introduction   *Chris Harrison*   1

1. Paul Black – A Reflection on the Journey to Educational Research (1930–1976)   *Simon Black*   11
2. An Appreciation of the Contribution of Paul Black to National Policy on Curriculum and Assessment   *Margaret Brown*   19
3. Putting Learners at the Heart of the Assessment System   *Dylan Wiliam*   29
4. Inspiring Change in Classroom Assessment   *Gordon Stobart, Jo-Anne Baird and Louise Hayward*   45
5. Unifying the Purposes of Teacher Assessment   *Wynne Harlen*   63
6. The Revolutionary International Transformation of Educational Assessment   *Rick Stiggins*   79
7. The Impact of Two Key Themes from Paul Black's Work on U.S. K-12 Policy and Practice   *Margaret Heritage and Caroline Wylie*   93
8. The Role of Teachers in Making and Moderating Assessment Judgements: Opening the Black Box to Challenge Paradigms in Australia   *Claire Wyatt-Smith and Lenore Adie*   109
9. Student Involvement in Assessment: Queensland Teacher Repertoires of Practice   *Valentina Klenowski and Jill Willis*   127
10. Assessment for Equity: The Role of Formative Assessment   *Dennis Alonzo, Chris Davison and Pasi Salhberg*   143
11. Changing the Culture of Classrooms, Changing the Responsibility of Students   *Jo Boaler*   163
12. Using Research to Inform Practice and Teaching to Shape Research   *Paul Spenceley and Chris Harrison*   181
13. Mapping the Roads of Learning: Linking Learning Progressions with Assessments   *Mark Wilson*   195

14 Certificating Learning on the Basis of Teacher Assessment
   Paul E. Newton 221
15 Braiding Research, Practice, Policy and Dissemination
   Bronwen Cowie 241
16 Research Design Principles for Dynamic Teacher-Researcher
   Collaboration: Two Stars and a Wish *Natasha Serret and
   Catarina F. Correia* 259

Chronological List of Paul Black's Key Publications 275
Index 276

Figures

1.1	Paul's academic publications (1952–77) by discipline	14
5.1	Formative assessment as a cycle of events	67
10.1	Selection process for articles	150
11.1	Rubrics used at St Alphonso School, Toronto	170
12.1	School biology 'A' level result improvement from 2010 to 2015	191
13.1	The traditional CPA triangle (left panel) and the 'vicious' triangle	197
13.2	The initial Structure of Matter roadmap	199
13.3	An example of a Changes of State task with two questions	200
13.4	The scoring guide for the open-ended Changes of State question in Figure 13.3	201
13.5	Twin Wright maps for the melting and evaporation tasks in Changes of State	202
13.6	Subsequent roadmap for the Structure of Matter	204
13.7	What we 'expected' to get (upper panel) and what we got (lower panel)	205
13.8	The revised set of constructs for Particulate Explanations of Chemical Changes	206
13.9	The Wright map for the three new constructs in Particulate Explanations of Chemical Changes	207
13.10	Latest roadmap for Structure of Matter	208

Tables

10.1	Summary of research studies linking FA and equity	152
11.1	Jordan Benedict's self-assessment/reflection/error analysis protocol	169
11.2	Teachers sharing their approaches to AfL	172
13.1	The generic construct map for Changes of State	198
13.2	The initial construct map for Particulate Explanations of Chemical Changes	203

Contributors

Lenore Adie is Associate Professor of Teacher Education and Assessment, and Senior Research Fellow at the Institute for Learning Sciences and Teacher Education, Australian Catholic University, Australia. Her research focuses on assessment and moderation processes as these contribute to quality assurance and improvement purposes for teaching and learning. Recent publications include an authored book *Professionalizing Teacher Education: Performance Assessment, Standards, Moderation, and Evidence* (2022) with Claire Wyatt-Smith, Michele Haynes and Chantelle Day. She currently leads an Australian Research Council project investigating the use of scaled annotated exemplars of achievement standards in online moderation to improve teacher assessment capability.

Dennis Alonzo is a lecturer in assessment, evaluation, and teacher education and development at the School of Education, University of New South Wales Sydney, Australia. He works with educational systems and schools nationally and internationally to lead their assessment reforms focused on articulating policies, developing assessment resources, implementing professional development and changing teachers' beliefs and practices. He also supports individual schools in designing and evaluating educational programmes to improve student outcomes.

Jo-Anne Baird is Professor of Educational Assessment at the University of Oxford, UK. Jo-Anne was specialist adviser to the UK parliament's Education Select Committee, is a member of Ofqual's (the English examination board regulator) Standards Advisory Group, the Assessment and Qualifications Alliance's Research Committee, the Scottish Qualifications Authority's Qualifications Committee and the Qualifications Wales' Academic Advisory Group. She is a member of the editorial board of the *Oxford Review of Education* and former lead editor of the journal *Assessment in Education: Principles, Policy & Practice*. Her research engages with system-level assessment issues, including policy reform, standard-setting and assessment structures.

Simon Black is a visiting academic at the University of Manchester, UK. Previously he worked as a crystallization scientist in industry. Published work ranges from scale inhibitors to drug development, including the book chapter *Crystallization in the Pharmaceutical Industry* (2019). He still enjoys learning about crystal structures.

Jo Boaler is the Nomellini-Olivier Professor of Mathematics Education at the Stanford Graduate School of Education. Jo completed her PhD at King's College London under the supervision of Paul Black. She is now known for promoting reform mathematics and working with teachers to establish equitable mathematics classrooms

Margaret Brown is Emeritus Professor of Mathematics Education, and a former head of the School of Education, at King's College London, UK. She has directed many research and development projects on mathematics learning, teaching and assessment in all phases, and has been a member of government advisory groups on the mathematics curriculum.

Catarina F. Correia is Lecturer in Educational Assessment in the Department of Curriculum, Pedagogy and Assessment at the Institute of Education, University College London's Faculty of Education and Society, UK. Her research interests focus on assessment literacies and participation in assessment, classroom-based assessment, teacher education and science education. She has published in the areas of formative assessment and teacher education.

Bronwen Cowie is Professor at the University of Waikato, New Zealand. Her research interests include assessment for learning, science education, culturally responsive pedagogy and assessment, and initial teacher education. Her research is characterized by collaboration with teachers, with this including co-authorship.

Chris Davison, a specialist in language education and school-based assessment, is Emeritus Professor of Language and Literacy Education in the School of Education, University of New South Wales (UNSW), Australia, and the former Head of School 2008–2019. She has worked in teacher education for over 40 years, including at the University of Hong Kong, Hong Kong (1999–2008) where she was Associate Dean (Research), the University of Melbourne, Australia (1988–1999) and La Trobe University, Australia (1985–89). Before that, Chris worked as an English and ESL teacher and consultant in Australia and overseas.

Wynne Harlen is Visiting Professor at the Graduate School of Education of the University of Bristol, UK. Before retirement she has been Professor of Education at the University of Liverpool, UK, and Director of the Scottish Council for Research in Education. In her long career in research and development in science education she has focused on enquiry-based pedagogy and the assessment of learning and has taken part in major national and international developments in these areas. Her many publications include *Assessment of Learning* (2007), *The Teaching of Science in Primary Schools* (2018) and *The Case for Inquiry-based Science Education* (2022).

Christine Harrison worked in secondary schools for 13 years before joining King's College London, UK, to run the Biology Education section, where she is now Professor in Science Education. Her teaching and research have centred on assessment, science education, cognitive acceleration and the use of text and TV in classrooms. In 1998, Christine began work on the King's-Medway-Oxfordshire Formative Assessment project (KMOFAP), where she developed action research work with science and mathematics teachers to help them focus on and improve their formative practice. This led to other national and international research projects and consultancies in the area of classroom assessment.

Louise Hayward is Professor of Educational Assessment and Innovation at University of Glasgow, UK, and Honorary Professor at the University of Wales Trinity Saint David, UK. She was a member of the Assessment Reform Group and has published widely on assessment. She founded the International Educational Assessment Network in 2018, where researchers and policymakers from twelve nations collaborate to tackle assessment challenges. Louise has recently worked with OECD and UNESCO. She is an advisor to governments in Wales and Ireland. She chaired the NEU-funded Review of Qualifications and Assessment in England and currently chairs the Independent Review of Qualifications and Assessment in Scotland.

Margaret Heritage, formerly an assistant director at the National Center for Research on Evaluation, Standards, and Student Testing at the University of California, Los Angeles, USA, is currently an independent consultant in education. Her present work focuses on teachers' implementation of formative assessment and on improving outcomes for English learners in the secondary grades. Her most recent book, co-authored with Caroline Wylie, is *Formative Assessment in the Disciplines: Framing a Continuum of Professional Learning* (2020).

Valentina Klenowski is Adjunct Professor at Queensland of Technology, Australia. Her research interests focus on teacher and classroom assessment. She has published on the use of portfolios for assessment, formative assessment and the use of standards.

Constant Leung is Professor of Educational Linguistics in the School of Education, Communication and Society, King's College London, UK. His research interests include academic literacies, additional/second language teaching and language assessment. He is editor of *Research Issues of TESOL Quarterly* and serves on a number of editorial boards, including Australian Review of Applied Linguistics, Language and Education, and the Modern Language Journal. His work in developing the English as an Additional Language Assessment Framework for Schools (funded by the Bell Foundation) was given the 2018 British Council ELTons International Award for Local Innovation. He is a Fellow of the Academy of Social Sciences.

Paul Newton is the Resaewarch Chair at OfQUAL and formerly Professor of Educational Assessment at the Institute of Education in London. He has an interest across the assessment spectrum and is known for his work on validity.

David Pepper is Senior Lecturer in International Education and Educational Assessment in the School of Education, Community and Society at King's College London, UK, and Programme Director of the MA in international education. His background is in research and development supporting school curriculum and assessment policy at national and international levels. His research interests are in educational assessment, international and comparative education, and STEM education, and he was a co-editor of *Becoming a Teacher: Issues in Secondary Education* (2018).

Pasi Sahlberg is Professor of Education and Co-director of the TeachLab at the Southern Cross University in Lismore, Australia. He is former mathematics teacher and served as director general at Finland's Ministry of Education. His latest books are *Let the Children Play: How More Play Will Save Our Schools and Help Children Thrive* (William Doyle, 2019), *In Teachers We Trust: The Finnish Way to World Class Schools* (with Tim Walker, 2021), and *Finnish Lessons 3.0: What Can the World Learn from Educational Change in Finland* (2021).

Natasha Serret was a primary teacher and is now Senior Lecturer working with the primary education team at the Nottingham Institute of Education,

Nottingham Trent University, UK, where she is the joint course leader for BA (Hons) in primary education. Over the last 20 years, she has collaborated on several research projects with King's College and other research teams across Europe. These have focused on assessment in science education, outdoor learning in science and Cognitive Acceleration in Science Education (CASE).

Paul Spenceley is a retired science teacher, who was originally involved in the KMOFAP, which led to the publication of *Working inside the Black Box* (2002). He has spoken at many conferences and schools on Assessment for Learning over the past 20 years. His book, *Successful Science Teaching – Improving Achievement and Learner Engagement by Using Classroom Assessment* (2022) summarized his work.

Rick Stiggins is the founder and retired President of the Assessment Training Institute, Portland, Oregon, USA, a professional learning institute devoted to understanding the task demands of classroom assessment and developing the classroom assessment literacy of teachers and school leaders. His most recent book, *The Perfect Assessment System* (2017), balances classroom, interim and annual assessments for maximum student academic success.

Gordon Stobart is Emeritus Professor of Education, Institute of Education, University College London and an Honorary Research Fellow at Oxford University, UK. Having worked as a secondary school teacher and an educational psychologist, he spent 20 years as a senior policy researcher in examination boards and government education agencies. He was a founder member of the Assessment Reform Group which has promoted Assessment for Learning (AfL) internationally. He is a former editor of the international journal *Assessment in Education: Principles, Policy and Practice* and author of *Testing Times, the Uses and Abuses of Assessment* (Routledge).

Dylan Wiliam is Emeritus Professor of Educational Assessment at the UCL Institute of Education, UK. In a varied career, he has taught in inner-city schools, coordinated a large-scale testing programme, served a number of roles in university administration, including Dean of a School of Education, and pursued a research programme focused on supporting teachers to develop their use of assessment in support of learning.

Jill Willis is Associate Professor in the Faculty of Education at Queensland University of Technology, Australia. Her research focuses on reflexivity and agency in classroom assessment and evaluation processes. She currently leads research on accessibility in assessment and student evaluations of vertical schools.

Mark Wilson is Distinguished Professor of Education at the University of California, Berkeley, USA, and also a professor at the University of Melbourne, Australia. He teaches courses on measurement in the social sciences, multidimensional measurement and applied statistics. He is also Director of the Berkeley Evaluation and Assessment Research (BEAR) Center. His research and development interests focus on the development and application of sound approaches for measurement in education and the social sciences, the development of statistical models suitable for measurement contexts, the creation of instruments to measure new constructs and scholarship on the philosophy of measurement.

Claire Wyatt-Smith is Professor of Educational Assessment and Evaluation at the Institute for Learning Sciences and Teacher Education, Australian Catholic University, Australia. Her research investigates assessment, teachers' evaluative expertise and standards. She examines teachers' use of learning evidence in moderation online and in person, in schools and universities. A related focus is digital disruption in schooling and approaches to data visualization to improve teachers' data literacy and students' learning opportunities. Her most recent books are *Professionalizing Teacher Education: Performance Assessment, Standards, Moderation, and Evidence* (2022) and *Digital Disruption in Teaching and Testing: Assessments, Big Data, and the Transformation of Schooling* (2021).

Caroline Wylie is a principal research scientist in the K12 Teaching, Learning and Assessment Research Center at ETS, Princeton, USA. Her research interests focus on the intersection of formative assessment practices, assessment literacy and teacher professional learning. Her publications include both research publications and more practitioner-oriented writing. Her most recent book *Formative Assessment in the Disciplines Framing a Continuum of Professional Learning* (2020) was co-authored with Margaret Heritage.

Introduction

Chris Harrison

This book is presented in the spirit of a Festschrift, which literally means 'celebration writing'. It has been organized to celebrate the research contributions that Paul Black has made to the research field of educational assessment from the 1970s to the present day. This volume draws together chapters from colleagues, collaborators, students, family and friends of a distinguished scholar, both piecing together some of the direct influences he has had on the field and capturing some of the more indirect ripples that he has initiated. As such, the contributing authors provide insights about the significant part played by Paul's research field through the reflective narrative journeys, which the chapters provide, and the proactive ideas. These accounts create a unique lens for interested parties to understand from both a historical and cultural perspective how various ideas arose and evolved in the research field, helping them make sense of the history, current-day issues, and future challenges and possibilities for the research area.

Paul is a world-leading researcher in educational assessment. In 1976, Paul moved from an academic career in physics to becoming Head of Department at the Centre for Science and Mathematics Education at Chelsea College, University of London. Prior to this, Paul had taken great interest both in innovative ways of using assessment in his own undergraduate teaching and in the ways physics was assessed in schools. Working closely with other educators at Chelsea College, Paul began to explore further how assessment might work more productively in schools through the graded assessment (GA) project and the assessment and performance unit (APU) work. Chapters 1 and 2 provide some of the background context that these more innovative approaches to assessment in schools arose. These chapters were written by Paul's eldest son, Simon Black, and a close colleague of Paul, Margaret Brown. It is interesting to note that Paul expanded his physics research methodology that traditionally employed quantitative methods concerned with investigating things which could be observed and measured in some way by taking account of qualitative research that explores meanings in social actions from the experiences and beliefs of the people involved. In fact, many of his projects married methodological approaches from both paradigms indicating that Paul's approach was both epistemologically broad and pragmatic. Using methods from both research paradigms enabled Paul to develop a greater understanding of cultural artefacts and social conduct, and more importantly, of the underlying cultural values and assumptions. This was important in the approach that he took as his research often involved communicating with a range of stakeholders including teachers and learners, head teachers and local authority advisors to examination officials and government ministers. While some of these groups appreciated the respectful way in which he engaged with teachers and their social reality in exploring educational phenomena, others relied on his skills in interpreting evidence rigorously.

Any assessment process in education generally involves a great deal of investment in terms of time and commitment from those concerned in making it function. This sometimes brings with it a reluctance to make changes as well as concerns that change may devalue established practices. Issues and concerns such as these can often make it difficult for those in the research area to raise questions or suggest alternatives and to encourage debates to facilitate movement in the field. Paul is a researcher who has always been willing to take risks and ask challenging questions in a manner that encourages others to stop and think rather than immediately dismiss new ideas. He is also very aware of the impact of assessment on education systems and people; he is respectful of the stakeholders' ideas and opinions. Paul has the professional stature nationally and internationally to bring together key stakeholders to consider and contribute to new ways of thinking and working without dismissing the values of previous ways of working. This aspect is highlighted in Chapters 3 and 4. In Chapter 3, Dylan Wiliam provides some of the educational context and history of how the King's College group began their epic series of studies on classroom assessment; he explains how Paul shaped both the research aims and methodological approach. In Chapter 4, members of the Assessment Reform Group (ARG), an advisory group that emerged from the British Education Research Association (BERA), provide further commentary on how the review paper on formative assessment by Black and Wiliam in 1998 set forth the momentum for change in the ways teachers used assessment in classrooms. Gordon Stobart, Jo-Ann Baird and Louise Hayward describe this change as 'one of the most successful classroom assessment initiatives of the past two decades … because it brought about changes in teachers' classroom practice but also because it offers a model of how to put theory into practice'. While the ARG group fostered change from a policy perspective, Paul's more pragmatic approach of working directly with teachers made it more possible to tackle the inertia and slowness to change that generally accompanies assessment practices.

Assessment for learning (AfL) is any assessment for which the first priority in its design and practice is to serve the purpose of promoting pupils' learning. The Black and Wiliam (1998) review on formative assessment and the King's-Medway-Oxfordshire Formative Assessment Project (KMOFAP) provided evidence of the practical relevance of research and this enabled teachers to begin to visualize how a more formative approach to assessment might function in their own classrooms. Paul's exposition of formative assessment practices was underpinned by a social constructivist view to learning that emphasizes the role of learners constructing their understanding through collaborative group work with others. This involved regular shifts between individual to group activities in the classroom offering opportunity for knowledge to be constructed and refined through dialogue. In Chapter 5, Wynne Harlen considers how and why such practices develop and function; her account describes a model that summarizes how classroom assessment events interact and build evidence of learning for both the teacher and the pupils. Encouraging pupils to take a more active role in assessment and greater responsibility for their future learning is also highlighted in Rick Stiggins' Chapter 6, Jo Boaler's Chapter 11, and Paul Spenceley and my Chapter 12.

Educational assessment has taken an increasingly prominent role on the agenda of many countries in the last few decades. National assessments have two main purposes. They are designed to give a reliable indication of attainment and ensure the consistency of standards at assessment points to promote public confidence. Because standards in most education systems are predetermined by policy and curriculum authorities, the design of assessment systems in schools tends to adopt a 'top-down' approach to try and ensure opportunities for students to demonstrate how their learning is moving towards the goals set in the standards. Some countries, such as Australia, have taken the approach of describing standards for each year level. At the same time, this has led many countries to regularly monitor student and school performance making schools more accountable for student performance. Teachers in most countries have little experience of mapping how their classroom assessments fit with curriculum-engendered final pupil attainment goals. This can create tensions between what is aspired to at policy and whole system levels and what happens within the classroom, particularly where teachers use assessment evidence to inform their teaching and provide guidance for learners on how to improve. While a top-down assessment approach helps teachers recognize expectations for a specific cohort it does not take into account the wide diversity in performance that students within that group may exhibit or the rate at which they might progress towards the final goals. It is therefore not surprising that the changes in classroom assessment associated with implementing AfL differ across a range of countries. A selection of the approaches, outcomes and challenges identified in the United States and Australia is exemplified across Chapters 7–9. Margaret Heritage and Caroline Wylie document the difficulties of making changes within the US assessment systems, particularly the development of a healthy relationship between summative and formative assessment purposes, and the move from transmission pedagogy to a more social constructivist approach to teaching and learning. Claire Wyatt-Smith and Lenore Adie focus on how researching and rationalizing national and classroom assessment have enabled them to gain better understanding of the role of teacher judgement-making, evaluative expertise and moderation across all stages of planning, teaching and learning in the Australian context. In Chapter 9, Valentina Klenowski and Jill Willis focus on how teachers and researchers in Queensland, Australia, have been inspired by more formative approaches to explore student-teacher interactions and co-regulation in assessment. This work highlights student involvement in assessment and the role of equity and technology use in assessment as new directions for assessment research.

Chapter 10 by Dennis Alonzo, Chris Davison and Pasi Sahlberg also focuses on equity issues in classroom assessment by revisiting the volume of literature that has arisen since the Black and Wiliam (1998) seminal review. They use a scoping technique to review research evidence on how formative assessment is used to address classroom equity issues in teaching and learning internationally, and some of the challenges in doing so.

To maximize learning benefit, students need to trust teacher guidance and be willing to reveal and explore difficulties they are having, and the assessment has to occur early enough in the learning sequence to be of use in the development of ideas and tailored to the needs of individual students. Student involvement in their own learning trajectory enables learners to be more self-regulating. Jo Boaler explains in Chapter 11 how her work brings together ideas developed from Carol Dweck's mindset ideas with formative assessment to create teaching-learning scenarios that have transformed mathematics classrooms. She explains how this innovative mathematics teaching approach initiates pedagogy and assessment that values the creative ways students think and encourages a more collaborative learning environment that allows students to share ideas as well as teachers recognize and provide the support learners need. Jo initially studied with Paul at King's and taught in the UK before moving to Stanford University in the United States; her work indicates some of the change that has happened in US classrooms from the scenarios Margaret Heritage and Caroline Wylie describe in Chapter 7.

When teachers move to a more formative assessment practice, it requires more than a marginal change in classroom activities because it relies on strengthening feedback loops between learners and teachers and within learning groups (Harrison, 2017). Common to all AfL practices is the active involvement of pupils, whose role changes from passive recipients of knowledge to active partners in the learning process (Swaffield, 2011). While it has been accepted for a while that pupils can share ideas and learn from one another (Heritage, 2007) the role of the teacher is key in helping pupils weigh up ideas and consolidate understanding. The teacher's role in a dialogic classroom (Alexander, 2006) is to decide which of the many diverse student ideas and experiences are productive starting points for navigating and guiding learners towards the accepted knowledge base of a subject domain (Bang & Medin, 2010). Importantly through AfL, pupils can use feedback from their teacher and peers to evaluate thinking, learn from their mistakes and reflect on understanding. When pupils make a mistake or realize something is incorrect, they often need some resilience to rethink an idea or make another attempt at revising an activity. This can be emotionally challenging for pupils, and teachers need to be mindful and support students in being more self-regulating.

Paul Spenceley, a project teacher from the KMOFAP, documents how his teaching, thinking and confidence evolved as he experimented and worked at establishing a more formative approach to his practice in Chapter 12. It makes clear how a teacher cannot simply add new strategies to their current practice in an instant. Instead, they need to gradually make changes to their current routines and activities to allow new ways of interacting and thinking while, at the same time, supporting their students in responding to feedback. Paul Spenceley describes and explains how AfL benefited students and colleagues from a practitioner viewpoint; he also highlights the importance of collaborative endeavour in changing and building professional knowledge, practices and routines.

AfL enables students to recognize their current thinking and is often explained in terms of a 'close the gap' metaphor; teachers and peers provide feedback that help learners progress. To put this in action, teachers need to have in mind a trajectory of learning that they expect learners to move through in any domain of learning. The stages or steps involved are called learning progressions. This helps teachers decide on the appropriate next pedagogical action to move student learning forward in that domain (Heritage, 2008). Implicit in learning progressions is a sequence along which students can move incrementally from being a novice to an expert. This allows teachers to focus on specific learning goals within the domain and so helps them shape movement and pace through a topic in relation to the evidence of learning and student needs. A study by Heritage, Kim and Vendelinski (2008) recognizes that it is essential that teachers know what learning needs to come before or after a learning goal in order to support progression. Over time, learning progressions support teachers in moving from using assessment as a means of deciding what is correct or incorrect within a student's work towards framing their use of assessment evidence to map and support developing understanding and documenting how ideas have moved (Alonzo, 2018).

Mark Wilson, who leads the Berkeley Evaluation and Assessment Centre (BEAR), provides a detailed account of the work he undertook with Paul on mapping learning progressions in physical science in Chapter 13. While Mark and other US researchers had already constructed assessments that helped map progression in some science topics, Paul brought his knowledge and experience of classroom assessment activities to the project. This helped the group adapt the learning progressions they had to fit with the ways the topics were being taught in schools and enabled them to collect empirical data to adjust their models of progression, moving from a broadly linear, hierarchical representation to ones that had some overlapping steps suggesting more flexible trajectories. The group called this new visualization of progression as construct maps within which teachers had assessment items that supported teachers in collecting and using evidence to inform teaching and learning.

System-wide formal tests are by their nature limited in scope. They inevitably sample the knowledge/skill curriculum more narrowly than any teacher might, and they therefore lack that ability to provide a truly holistic view of development and achievement. The principal advantage of teacher assessment over formal testing is generally acknowledged to be the fact that teachers are with their pupils for long and continuous periods of time, constantly interacting with them inside and outside the classroom, posing questions to develop their thinking and observing them as they carry out assigned tasks and activities. In consequence, teachers are assumed to have a more comprehensive, and by default more valid, picture of their pupils as learners and achievers than any set of test results can alone provide. Harlen (2007) shares this view: *Teachers' judgements can, when moderated, provide more accurate information than external tests because they can cover a much wider range of outcomes and so provide a more complete picture of students' achievements* (Harlen 2007, 138). Paul has advocated and explored teachers' capabilities to design assessment activities, assess and moderate student performance in the King's Oxfordshire Summative Assessment Project (KOSAP).

Chapter 14, written by Paul Newton, outlines some of the reasons why teacher assessment (TA) is not considered an appropriate approach to summative assessment and why this opposition to TA has grown over the last two decades in England. He suggests that a reason why some stakeholders take such strong opposition to the inclusion of TA is related to a lack of understanding that assessment data can be used for multiple purposes. As well as unpacking reasons why recent changes in UK assessment have settled or faltered, Paul's chapter provides insights into the importance of stakeholders' 'buy-in' of validity claims especially in a high-stakes assessment environment.

While Paul was developing his thinking on classroom assessment in England, Beverley Bell and Bronwen Cowie were already working with teachers on connecting teaching and assessment, building on the Learning in Science Project (LISP) in New Zealand. Chapter 15, written by Bronwen Cowie, is a reflection on the evolution of formative assessment practices in NZ classrooms and the convergences that occurred with the work of the King's team. More importantly, she frames how paying attention to and interweaving research, practice, policy and dissemination were at the heart of making AfL accepted, effective and productive. As such, this chapter provides further evidence of the reach of Paul's influence on classroom assessment.

One of the aspects that stands Paul's work apart is the importance he gives to professional learning and the trust he has that teachers can make changes to their practice. The final chapter by Natasha Serret and Catarina Correia focuses on the collaborative action research approach that the King's team takes when exploring classroom assessment. They document and discuss Paul's contribution to the development of collaborative teacher-researcher practices. They take the AfL principle of 'starting from the position of the learner' and relate it to teachers as professional learners, who draw on assessment theory as well as their lived experiences as they translate research ideas into meaningful classroom practice.

For reasons of space and scope, it has not been possible for this volume to cover the full range of research and development in many curriculum areas that draws on Paul's pioneering work. While initially focused on school science and mathematics in the KMOFAP project, the ideas were adopted and adapted for assessment across a range of other school curricular areas and also into other phases of education, including higher education. AfL also transferred to other educational initiatives such as English as an additional language for schools, taking on the same ideas that promoting pupil learning is front and centre in the classroom-based formative assessment framework (Leung et al., 2021). This assessment framework locates the assessment of English language proficiency of linguistic minority pupils at the teaching-learning interface – therefore supporting pupil language development across different curriculum areas.

As a compilation of chapters by leading researchers in the field of educational assessment, this book provides a plethora of insights and journeys into the research field. One advantage of a volume like this is that some of the chapters allow a close-up view of specific studies while others inform on how some research trajectories emerged and grew from earlier work, thus providing a fuller picture of the historical and cultural reality. Paul has played a major role in shaping the assessment field for many decades through his own research and scholarship and through the responses to his ideas by many other scholars. He has also been a key influencer on how teachers think about and carry out assessment in the classroom, resulting in both introduction of new policies and implementation of innovative assessment in many countries. His ideas have been revolutionary in reconsidering paradigms of assessment even when the educational context makes change difficult. Perhaps, more importantly, it is Paul's realization that new ways of working need to be approached through development of and support by collaborative partnerships to ensure better understanding between and within researcher and practitioner groups. This approach to research is akin to 'Close to Practice' research recently highlighted by BERA as a growing and important area; Paul's ways of working, throughout his many projects, emphasize the cyclic and dynamic iterative processes that needed to be employed as well as recognize the importance of a strong trusting relationship between researchers and teachers (Wyse et al., 2020). This enables research to explore and influence practice as practice informs research.

References

Alexander, R. (2006). *Towards Dialogic Thinking: Rethinking Classroom Talk*. York: Dialogos.

Alonzo, A. (2018). 'An argument for formative assessment with science learning progressions'. *Applied Measurement in Education*, 31(2): 104–12.

Bang, M. & D. Medin (2010). 'Cultural processes in science education: Supporting the navigation of multiple epistemologies'. *Science Education*, 94(6): 1008–26.

Black, P. J. & D. Wiliam (1998). 'Assessment and classroom learning'. *Assessment in Education: Principles Policy and Practice*, 5(1): 7–73.

Harlen, W. (2007). *Assessment of Leaning*. London: Sage.

Harrison, C. (2017). 'Adapting pedagogy for formative assessment'. *Encyclopedia of Educational Philosophy and Theory*, 1–5: Springer.

Heritage, M. (2007). 'Formative assessment: What do teachers need to know and do?' *Phi Delta Kappan*, 89(2): 140–5.

Heritage, M. (2008). *Learning Progressions: Supporting Instruction and Formative Assessment*. Washington, DC: Council of Chief State School Officers. http://www.ccsso.org/Documents/2008/Learning_Progressions_Supporting_2008.pdf

Heritage, M., J. Kim, T. Vendlinski & J. Herman (2009). 'From evidence to action: A seamless process in formative assessment?' *Educational Measurement: Issues and Practice*, 28: 24–31.

Leung, C., M. Evans & Y. C. Liu (2021). 'English as an additional language assessment framework: Filling a void in policy and provision in school education in England'. *Language Assessment Quarterly*, 18(3): 296–315.

Swaffield, S. (2011). 'Getting to the heart of authentic 331 assessment for learning'. *Assessment in Education*, 332 18 (4): 433–49.

Wyse, D., C. Brown, O. Sandy & X. Poblete (2020). 'Education research and educational practice: The qualities of a close relationship'. *British Educational Research Journal*, 47: 1466–89.

1

Paul Black – A Reflection on the Journey to Educational Research (1930–1976)

Simon Black

My father, Paul Black, changed academic disciplines from crystal physics to educational research in his forties. This personal perspective on the first half of his life reflects on how his faith, physics and family influenced this move. The overlaps with Paul's own account Black (2003) are indicated, although these reflections are based on my own experiences and family conversations.

Paul Joseph Black was born in Colombia on 10 September 1930. His parents, Walter and Susie Black, were both from the north-west of England, both Roman Catholics of partially Irish descent and both without a university education. They had moved to Colombia to set up a clothing business and returned to Britain in 1933, at which time Paul allegedly spoke fluent Spanish. He had most of his schooling in Rhyl in North Wales. His early memories are of the drapery store his mother ran, enjoying his academic studies and walks with his older brother Stephen. His father found work in a relocated civil service department during the war, and Paul often recalled the glow in the eastern night sky from the 'Liverpool Blitz' in 1940–41.

He attended Rhyl Grammar School, where he soon stood out as an avid and confident learner. After briefly flirting with self-taught classical Greek, he specialized in mathematics, physics and geography. He showed less interest in team sports and PE generally, which was spotted by a new PE teacher. When asked what physical activities he enjoyed, he replied 'walking'. The attentive teacher had him walking around a local field, saw potential and coached and encouraged Paul, who later won a Flintshire County Schools walking race. Subsequently he took us on many long family walks; he always preferred stairs to lifts; and he has recently, at the age of 90+, embraced the technology that allows him to count and record his daily steps.

Soon after the end of the war, Paul's father and older brother emigrated permanently to South Africa. Paul was expected to follow, with his mother and younger brother Peter. Paul had other ideas and was encouraged by his school to apply to Cambridge. They responded that he was too young and should try again in one year's time. He returned to school in early September 1947 to study for Cambridge Entrance, but Manchester University offered him a place to start immediately to study physics, which he accepted.

At Manchester, some of Paul's fellow students were considerably older, having deferred their studies to fight in the war. Their more mature perspective made a deep impression on him, just 17 at the start of his course and with all of his immediate family overseas. Paul graduated with a first in 1950 and was encouraged to apply for a doctorate in crystallography. A visit to London was unsuccessful, as J. D. Bernal, a pioneer of X-ray crystallography in molecular biology, mysteriously failed to appear for the scheduled interview. However, he was accepted at the Cavendish Laboratory in Cambridge.

Here he spent six years learning and practising crystallography of iron-aluminium alloys. This was relevant to the construction of ships with steel hulls and aluminium superstructures, allowing Paul to avoid National Service. Lawrence Bragg, the founder of X-ray crystallography, was head of department and Paul's contemporaries included Francis Crick, James Watson, Max Perutz and Peter Pauling. Paul remained focused on alloys, received his doctorate in 1954 and continued his research there with a Royal Society Research Studentship until 1956.

Paul's studies presented him with an early problem – his meticulous X-ray crystal structure analysis did not agree with previous X-ray analyses of the same alloy. Paul showed that this inconsistency was due to persistent 'twinning' of the material, which earlier X-ray studies had overlooked. He also found that studies of the same alloy half a century earlier, using precise methodologies of *optical* crystallography, had observed the same 'twinning', albeit differently described (Black, 1955). Paul recounted this study frequently in later years, articulating 'the flavour of doing science' (Black 2003).

Paul also led small group tutorials for undergraduates at his college, Trinity Hall. In one of these groups, he noticed that one student was considerably more capable than the other two. Paul addressed this by arranging to give that student separate individual tutorials, tailored to his needs. The student was David Thouless, who went on to win the 2016 Nobel Prize for physics.

Paul's Catholic faith grew during his time in Cambridge: he was deeply involved in the Catholic chaplaincy at Fisher House and in the national Catholic student activities, serving as president of the Union of Catholic Students. For several years, he lived in a mixed lay Franciscan house on Trumpington Street and was intrigued to stay there again more recently in its new guise as the Hotel du Vin. He consulted the then chaplain at Cambridge, Monsignor Gilbey, about a possible vocation to the priesthood, and was wisely advised to be patient. Fate, through the auspices of the committee of the Union of Catholic Students, then introduced him to Mary Weston.

In 1957, Paul and Mary married. Mary's father Geoffrey, a shrewd banker, soon assessed his new son-in-law's scientific ability thus: 'Paul is a *very* clever man. He tells *me* that glass is a liquid.' Years later, at the celebration of Geoffrey and Elaine's golden wedding anniversary, Paul spoke movingly – under cover of pretending to be inebriated – of how he had benefited, directly and indirectly, from the role model of their marriage.

In 1956, Paul was appointed as a lecturer in crystal physics at Birmingham University. The head of department was Professor P. B. Moon and this was a time of limitless optimism in what science and technology would achieve. Paul was fond of recounting the day a staff member pinned up a newspaper cutting in the department: 'Moon Shot Soon'. When Paul acquired reading glasses years later, his daughter asked if he would become 'Professor Half Moon'.

At Birmingham, Paul's crystallographic investigations broadened to a wider range of alloys, using a wider range of techniques (anomalous dispersion, multiple wavelength methods and Mössbauer spectroscopy) to supplement standard X-ray approaches. Paul's most prestigious crystal physics publications (Black & Moon, 1960; Black, Evans & O'Connor, 1962; Black, 1965) dealt with the initially controversial proposal that nuclear resonance excitation by the Mössbauer effect gives coherent scattering with diffraction. Paul verified this claim by painstaking experimental design, construction and execution, followed by rigorous data analysis. Paul would fondly recall the fine details of this study forty years later – 'the sense of interrogating reality was clear and strong' (Black 2003). Later work on Mössbauer spectroscopy led Paul deeper into statistical methodologies to investigate which standard profile (Gaussian, Lorenzian or Voigt) was most appropriate and what this revealed about the underlying physics (Evans & Black, 1970). Here he had 'experienced the excitement of searching for a model that gave the best fit to one's data' (Black 2003).

Paul's appointment at Birmingham resulted in a heavy teaching load, as well as considerable freedom in what and how to teach (Black 2003). He was soon troubled by observing that university examinations gave unexpected outcomes on student performance. Paul also started marking 'A'-level examination papers, exposing him to a wider range of teaching outcomes than he had hitherto

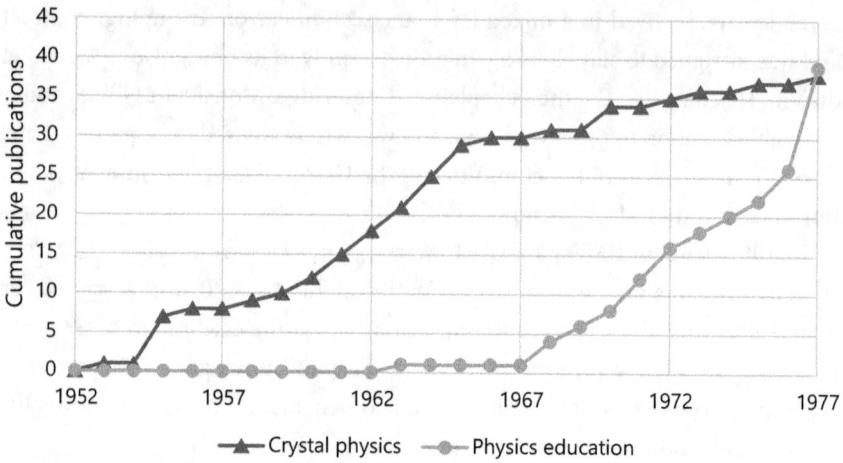

Figure 1.1 Paul's academic publications (1952–77) by discipline.

considered possible. From 1963 onwards, this led to his increasing involvement in educational activities, including the Institute of Physics group study of university examinations (1963–7) and joining the governing board of the Joint Matriculation Board (1965–76). A further step came in 1967 with Paul's part-time secondment to join the Nuffield 'A'-level physics project. Yet Paul remained active in crystal physics: Figure 1.1 expresses the gradual transition from crystal physics to physics education by total number of publications over time.

At the same time, Paul's life at home was also changing rapidly. Mary went straight from completing her degree in history at Queen Mary's College, London, into teaching – an experiment which was terminated after a year in favour of raising a family. My arrival in 1959 was quickly followed by John, Jeremy and Michael over the next six years and then Mary Jane in 1970. We all attended the local state (voluntary aided) Catholic primary school. Through the filter of parents' evenings, Paul experienced anew the positive influence of supportive teaching, this time for his own children, particularly when we found our studies challenging.

As a committed Catholic with an increasing interest in education (Black, 1960), Paul became a school governor and then chair of governors at the local Catholic grammar school. He also served on the Laity Commission, which he later chaired (Black, 1971). This national group, sponsored by the bishops of England and Wales, proposed new ways for Catholics to become more involved in the activities of the Catholic Church. For this work, Paul was appointed a Knight of Saint Gregory (KSG) in 1974 by Pope Paul VI.

Meanwhile, mealtimes at home developed into intellectual jousting competitions. We all studied more traditional physics courses in our respective schools, so occasionally we would take a tilt at Nuffield courses or the extent of Dad's baldness. Dad observed quietly, only occasionally intervening, always gently, with a pointed rebuke or comment that would calm the moment and make us think afterwards. As our mathematical and scientific studies progressed, we quickly worked out how best to obtain help. We learnt to ask each other first and only 'ask Dad' as a last resort. Dad would not simply tell us the answer. He would insist patiently and firmly that we first explained our own understanding of the problem. He would then interrogate this understanding forensically until we had sufficient insight to go away and solve the problem ourselves. As our interest in science increased, Mary joined in by doing a general science degree with the Open University. This provided an early opportunity for all of us to test our capability to communicate fundamental scientific principles – with mixed results.

There were always books, and more books at home, and bedtime stories read by Dad – he particularly relished reading out loud the part of Gollum from 'The Hobbit'. Weekend trips included visiting nearby Henley-in-Arden for ice cream, although one of these turned into a somewhat longer drive to marvel at the newly opened Severn Bridge. We also had a family outing to Worcester for lunch with a local teacher called Jon Ogborn – who was then working with Dad on Nuffield Physics (Black 2003). On Saturdays, Dad might take one or two of us with him into 'The Department' – a collection of mysterious, cavernous, quiet and cold red-brick buildings. We were led to a small, hot, noisy room housing a PDP-11 computer, which we were encouraged to programme to generate prime and perfect numbers, using yellow ticker-tape. On one occasion, we had to make way for some of Dad's colleagues to analyse data from 'The Apollo Programme'.

Dad was awarded the Lawrence Bragg Medal and Prize of the Institute of Physics in 1973. The chunky medal was passed around at home with a sense of awe. Yes this was the same Lawrence Bragg that Dad knew from Cambridge, although the award was for Dad's work in physics education, not crystal physics. The award was shared with the aforementioned Jon Ogborn, who by then had moved to Chelsea College in London. Paul and Jon were collaborating again, this time on the Higher Education Learning Project (HELP) on small group teaching in undergraduate science. We were amused that the first case study (Black, 1977) featured two students called Simon and John.

A further milestone in this transformation came with Dad's appointment in 1974 to a personal chair in physics (Science Education). We attended his inaugural lecture the following year – at the time I was considering what subjects to study for 'A' level. I was consulted about a possible family move to Leeds in the summer of 1975. This was just a prelude to the 'final discontinuous step'[1] of Dad accepting the post of Professor and Head of Department at the Centre for Science and Mathematics Education at Chelsea College in London (Black 2003).

The family relocation from Birmingham to London over the summer and autumn of 1976 was disruptive on many levels. Dad's mother moved with us – her increasingly erratic and illogical interventions were a sore trial to Dad's rational approach. Mum's regret at leaving many Birmingham friends was tempered with joy at returning to her home city and being closer to her parents. John (16) and Jeremy (14) switched secondary schools, Michael (11) transferred to a 'Middle School' and Mary Jane (6) switched primary schools. I opted to stay in Birmingham for my final school year. We all took these changes in our stride. We all passed our physics 'A' levels. We all went on to study science/engineering at Cambridge University.

Paul's academic life in crystal physics had involved close collaboration with one or two fellow researchers. Starting with the Nuffield Project, the nature of his educational research involved project leadership of collaborations with large and diverse groups of educational researchers and teachers. By 1976, his transition from crystal physicist to educational researcher was almost complete. Dad reflected later that the biggest challenge of the 1976 move was the step into leading a department. The whole of the first half of Dad's life, as described here, motivated and prepared him for this challenge.

Acknowledgements

John Black, Jeremy Black, Michael Black and Mary Jane O'Sullivan are thanked for their helpful comments on an earlier draft, as are Consilia Black, Caroline Black and Jim O'Sullivan.

References

Black, P. J. 'The structure of FeAl3: I'. *Acta Cryst* (1955): 8, 43–8 https://doi.org/10.1107/S0365110X5500011X

Black, P. (1960). 'The religious scene: Belief and practice in universities'. *The Dublin Review* 484: 105–25.

Black, P. (1965). 'Use of nuclear and electronic resonance scattering in crystallography'. *Nature*, 206: 1223–6.

Black, P. J. (1971). 'Report to the Laity: The work and experience of the Laity Commission 1967–1971' (1971). London: Living Parish Pamphlets.

Black, P. J. (1977). 'John's Pen'. In J. Ogborn (Ed.), *Small Group Teaching in Undergraduate Science*. London: Heinemann, 2–4.

Black, P. J. (2003). 'Paul's Stories'. pp. 15–21 and Timeline pp. 175–6. In J. M. Atkin & P. Black (Ed.), *Inside Science Education Reform*: A History of Curricular and Policy Change. Buckingham, England: Open University Press.

Black, P. J. & P. B. Moon (1960). 'Resonant scattering of the 14-kev iron-57 gamma-ray and its interference with Rayleigh scattering'. *Nature*, 188: 481–2.

Black, P. J., D. Evans & D. A. O'Connor (1962). 'Interference between Rayleigh and nuclear resonant scattering in crystals'. *Proc. Roy. Soc.* A., 270: 168–85.

Evans, M. J. & P. Black (1970). 'The Voigt profile of Mossbauer transmission spectra'. *J. Phys.* C 3: 2167–77.

2

An Appreciation of the Contribution of Paul Black to National Policy on Curriculum and Assessment

Margaret Brown

Introduction

We have seen over the course of two pandemic-dominated summers an inability of the national education system in England to manage a fair system of summative assessment without final national written examinations. When in 2020 a centralized algorithmic system collapsed under the impossibility of delivering fair results to individual students, it was replaced by one which could not promise equality of standards across schools, and often put teachers under pressure from schools, students and families to raise results.

No one is suggesting that we design our summative assessment system to give priority to its degree of resilience in times of pandemic, yet the unusual situation highlights the weaknesses of the national assessment arrangements currently in place in England, which scarcely differed from those used in the 1950s. In the area of government policy there seems to be no institutional memory for successful developments in the interim period which if continued would not only have avoided these situations which have seriously affected thousands of students, teachers and parents, but more importantly would also have significantly improved the quality of day-to-day educational experiences and learning across the primary and secondary school.

As someone who was also involved, I want to explain why I believe Paul's achievements, culminating in the late 1980s in designing a structure for the first comprehensive national curriculum and its assessment in England and Wales, are so significant.

Building assessment expertise

Paul's previous experience was essential in leading up to his work on the national curriculum. My memory is that Paul said he first became interested in the validity of assessment as a physics lecturer at Birmingham University in the 1960s, trying out forms of assessment which differed from the traditional timed written papers. Broader insight came from his membership of a committee of the Northern Universities Joint Matriculation Board, and his role as co-director of a cross-university study of physics teaching and assessment. The university context was helpful in that since universities set their own curriculum, standards and assessment, subject only to guidance of external examiners, there was considerable freedom and autonomy to allow experiment.

A greater challenge on a national scale was then presented when, still as a physics lecturer at Birmingham, he became joint organizer with Jon Ogborn of the Nuffield 'A'-level physics project, published during the 1970s. This had broad aims reflected in the advanced-level (age 18) examinations offered nationally by the Oxford and Cambridge Schools Examination Board.

> ... an end-of-course examination that was not only technically 'reliable' but was also 'valid', in that it tested the stated aims of the course ... Accordingly, the examination had six distinct elements including an investigation ... (which) lasted for two weeks.
>
> (Dobson, 1985:5)

This variety of assessment methods in the 1970s illustrates the degree to which curriculum and assessment in the UK have now returned to the dark ages, having earlier experienced such enlightenment.

On his appointment as Professor of Science Education and Director of the Centre for Science and Mathematics Education at Chelsea College in 1976, Paul took over from his predecessor, Professor Kevin Keohane, as co-director of a five-year research project Concepts in Secondary Mathematics and Science (CSMS). Results for both science (Shayer & Adey, 1981) and mathematics (Hart(ed.), 1981), in which I led the team for two years under the overall direction of Professor Geoffrey Matthews, provided convincing evidence of a wide attainment spread and slow development of understanding of key concepts in these subjects among secondary students, describable by identified stages of learning.

The next large project which Paul was successful in bidding for, and co-directing, was the Assessment of Performance Unit (APU) in science.

Starting in 1975, this was a government-funded attempt to regularly assess student performance by large-scale survey, for the overt purpose of monitoring changes in national performance over time. What was new here was the move into the primary as well as secondary age group, together with a more developed use of models of curriculum specification, including a variety of both content and process. As an advisory group member for the earlier maths APU project, I could appreciate how much better designed was the science work.

The last major project which prepared Paul for his major national role was as Director of the Graded Assessment in Science Project (GASP), starting in 1985. The background to this was an agreement between the well-respected Chief Education Officers of London, Manchester and Oxford that the 'O'-level/CSE system did not provide evidence of progress capable of motivating students across all attainments and year groups in the secondary school. The three authorities each went on to develop their own 11–16 school-based assessment schemes using their local universities and school examining boards but to inform each other along the way. They were informed by the criterion-referenced movement in the United States which was being introduced to the UK through vocational education in FE Colleges, but more particularly by the Records of Achievement which were starting to be planned by some Local Education Authorities to celebrate the successes of school leavers, focusing on those whose traditional academic achievement was weak.

In the case of London, the University of London Examinations and Assessment Council, running General Certificate of Education (GCE) examinations for more able students at age 16 and 18, had had considerable success in stimulating modern foreign language study by introducing a series of graded tests modelled on instrumental music examinations which could be taken at any stage in the secondary school (Harrison, 1982). These were not only motivating students who had intended to give up languages at an early stage but were also significantly increasing the numbers continuing to participate. The tests were practical and the objectives carefully specified, so that teachers and students could see the usefulness of the knowledge and what they were aiming for at each stage. The Inner London Education Authority (ILEA) asked Chelsea College to work on an equivalent scheme in science and mathematics with Paul and David Johnson, then Professor of Mathematics Education, to respectively lead. English, design technology and modern foreign languages were included using other constituent colleges of London University. Many of the development staff would be seconded London secondary teachers, working alongside academic researchers.

It was agreed that one of the higher levels in the scheme would be designed to be equivalent to a basic pass grade at age 16 in GCE. Battles were then fought with the GCE and with the London Certificate in Education (CSE) boards, serving average and below-average students, to ensure moreover, as a result of achieving specific levels in the schemes, the full set of GCE/CSE grades would be awarded by the examining boards. (As the two examinations were merged into the General Certificate of Secondary Education (GCSE) from 1988, these would become GCSE grades.) This was a major step, since by then it was being agreed between the ILEA and the developers that graded tests would evolve from pre-specified tests into a broader scheme of graded assessment, with much of the assessment being done formatively by teachers in classrooms against agreed criteria and with some standardized investigational tasks. A precedent had been set at lower levels by part- or wholly-teacher-assessed CSE examinations and at higher levels by a single widely adopted GCE 'O'-level English examination which was assessed by teachers, with board-set questions and strict moderation procedures.

In the GASP the levels for 11–16-year-olds were defined by three components: practical skills, inquiry processes and content knowledge, and were assessed respectively by short practical tests, sustained inquiries and written tests. There were over a hundred schools involved in trialling the scheme, in the Inner London area and more widely, and it was being very well received, as were those in other subjects, including the Graded Assessment in Mathematics (GAIM) project, of which I was the executive director. To differing extents, both Chelsea projects incorporated the results of the CSMS research into level definitions. All subjects used experts, mainly advisory teachers, as leaders of teacher meetings to moderate GCSE grades between teachers and schools. Although later adapted to the national curriculum, these graded assessment schemes were abandoned in the early 1990s, when teacher assessment was limited by John Major's government to constitute at most 20 per cent of GCSE assessment.

So, to summarize, this remarkable sequence of projects provided Paul with experience of formative and summative assessment by teachers, a variety of forms of assessment, working with assessment criteria arranged according to evidence-based learning progressions in content and process, national-scale surveys and national examinations, and working in partnership with teachers, Local Education Authorities, awarding bodies and government. This was a perfect apprenticeship for Paul's most important role of Chair of the National Curriculum Task Group on Assessment and Testing (TGAT).

The TGAT work

Since the 1960s, the momentum for a national curriculum and national tests had been steadily building and had been given a strong push in a speech given at Ruskin College Oxford in 1976 by the then Labour Prime Minister James Callaghan, reflecting dissatisfaction by employers at the educational standards of their recruits. It was later fuelled by both disappointing international comparisons (of variable quality) with standards of our industrial competitors and a (mainly) mistaken fear among members of the post-1979 Thatcher government that schools were being taken over by radical left-wing teachers more interested in liberation politics than in English grammar and times table. This led to an outpouring of official reports laying groundwork for national curriculum objectives, some general (e.g. DES/HMI, 1985) and some subject based.

National criteria for the new GCSE, of varying quality, achieved some degree of commonality in the final years of compulsory schooling, but the Tory Secretary of State for Education and Science (1981–1986), Sir Keith Joseph, was also keen to have more uniformity at primary level, especially following the removal of 11+ examinations in most areas, consequent on the introduction of comprehensive schools. The method first proposed was a set of attainment targets (objectives) in English, mathematics and science and related tests for pupils at the end of the primary stage (DES/WO, 1985).

But the next Secretary of State for Education, Kenneth Baker, was considerably more ambitious and lost no time in getting things moving. In spring 1987, based on a system being administered in the London Borough of Croydon to measure children's attainment at four different stages of the primary and secondary school, introduced to compare school performance, Baker proposed, in each subject, attainment targets (objectives) and related national tests for ages 7, 9 (later abandoned), 11, 14 and 16 (later combined with GCSE), together with programmes of study which specified 'what was to be taught' in each between the ages of 5 and 16. Three working groups, developing the detailed structures and content, were to be appointed at the earliest possible moment, to work on generic assessment structures and methods, and the content respectively for mathematics and science. This was announced even before the rushed post-election publication in July of a consultation document (DES/WO, 1987), which led to a huge and heavily critical response from teachers and educationists, largely ignored by government (Haviland, 1988). The timetable was tight: the new national curriculum and assessment was to be combined with school league tables to inform parental choice in a competitive educational market, and with new school organization and funding systems, into an Education Reform Bill to be published that November (1987). Paul was interviewed and chosen from a secret shortlist to chair the Task Group on Assessment and Testing (TGAT) and then had just over four months from the first meeting of the newly formed and diverse committee, reflecting a broad span of both degrees of assessment expertise and of political opinion, to deliver a report to ministers by 31 December. This was a truly Herculean task.

The Mathematics and Science Groups would report progress in November and then, making use of the agreed TGAT structures, would deliver a full assessment structure and teaching programme by the following May.

The reason this was thought to be a reasonable timetable may have been because ministers and civil servants generally believed that writing learning objectives was a relatively straightforward process, involving outcomes like 'knows the names of parts of plants' or 'can wire an electric circuit', with straightforward tests showing whether or not these are achieved. It was not easy to explain that with computers and calculators, including the forerunner of Wikipedia, now readily available, more complex notions, like designing experiments and understanding about the science and politics of nuclear power, were both more important and more difficult to assess than passive recall and routine skills.

It was clear that Paul would have a difficult task explaining to the Secretary of State that finding a structure to describe developing learning, and designing related assessment structures and methods, was not so simple even in one discipline; trying to get agreement across the ten subjects to be included in this new national curriculum appeared nigh impossible on this timescale.

The first model presented by Kenneth Baker was a set of objectives ('attainment targets') and matching tests for each subject at ages 7, 11, 14 and 16 and a detailed teaching programme based on these. But it was pointed out that given the huge range of attainment in maths and science, a single set of objectives aimed at average students would be unduly limiting for high achievers and lead to repeated failure at each testing point for lower achieving students.

Hence the brief for the three committees was amended to require criteria describing low, average and high levels of attainment in each attainment target at each testing age. This was accepted by the National Curriculum Science Working Group, but the parallel Mathematics Working Group rejected the model arguing that CSMS, GAIM and other data demonstrated for example that low-attaining 14-year-olds were similar in mathematical attainment to average 11-year-olds and high-attaining 7-year-olds. Thus, a single set of progressive levels spanning all age groups through which each child could travel would be a better model and would avoid a rigid low/average/high labelling of children. Having taken evidence from graded test and graded assessment developments across the country, Paul guided TGAT to opt for the progression structure, with ten levels in each attainment target, each representing about two years of progress. This meant an average child would be at level 2 at age 7, level 4 at age 11, and between levels 6 and 7 at age 16. At each level in each target there would be multiple 'statements of attainment' representing assessable criteria.

Both science and maths groups were by mid-Autumn wildly proliferating the numbers of attainment targets beyond what was realistic to report (originally twenty-five in maths), so the TGAT group had to invent a requirement to group attainment targets together into reportable 'profile components' (e.g. in maths these were initially 'Number, Algebra and Measures', 'Shape and Space and Handling Data' and 'Practical Applications'). Thus, Paul would have to convince the Secretary of State that a very different assessment structure from that he had proposed would be optimal.

As noted earlier, as a result of experience in previous projects, Paul was convinced that national short-answer standard written tests, of the sort expected by ministers, taken on their own would be insufficiently valid attainment measures: they could not cover the extent or the variety of types of knowledge that were important in the curriculum. High-stakes testing on a narrow base was known to drive the curriculum towards continual practice of a narrow set of routine skills. But clearly ministers were not going to be willing to sacrifice completely this type of testing, which was also widely perceived to be 'fair', providing a common standard for school comparisons. Teacher assessment using either standard tasks or standard criteria, as in GAIM and GASP, rendered more reliable and valid by being communicated clearly and by exemplars, and supported by professional development and teacher moderation groups, would not only lead to greater validity in assessing summative pupil performance but also drive teacher development, lead to a broader curriculum, and raise standards by supporting continual formative assessment. Thus, Paul had the challenge of convincing first TGAT and then ministers that it was possible to put well-designed teacher assessment at the heart of national assessment but also to use standard attainment tasks (SATs) alongside, not necessarily in the form of short written tests but more often in the form of extended tasks, to help standardize the teacher-assessed results across schools. These tasks only needed to lightly sample the statements of attainment.

During the TGAT process, it was clearly important to not only convince the Secretary of State and other ministers that changing their brief would lead to better results but also to persuade an increasingly angry and cynical population of teachers (represented by unions and professional associations), educationists and researchers, that the proposed system would be workable, and if not positively beneficial, at least the best that could be agreed under the political circumstances.

Of course, in the end, due to failures to understand the TGAT recommendations (National Curriculum: TGAT, 1987) and right-wing political ideology in roughly equal measure, the implementation fell short of the design (Daugherty, 1995). In particular, pilot extended tasks at age 14 which had positive evaluations were rejected by the next Secretary of State as 'elaborate nonsense' in his haste to return to short written tests. Nevertheless, a levels-based curriculum and assessment structure, unique in the world but later copied by other countries, survived for more than 20 years, and only after a Tory-led coalition replaced the Labour government in 2010 was the traditional 1950s model re-instated. I still believe that the TGAT model is optimal and provides a system which could work a great deal better than what we currently have.

Afterwards I was lucky enough to work closely with Paul in co-directing a project to demonstrate the validity of the age-independent progressive-level structure in aspects of science and mathematics. After being Deputy Chair of the new National Curriculum Council (but interestingly not invited to be a member of the parallel assessment committee), he then went on to achieve international success in describing and implementing assessment for learning, as described in the rest of the book.

But in terms of TGAT, I am not sure which is the greater achievement:

- leading a disparate group within a matter of a few months to devise complex, coherent and internationally trend-setting proposals for a national assessment system across the full 5–16 age group which are valid, reliable and practicable, based on experience and research, and capable of improving education for all stakeholders,

  or

- persuading everyone from right-wing ministers to left-wing union leaders that this is something they can and should for good reasons sign up to.

Several well-respected educationists tasked with designing educational initiatives have failed on either or both of these hurdles; it demanded someone with the exceptional qualities of Paul Black to be able to succeed.

And finally...

Paul was and is in the nicest possible way just very intelligent – extraordinarily rational and clear-sighted. Yet he is also remarkable for his humility and lack of ego, and his sensitivity to others' positions, and being ready to listen to and to learn from a variety of lesser mortals. During the TGAT development especially, he worked hard to anticipate and to understand other people's points of view and arrive at solutions to complex problems that could be rendered mutually acceptable but were still entirely coherent, beneficial and workable, presenting them in such a way that they seemed like the only reasonable way ahead. This required great courage and inner strength, respect for those with alternative stances, deep and transparent integrity which inspired trust, clear focus and the drive to fuel extreme degrees of selfless hard work.

Paul was for many years my head of department, and later friend, colleague and fellow researcher, but he was above all always my role model whom I tried to observe carefully and forever strove to emulate. It has been my huge good fortune to have known and worked alongside Paul – indeed it has been one of the greatest gifts of my life. I have the feeling that in this I am not alone!

References

Daugherty, R. (1995). *National Curriculum Assessment: A Review of Policy 1987-94*. London: Routledge.

Department for Education/Her Majesty's Inspectorate (DES/HMI) (1983). *The Curriculum for 5-16 (Curriculum Matters 2)*. London: HMSO.

Department for Education/Her Majesty's Inspectorate (DES/HMI) (1985). *Curriculum 11-16: Towards a Statement of Entitlement*. London: HMSO.

Department for Education/Welsh Office (DES/WO) (1985). Better Schools (Cmnd. 9469). London: HMSO.

Department for Education/Welsh Office (DES/WO) (1987). *The National Curriculum 5-16: A Consultation Document*. London: DES/WO.

Dobson, K., Ed. (1985). *Revised Nuffield Advanced Science: Physics Examinations and Investigations*. Harlow: Longman Group.

Harrison, A. (1982). *Review of Graded Tests – School Council Examination Bulletin 41*. Methuen Education.

Hart, K., Ed. (1981). *Children's Understanding of Mathematics 11–16*. London: John Murray.

Haviland, J., Ed. (1988). *Take Care, Mr. Baker*. London: Fourth Estate.

National Curriculum: Task Group on Assessment and Testing (1987). *A Report*. London: DES.

Shayer, M. & P. Adey (1981). *Towards a Science of Science Teaching*. London: Heinemann.

3

Putting Learners at the Heart of the Assessment System

Dylan Wiliam

Introduction

My first teaching job was in a private, residential sixth-form college providing intensive coaching to help students improve grades on public examinations. Most of my teaching was to two or three students (my largest group was four) and so unlike most teachers, I learned a lot about teaching individual students before I learned about classroom management. What this meant was that, for most of my working week, I was engaged in what Benjamin Bloom (1984) regarded as the most effective form of education, namely one-to-one tutoring.

My next teaching job was at a school that was closely involved in the Secondary Mathematics Individualized Learning Experiment (SMILE). Students would complete a number of individually assigned tasks and then check their answers in freely available answer books. Then, the student would complete a test, typically involving two or three questions on each assigned task, which the teacher then marked. The teacher then selected the next batch of tasks, taking into account the student's performance on the tests. Echoing the thinking of Benjamin Bloom on mastery learning some years earlier, with SMILE, teaching was conceived of as a *contingent*, rather than *linear* process (Bloom, 1968). The next steps were decided only once there was evidence about what students had learned. Although I never heard anyone use this term at the time, this was formative assessment in action.

After seven years teaching in West London, I took up a research fellowship at Chelsea College, working with the Graded Assessment in Mathematics (GAIM) project, along with associated projects in science (the Graded Assessment in Science Project) and design and technology (the Graded Assessment in Craft,

Design and Technology Project), which were explicitly focused on providing information assessment information that could be used both summatively and formatively, though, again, these terms were hardly ever used.

In particular, building on then novel work by Carol Dweck and her colleagues (e.g. Dweck, 1986), each of the schemes sought to assess student achievement in terms of a developmental continuum, rather than a snapshot in time, so that students would see their current achievement not as a limit on their potential but rather as an indication of the level of achievement they had currently reached. The intended implication was that further effort would lead to further progress, so that, in Dweck's terms, ability was conceived of as incremental rather than fixed.

For example, in their work on young children's acquisition of number skills, Denvir and Brown (1986) found that the following skills formed a hierarchy, in the sense that students who could demonstrate one of these skills could almost always demonstrate the skills above them:

> Models two-digit addition without regrouping using physical base ten apparatus
> Models two-digit subtraction without regrouping using physical base ten apparatus
> Knows answer when adding or subtracting ten from a two-digit number
> Mentally carries out two-digit subtraction without regrouping
> Mentally carries out two-digit subtraction with regrouping

Such learning hierarchies provide a way of establishing where learners are in their learning, but also, importantly, provide suggestions about 'where next?'

Over the next three years, the three graded assessment teams, and a related project in English, funded by the Inner London Education Authority, developed assessment systems for secondary schools that would both provide information that could be used to inform next steps in teaching and, at the same time, lead to certificates equivalent to those provided by public examinations. The work undertaken by these projects on age-independent levels of achievement played an important role in national policy when, in the summer of 1987, the British government announced its intention to introduce a national curriculum for all students of compulsory school age in England and Wales.

National curriculum assessment

In addition to establishing a national curriculum, the government proposed national testing at the ages of 7, 11, 14 and 16 – the ends of what were called 'key stages' of schooling (Department of Education and Science and Welsh Office,

1987). Although the relevant legislation – the Education Reform Act – was not enacted until July 1988, a year earlier, the Department of Education and Science (DES) established working groups to develop proposals for the national curriculum in mathematics and science (chaired by Roger Blin-Stoyle and Jeff Thompson, respectively) with a request that the groups produce interim reports by November 1987. In addition, over the summer, Paul Black had been asked to chair a third group – the National Curriculum Task Group on Assessment and Testing (TGAT) – to advise the Secretary of State 'on the practical considerations which should govern all assessment including testing of attainment at age (approximately) 7, 11, 14 and 16, within a national curriculum' (National Curriculum Task Group on Assessment and Testing, 1988: Appendix A).

From statements made at the time, it seems that Kenneth Baker, then Secretary of State for Education and Science, expected a simple reporting system with 'benchmarks' specified for the desired level of achievement at the end of each key stage (Nuttall, 1989). The difficulty with a single benchmark, of course, is that if they are sufficiently demanding to provide challenging targets for higher achievers, they are likely to be beyond the reach of many students, while more realistic benchmarks would not motivate higher achieving students who would be aware that they could achieve the benchmark level with little effort (Wiliam, 1995).

The authors of the original consultation document appear to have been aware of this inherent contradiction because it was made clear that the attainment targets were to be differentiated in some way:

> [T]he range of attainment targets should cater for the full ability range and be sufficiently challenging *at all levels* to raise expectations, particularly of students of middling achievement who are frequently not challenged enough, as well as stretching and stimulating the most able.
> (Department of Education and Science and Welsh Office, 1987: 9–10, original emphasis)

The task group did examine the possibility of age-specific scales – i.e. a separate scale, such as A, B, C, D and E (as was common in many schools in England), or grades 1 to 6 (as used in Germany), at the end of each of the key stages – and noted that such an arrangement did 'have the attraction of apparent uniformity across all ages' (National Curriculum Task Group on Assessment and Testing, 1988 paragraph 98). However, the report noted that such scales had specific drawbacks. In particular, the report noted that a child might be reported as level 2 at the end of one key stage and at level 1 in the next, despite having made progress in absolute terms.

The task group concluded that the only way to satisfy the consultation document's requirements was to adopt age-independent levels of achievement similar to those in use in the graded assessment schemes. Drawing on the work that Margaret Brown, Alice Onion and I had done on rates of progression, the task group concluded that a system with ten levels would mean that each student would have a good chance of reaching a new level each key stage.

The main recommendations of the report were accepted on 7 June 1988 (Secretary of State for Education and Science, 1988), and although the scale was the subject of much criticism over subsequent years, a major review chaired by Ron Dearing (1994) concluded that most of the criticisms of the scale were in fact criticisms of the way that assessment against the scale had been carried out, rather than of the scale itself. However, the Dearing report did recommend that the scale should be used only for assessment at the end of the first three key stages, so that only eight levels would be needed.

While the system of age-independent levels proposed by the first TGAT report clearly supported a focus on progression in students' learning, most of the discussions of assessment at that time were concerned with how teachers might reach sound conclusions about students' levels of achievement. The role that assessment might play in improving learning was limited to the idea that suitable assessment arrangements might motivate students, and a concern to avoid negative backwash.

The Assessment Policy Task Group

While the idea of a national curriculum was welcomed by many, some of the provisions of the Education Reform Act were not. Within the academic community in particular, reaction was largely hostile to the proposed reforms (e.g. see Torrance, 1988). However, as Richard Daugherty (2008: 25) points out, these responses had 'every appearance of being a debate amongst educational researchers rather than a dialogue between researchers and policy-makers'. In an attempt to make educational research more relevant to policy and practice, in 1989 the British Educational Research Association (BERA) established five policy task groups – on assessment, curriculum, local management of schools, teacher education and, later, on adult and continuing education – to facilitate discussion between educational researchers, civil servants and other policymakers on issues of educational policy.

As Daugherty (2008: 27) notes, the Assessment Policy Task Group (APTG) produced a number of critiques of the many new educational policies that were being implemented in England and Wales and, over time, adopted 'a more strategic approach in its attempts to influence policy on assessment'. In particular, the group had secured funding from the Nuffield Foundation for a review of research on the effects of classroom assessment.

Due to pressure of other commitments, none of the members of the APTG had time to undertake the review, so they asked Paul, who had recently retired, if he was able to undertake the review with a specific brief to update the reviews of classroom assessment that had been conducted almost a decade earlier by Gary Natriello (1987) and Terry Crooks (1988).

In 1993, Paul had written a paper titled 'Formative and summative assessment by teachers' (Black, 1993). Paul and I had been working more and more closely together since his appointment as my appraiser in 1989, and reading this paper crystallized for me how several disparate strands of my work, going back to my experiences with one-to-one tuition and SMILE teaching, and my attempts to make sense of the judgements that teachers made when they agreed on the value in students' work, might come together. The key was to conceive of all the ways that teachers made sense of evidence from their students – whether that was to draw conclusions about the value of a student's portfolio of work or to draw conclusion about what kinds of teaching activities might be most appropriate – as a process of *evidentiary reasoning*. While many people regarded what teachers did in listening to their students and adjusting what they did as 'just good teaching', thinking of these processes as examples of evidentiary reasoning immediately highlighted issues about the adequacy and appropriateness of the inferences drawn and, in particular, the breadth and the depth of the evidence.

Over the next year or so, Paul and I worked both independently and together on formative assessment and, together with Christine Harrison and Robert Fairbrother, organized a symposium on formative assessment at the joint conference held by BERA and the European Educational Research Association in September 1995. Paul and I summarized our conversations in a paper titled 'Meanings and consequences: A basis for distinguishing formative and summative functions of assessment' (Wiliam & Black, 1996). With characteristic generosity, Paul told me that he would be more comfortable if my name preceded his, although as far as I can recall, the ideas in the paper were developed jointly.

Presumably because of our existing work on formative assessment, Paul told the APTG that he would be happy to accept the task only if the work could be done as a collaboration between him and me.

When we began our work, we quickly realized that no single approach was likely to be successful in identifying all or even most of the relevant studies. The 1989 edition of *Educational Measurement* contained just two references to the term 'formative assessment' – both in a chapter by Nitko (1989). The reviews by Natriello and Crooks cited 91 and 241 references respectively but had only 9 references in common, and neither cited an earlier meta-analysis of research on formative assessment in special education (Fuchs & Fuchs, 1986).

We therefore decided to identify relevant studies in four ways. First, we used online databases such as ERIC and PsychLit – then rather a novelty. However, we discovered that automated searches either missed out publications that we knew from our own previous reading were relevant and important or produced large numbers of irrelevant hits.

Second, we identified papers that had cited the reviews by Natriello and Crooks, Paul's 1993 paper, and reviews on the effects of testing by Bangert-Drowns and his colleagues (e.g. see Bangert-Drowns et al., 1991).

Third, in a kind of 'snowball' approach, we identified studies from the reference lists of the papers we had already found and looked at those studies, and other studies that cited them.

Finally, we undertook a manual search of seventy-six education and psychology journals likely to contain relevant studies. Paul had reviewed a number of the most relevant journals for his 1993 paper and so we read titles and abstracts in issues of these journals from 1992 to 1997 and issues of other relevant journals from 1988 to 1997.

This yielded 681 publications that appeared relevant to the review, approximately 250 of which were read in full and coded using a total of 47 codes. From our preliminary reading, we identified seven main sections for our review and allocated each of the 47 codes to a section (one code was allocated to two sections). Each section was allocated to one of us to prepare a draft, which was then revised jointly. Further details of the writing process are described in the paper itself.

When we presented the report to the APTG, members of the group suggested that the report should be more widely circulated. Two of the members of the group were on the editorial board of the journal *Assessment in Education* so, given the focus of the journal, and of the report, it seemed a natural choice. Our report, with minor revisions, was published as the focal article of a special issue of the journal together with commentaries by authors from Africa, Australia, Europe and North America.

Although publication in an academic journal was an appropriate forum for our report, Paul and I felt that such an article would have limited impact. Paul suggested that we write something explicitly for practitioners and policymakers. The APTG members indicated that this was not something that they were particularly interested in, but they were happy for us to do this if we thought it was worthwhile.

The paper we eventually produced differed from the report to APTG in several ways:

- It was much shorter (one-fifth of the length of the academic journal article).
- It was written so as to be accessible to practitioners and policymakers, avoiding technical language as far as possible.
- The paper took the research summarized in the ARG report as a starting point and, going beyond the evidence, speculated about what these findings might mean for practitioners and policymakers, and in particular how the most important findings from our review might be implemented in classrooms.
- In drawing conclusions, the paper adopted a stance of practical, rather than analytic rationality (Flyvbjerg, 2001) using a standard of *reasonableness* as advocated by Stephen Toulmin (2001).
- The paper was published as a twenty-four-page pamphlet and sold with a substantial discount for bulk copies to encourage schools to buy a large number of copies.

We were attracted to the idea of the eventual title – *Inside the Black Box* – because it seemed to us, as we noted in the introduction, that

> present policy seems to treat the inside of the classroom as a *black box*. Certain *inputs* from the outside are fed in or make demands – students, teachers, other resources, management rules and requirements, parental anxieties, tests with pressures to score highly, and so on. Some *outputs* follow, hopefully students who are more knowledgeable and competent, better test results, teachers who are more or less satisfied, and more or less exhausted. But what is happening inside?

Inside the Black Box was released on 5 February 1998 at a special event funded by the Nuffield Foundation. The previous day we hosted a series of briefings with journalists and almost all the national daily newspaper in the UK carried some reference to the publication on the day of the launch.

Since its publication, at least 50,000 copies of the booklet have been sold, and data from the Authors' Licensing and Collecting Society suggest that at least many copies have been made in educational institutions in the UK. A slightly amended version of the text was published in the United States in *Phi Delta Kappan*, a professional journal (Black & Wiliam, 1998), and at one point was its most downloaded publication from that journal's website. For our reflections on the success of the booklet, see Black and Wiliam (2003).

The year after the publication of *Inside the Black Box*, the Assessment Reform Group (which took over from APTG when BERA wound up its policy task groups at the end of 1996) published a booklet titled *Assessment for Learning: Beyond the Black Box* that argued that the term 'formative assessment' was 'open to a variety of interpretations' (Broadfoot et al., 1999: 7) and instead proposed the use of 'assessment for learning' (for the origin of this term, see Wiliam, 2011). While the contrast between assessment of learning and assessment for learning has appeal, Paul and I and our colleagues continued to use the term 'formative assessment', not least because we thought it was important to focus on the function the assessment actually served rather than the purpose for which it was given; assessments that were designed originally for summative purposes might well be used formatively. In a follow-up publication we wrote:

> Assessment for learning is any assessment for which the first priority in its design and practice is to serve the purpose of promoting students' learning. It thus differs from assessment designed primarily to serve the purposes of accountability, or of ranking, or of certifying competence. An assessment activity can help learning if it provides information that teachers and their students can use as feedback in assessing themselves and one another and in modifying the teaching and learning activities in which they are engaged. Such assessment becomes 'formative assessment' when the evidence is actually used to adapt the teaching work to meet learning needs.
>
> (Black et al., 2004: 10)

Reflecting on these events, it now seems likely that one of the reasons for the differences in approach between Paul and me on the one hand, and the Assessment Reform Group on the other, was that Paul and I were more interested in practice in classrooms, while the members of the ARG had their roots in education policy and, specifically, in various efforts over the years to provide students with 'records of achievement' (e.g. see Wiliam, 2020). While Paul and I shared with members of ARG similar visions of what effective classroom assessment would look like, we differed on how we might get there. We had little doubt that policy changes, if implemented effectively, might well produce substantial improvements, but our experience of previous attempts to improve education through policy changes made us sceptical that such an approach would succeed. Working with teachers, while much messier, held out the hope of profound changes in classrooms, though would of course be much harder to implement at scale.

Implementation in classrooms

Inside the Black Box, and the research review on which it was based, presented a strong case that increased use of classroom formative assessment could improve students' learning, but it was not at all clear that such practices could be implemented in typical classrooms, especially in countries like England, where teachers were under pressure to increase their students' scores on national examinations.

Paul and I, together with Christine Harrison, one of our colleagues at King's, therefore sought, and received, funding from the Nuffield Foundation to undertake work in schools to find out whether the kinds of practices we had envisaged in *Inside the Black Box* were viable in schools and also to see if those practices, when implemented, did, indeed, improve student achievement. We were fortunate to partner with two local education authorities, Oxfordshire and Medway, where we knew there was strong support for developing teachers' assessment practices, and three schools in each authority agreed to work with us.

Each school participating in the King's-Medway-Oxfordshire Formative Assessment Project (KMOFAP) nominated two mathematics teachers and two science teachers, and we met with the participating teachers for a series of one-day workshops organized by Paul, Chris, Clare Lee and me. We presented some of our findings and encouraged the teachers to explore what these ideas might mean for their practice. As we wrote later, it seems that some of the teachers thought we were operating a rather perverted model of discovery learning in which we knew what they should be doing but we wanted them to discover it for themselves. However, after a couple of months, the teachers realized that we really had little idea of how formative assessment would best work in their classrooms and that it would be up to them to work out the implications for their own practice.

The quantitative findings of the project – indicating that students taught by the participating teachers made substantially more progress than other students in the same school, as measured using national tests and examinations – were published in an academic journal article (Wiliam et al., 2004). However, the main output from the project was a book for teachers (Black et al., 2003) and a follow-up to *Inside the Black Box*, titled, perhaps predictably, *Working inside the Black Box*, again published as a booklet in the UK (Black et al., 2002), and as a journal article in the United States (Black et al., 2004).

The work in Oxfordshire and Medway convinced us that classroom formative assessment practice was a valuable focus for teacher professional development because of its impact on student achievement and because it was clear that teachers could, with relatively little external support, make significant improvements in their practice. However, we were also aware that meeting with teachers for five or six days each year would be a model that would be impossible to scale up with any fidelity.

Between 2001 and 2003, we explored, with colleagues at the Open University, the University of Reading and the University of Cambridge, a number of approaches to scaling up classroom assessment practices in a large project funded by the Economic and Social Research Council (ESRC) as part of its Teaching and Learning Research Programme and titled 'Learning how to learn: In classrooms, schools and networks'. While the project generated much useful information about teacher professional development (see James et al., 2007 for a summary), the focus on 'learning how to learn' was ultimately rather too diffuse to generate clear evidence of how to improve schools. While Paul and I agreed about the importance of helping students to learn how to learn, we ended up calling it 'the swamp' in our frustration at our inability to define and measure the idea with any precision.

After the 'Learning how to learn' project, Paul's priorities and mine diverged. I had moved to the United States to work at the Educational Testing Service in Princeton, New Jersey, to explore ways of supporting teachers in developing their practice of formative assessment that could be implemented at low cost not just in a few dozen classrooms, as was the case with KMOFAP but in tens of thousands of classrooms. Paul continued collaboration with colleagues at King's helping teachers find ways in integrating formative and summative assessment (Black et al., 2011a, 2014) and also explored the use of sophisticated models for understanding student progression, particularly in science (Black et al., 2011b; Morell et al., 2017; Wilson et al., 2013).

However, we continued to work together on a number of projects. The most important of these was to try to clarify the foundations of our work through a series of articles and chapters on the theory of formative assessment. Our first paper together (Wiliam & Black, 1996) had established that since the same assessment, and even the evidence yielded by the assessment, could be used both summatively and formatively, to describe something as 'a formative assessment' was meaningless. Rather, formative and summative were better thought of as descriptions of the inferences that assessment outcomes support. The results of an assessment might be interpreted summatively, as for example, when a student is described as having mastered, or not mastered a given body of material, or formatively, when the student, a peer or a teacher interprets the results of the assessment in terms of what needs to be done next.

Some of these publications were produced for specific collections, such as two contributions to a National Society for the Study of Education Yearbook (Black & Wiliam, 2004a, b) and three contributions to a collection titled 'Assessment and learning' edited by John Gardner (Black & Wiliam, 2005a, b, c) and were therefore produced to deadlines. However, others, such as a paper titled 'Developing the theory of formative assessment', were papers that we had been discussing for years until we eventually decided that we might as well publish them since we would be unlikely to be able to improve them further ourselves. The most extreme example of this was our third attempt at a comprehensive theory of formative assessment which Paul first drafted in 2010 and was ultimately published eight years later as 'Classroom assessment and pedagogy' (Black & Wiliam, 2018). However, probably the most important vindication of our work on formative assessment came in 2018 with the publication of a report by the Education Endowment Foundation (EEF) of an independent evaluation of a professional development programme titled 'Embedding formative assessment' (EFA).

During our time together at ETS, Siobhan Leahy and I had explored how we might support groups of teachers in working on developing their practice of formative assessment without access to external support (since such support was often of poor quality and was vulnerable to shifts in funding). We developed the idea of teacher-led groups called 'teacher learning communities' and, when we returned to the UK in 2006, we produced materials that these groups could use to support each other, consisting of protocols and handouts for meetings, guidance for peer observations and so on. Partnering with the Specialist Schools and Academies Trust (SSAT) these resources were supplemented with videos of classroom practice, interviews with teachers and students, and a range of other materials that might help teachers improve their classroom formative assessment practice (Leahy & Wiliam, 2009).

In the first year of its availability, the EFA programme was acquired by approximately 30 per cent of all secondary schools in England, and since then it has been adopted as a state-wide model in South Australia, is in use in three quarters of the primary schools in Singapore, and in twenty-eight of the thirty-two LEAs in Scotland.

However, while schools that were using the materials were positive about the impact on student achievement, there was little hard evidence that such a 'light touch' approach was making any difference to student achievement. To address this, the EEF commissioned the National Institute for Economic and Social Research (NIESR) to undertake a large-scale, pre-registered, cluster-randomized trial of the EFA programme. Put simply, the NIESR recruited 140 schools, gave half of them, at random, the EFA materials and half of them the cash equivalent, and then analysed the grades students achieved in their GCSEs two years later.

The details of the study, and the analysis of the results, can be found in Speckesser et al. (2018) and a guide to interpreting the results can be found in Wiliam (2019). However, the main conclusion is that students taught by the teachers in the schools receiving the EFA materials made approximately 25 per cent more progress during key stage 4 than students in the other schools. According to the EEF's estimates, the cost of the intervention was approximately £1.20 per student and took up approximately 1 per cent of teachers' time. Supporting teachers in developing their practice of classroom formative assessment appears to be the most cost-effective way of improving student achievement.

Reflections

Looking back at the three decades over which Paul and I have been collaborating, what seems most striking is how far from inevitable the development of formative assessment in classrooms has been. Of course it is likely that had Paul and I and our colleagues not been engaged in this work, then others would, but I doubt that my career would have followed the path it has but for Paul. The idea that formative assessment would provide a way of bringing together my own work as a school teacher, as a researcher and as a teacher educator was not even on my horizon in the early 1990s. But for a series of coincidences – Paul's appointment as my appraiser, his invitation to me to work with him on the APTS's review and his unerring focus on keeping the interests of students at the heart of the education process – my career would certainly have followed a different path. For that, I am profoundly grateful and forever in his debt.

What is perhaps most surprising in all this is that my work with Paul over the last thirty years has been regarded as in any way innovative or groundbreaking.

After all, what we have done is simply to suggest to teachers that as long as they keep inquiring into the relationship between what they do in their classrooms and what their students learn as a result, then they will be able to improve their practice. To be sure, we have, through our empirical work, provided evidence that such a focus is probably the most powerful way to improve learning, and through our theoretical work, we have given teachers tools to reflect on and improve their practice. However, the most important message in all this is a theme common to all Paul's work. In education, good things happen when we keep the learner at the heart of all that we do.

References

Bangert-Drowns, R. L., C. L. C. Kulik, J. A. Kulik & M. Morgan (1991). 'The instructional effect of feedback in test-like events'. *Review of Educational Research* 61(2): 213–38.

Black, P. & D. Wiliam (1998). 'Inside the black box: Raising standards through classroom assessment'. *Phi Delta Kappan*, 80(2): 139–48.

Black, P., C. Harrison, C. Lee, B. Marshall & D. Wiliam (2002). *Working inside the Black Box: Assessment for Learning in the Classroom*. London, UK: GL Assessment.

Black, P., C. Harrison, C. Lee, B. Marshall & D. Wiliam (2003). *Assessment for Learning: Putting It into Practice*. Buckingham, UK: Open University Press.

Black, P. & D. Wiliam (2003). 'In praise of educational research: Formative assessment'. *British Educational Research Journal*, 29(5): 623–37.

Black, P., C. Harrison, C. Lee, B. Marshall & D. Wiliam (2004). 'Working inside the black box: Assessment for learning in the classroom'. *Phi Delta Kappan*, 86(1): 8–21.

Black, P. & D. Wiliam (2005a). 'Assessment for learning in the classroom'. In J. Gardner (Ed.), *Assessment and Learning*, 9–25. London, UK: Sage.

Black, P. & D. Wiliam (2005b). 'The reliability of assessments'. In J. Gardner (Ed.), *Assessment and Learning*, 119–31. London, UK: Sage.

Black, P. & D. Wiliam (2005c). 'Developing a theory of formative assessment'. In J. Gardner (Ed.), *Assessment and Learning*, 81–100. London, UK: Sage.

Black, P., C. Harrison, J. Hodgen, B. Marshall & N. Serret (2011a). 'Can teachers' summative assessments produce dependable results and also enhance classroom learning?' *Assessment in Education: Principles, Policy & Practice*, 18(4): 451–69.

Black, P., M. Wilson & S. Y. Yao (2011b). 'Road maps for learning: A guide to the navigation of learning progressions'. *Measurement: Interdisciplinary Research and Perspectives*, 9(2–3): 71–123.

Black, P., C. Harrison, J. Hodgen, B. Marshall & N. Serret (2014). *Inside the Black Box of Assessment: Assessment of Learning by Teachers and Schools*. London, UK: GL Assessment.

Black, P. & D. Wiliam (2018). 'Classroom assessment and pedagogy'. *Assessment in Education: Principles, Policy & Practice*, 25(6): 551–75.

Black, P. J. (1993). 'Formative and summative assessment by teachers'. *Studies in Science Education*, 21(1): 49–97.

Black, P. J. & D. Wiliam (2004a). 'Classroom assessment is not (necessarily) formative assessment (and vice-versa)'. in M. Wilson (Ed.), *Towards Coherence between Classroom Assessment and Accountability: 103rd Yearbook of the National Society for the Study of Education (Part 2)*, 183–8. Chicago, IL: University of Chicago Press.

Black, P. J. & D. Wiliam (2004b). 'The formative purpose: Assessment must first promote learning'. In M. Wilson (Ed.), *Towards Coherence between Classroom Assessment and Accountability: 103rd Yearbook of the National Society for the Study of Education (part 2)*, 20–50. Chicago, IL: University of Chicago Press.

Bloom, B. S. (1968). 'Learning for mastery'. *Evaluation Comment*, 1(2): 1–12.

Bloom, B. S. (1984). 'The search for methods of instruction as effective as one-to-one tutoring'. *Educational Leadership*, 41(8): 4–17.

Broadfoot, P. M., R. Daugherty, J. Gardner, C. V. Gipps, W. Harlen, M. James & G. Stobart (1999). *Assessment for Learning: Beyond the Black Box*. Cambridge, UK: University of Cambridge School of Education.

Crooks, T. J. (1988). 'The impact of classroom evaluation practices on students'. *Review of Educational Research*, 58(4): 438–81.

Daugherty, R. (2008). 'Mediating academic research: The Assessment Reform Group experience'. In J. Furlong and A. Oancea (Eds.), *Assessing Quality in Applied and Practice-Based Research in Education*, 21–35. London, UK: Routledge.

Dearing, R. (1994). *The National Curriculum and Its Assessment: Final Report*. London, UK: School Curriculum and Assessment Authority.

Denvir, B. and M. L. Brown (1986). 'Understanding of number concepts in low-attaining 7–9 year olds: Part 1. Development of descriptive framework and diagnostic instrument'. *Educational Studies in Mathematics*, 17(1): 15–36.

Department of Education and Science and Welsh Office (1987). *The National Curriculum 5–16: A Consultation Document*. London, UK: Department of Education and Science.

Dweck, C. S. (1986). 'Motivational processes affecting learning'. *American Psychologist*, 41(10): 1040–8.

Flyvbjerg, B. (2001). *Making Social Science Matter: Why Social Inquiry Fails and How It Can Succeed Again*. Cambridge, UK: Cambridge University Press.

Fuchs, L. S. and D. Fuchs (1986). 'Effects of systematic formative evaluation: A meta-analysis'. *Exceptional Children*, 53(3): 199–208.

James, M., R. McCormick, P. Black, P. Carmichael, M. J. Drummond, A. Fox, J. MacBeath, B. Marshall, D. Pedder, R. Procter, S. Swaffield, J. Swann & D. Wiliam (2007). *Improving Learning How to Learn: Classrooms, Schools and Networks*. London, UK: Routledge.

Leahy, S. & D. Wiliam (2009). *Embedding Formative Assessment*. London, UK: Specialist Schools and Academies Trust.

Morell, L., T. Collier, P. Black & M. Wilson (2017). 'A construct modelling approach to develop a learning progression of how students understand the structure of matter'. *Journal of Research in Science Teaching*, 54(8): 1024–48.

National Curriculum Task Group on Assessment and Testing (1988). *A Report*. London, UK: Department of Education and Science.

Natriello, G. (1987). 'The impact of evaluation processes on students'. *Educational Psychologist*, 22(2): 155–75.

Nitko, A. J. (1989). 'Designing tests that are integrated with instruction'. In R. L. Linn (Ed.), *Educational Measurement*, 447–74. Washington, DC: American Council on Education/Macmillan.

Nuttall, D. L. (1989). 'National assessment: Complacency or misinterpretation?' In D. Lawton (Ed.), *The Educational Reform Act: Choice and Control*, 44–66. London, UK: Hodder & Stoughton.

Secretary of State for Education and Science (1988). 'Assessment and testing: A reply to Mr Key'. In (Ed.), *Parliamentary Written Answers, Hansard, 7 June 1988*. London, UK: Her Majesty's Stationery Office.

Speckesser, S., J. Runge, F. Foliano, M. Bursnall, N. Hudson-Sharp, H. Rolfe & J. Anders (2018). *Embedding Formative Assessment: Evaluation Report and Executive Summary*. London, UK: Education Endowment Foundation.

Torrance, H., Ed. (1988). *National Assessment and Testing: A Research Response*. Keswick, UK: British Educational Research Association.

Toulmin, S. (2001). *Return to Reason*. Cambridge, MA: Harvard University Press.

Wiliam, D. (1995). 'The development of national curriculum assessment in England and Wales'. In T. Oakland, R. K. Hambleton & D. L. Stufflebeam (Eds.), *International Perspectives on Academic Assessment*, 157–85. Boston, MA: Kluwer Academic Publishers.

Wiliam, D. & P. J. Black (1996). 'Meanings and consequences: A basis for distinguishing formative and summative functions of assessment?' *British Educational Research Journal*, 22(5): 537–48.

Wiliam, D., C. Lee, C. Harrison & P. Black (2004). 'Teachers developing assessment for learning: impact on student achievement'. *Assessment in Education: Principles Policy and Practice*, 11(1): 49–65.

Wiliam, D. (2011). 'What is assessment for learning?' *Studies in Educational Evaluation*, 37(1): 2–14.

Wiliam, D. (2019). 'Why formative assessment is always both domain-general and domain-specific and what matters is the balance between the two'. In H. Andrade, R. E. Bennett & G. J. Cizek (Eds.), *Handbook of Formative Assessment in the Disciplines*, 243–64. New York, NY: Routledge.

Wiliam, D. (2020). 'Research into practice: The case of classroom formative assessment'. In S. Gorard (Ed.), *Getting Evidence into Education: Evaluating the Routes to Policy and Practice*, 119–35. London, UK: Routledge.

Wilson, M., P. Black & L. Morell (2013). 'A learning progression approach to understanding students' conceptions of the structure of matter. In *Annual Meeting of the American Educational Research Association*. San Francisco, CA: University of California Berkeley.

4

Inspiring Change in Classroom Assessment

Gordon Stobart, Jo-Anne Baird and Louise Hayward

If a journal or professional article on classroom assessment does not mention Paul in the opening paragraphs, we immediately become concerned about what the author knows. Equally, only casually referencing 'Black & Wiliam' (1998a), the most downloaded article to this day in the international journal *Assessment in Education; Principles, Policy and Practice* raises suspicions. And why is 'Classroom assessment and pedagogy', an article Paul wrote with Dylan Wiliam twenty years later, the journal's most popular download of the last three years?

How Paul came to lead one of the most successful classroom assessment initiatives of the past two decades is a story worth telling – not only because it brought about changes in teachers' classroom practice but also because it offers a model of how to put theory into practice.

The Prologue

The story begins much earlier than the seminal 1998 article on classroom assessment, and these earlier accounts will be found elsewhere in this book. Their importance was in Paul's immersion in the literature and politics of educational assessment. His work with the Assessment of Performance Unit (APU, run by the official Department of Science and Education) in the 1980s showed the importance of finding out in depth what learners know and how they think. The King's College London Graded Assessment programmes demonstrated how assessment can be used to encourage learner progress. This experience led to his government-commissioned Task Group on Assessment and Testing (TGAT) report. In this Paul sought to give primacy to formative assessment in the educational system – not something the government of the day wanted to hear.

Another group of assessment academics, later known as the Assessment Reform Group, was also concerned about the push towards national testing. The fear, soon to be realized, was that testing would be used primarily for school accountability. The formative role of classroom assessment, which TGAT had argued should be the primary purpose of national curriculum assessments, would therefore be neglected. To counter this the group, at this stage the British Education Research Association's (BERA) Assessment Policy Task Group obtained funding from the Nuffield Foundation to update Natriello's (1987) and Crooks' (1988) decade-old reviews of research into formative assessment.

Researching the field

Paul Black and Dylan accepted this invitation to conduct an updated review of the literature. They knew this was not going to be a simple computer-generated study – there were too many differing terms in play and too much loose thinking around terms such as 'formative' and 'assessment'. A measure of this was that while Natriello had reviewed 91 studies and Crooks 241 studies, they only identified 9 studies in common.

Anyone who has conducted computer-based literature searches would know the frustrations of entering key words which generate hundreds of articles, most of which are then eliminated as the quality and scope of the research are evaluated. Paul and Dylan's initial ERIC, and other, database searches identified the further problem of finding that relevant and familiar studies were not being identified. The researcher's temptation at this stage is to widen the search criteria until they netted these and other articles – followed by the thankless task of whittling down most of these newly found, but often irrelevant or methodologically flawed, studies.

Instead, Paul and Dylan took the more demanding route: a manual search of the 76 journals most likely to carry relevant articles. This generated 681 publications from the previous ten years. These were reduced to 250 after reading the abstracts and sometimes the full articles. The next decision was how to process the findings. They opted for a 'best evidence synthesis' of the kind proposed by Robert Slavin. They accepted there was a subjective element in this – others may have construed the findings differently (though in retrospect nobody has).

The power of the review was that it offered an authoritative synthesis of a complex area which would lead to changes in how teachers approached classroom assessment. This account has been, and still is, the foundation of much research and policy to this day. The full review was published in *Assessment in Education* (1998, 5, 1:7–74) and online in 2006 where it has been viewed over 66,000 times.

This was no dry technical review, it was deliberately written to capture the complexities of classroom teaching and learning and of the scope of formative assessment. In doing this Paul and Dylan sought 'ecological validity'. The article began with examples of classroom studies which illustrated some of the features of formative assessment. These eight case studies exemplified three broad areas: student involvement in their own learning; the role of teachers' dialogue, diagnostics and classroom assessments; and the importance of effective feedback.

Already some of the central tenets of formative assessment/assessment for learning were being articulated: finding out where learners are in their learning, clarifying what is being learned, providing feedback and encouraging learners to become more self-regulated and independent. It was recognized that, if put into practice, this would have profound effects on pedagogy and the classroom, rewriting the contract between students and teachers. This was not going to be easy, especially in assessment cultures in which the focus was on summative testing and didactic teaching. It was also recognized that much labelled 'formative' fell short of contributing directly to the learning process.

Elaborating these elements raises further questions: what other factors are at work in the classroom? Is there an underlying theory of formative assessment? What are the cultural factors at work? These are questions which still occupy debates around formative assessment – and ones with which, as we will see, Paul is still grappling.

In interpreting the research findings, it was recognized that other factors will confound them. Ecological validity means we are dealing with complex and messy settings. It makes randomised control trials (RCTs), which are so effective in evaluating the efficacy of medicines, problematic in classroom research. Are the teachers in the control group as good as those in the experimental group? What else is happening in the classrooms? When research on mastery learning produced paradoxical findings about the efficacy of more frequent classroom testing (Martinez & Martinez, 1992) the researchers realized that it was the quality of the teacher that could account for the differences between groups rather than the frequency of tests. The centrality of the teacher-pupil interaction to effective classroom learning is a theme which Paul has continued to develop.

The review drew on work from a variety of theoretical perspectives ranging from the behaviourist mastery learning tradition to more constructivist and sociocultural approaches. At this stage Paul and Dylan offered no more than a few 'notes towards a theory of formative assessment' (p.54), drawing on the work of Sadler (1989) and of Tittle (1994). They noted that a development of any theory seemed to call for links to compatible learning theories and to theories of meta-cognition and the locus of control of the learner. Over the next twenty years, they would progressively articulate the theoretical basis of formative assessment.

Welcome critique

The editor of *Assessment in Education* was, at that time, Patricia Broadfoot, a founder of the journal and a key mover in developing assessment for learning. The review was largely her idea, as was inclusion of responses in the same issue from a range of international scholars. These influential responses offered both support and critique, foregrounding many of the issues still with us today. Some scholars respond badly to critique, taking it as a personal attack. Paul is not one of these; he recognized the importance of these reviews and has continued to incorporate and develop the observations that were made.

For example, the French scholar Philippe Perrenoud offered a theoretical critique which suggested that the focus on the classroom and on feedback was too narrow and introduced the concept of *regulation*, a term that does not translate easily into English. Regulation involves the bigger context of 'what goes on "upstream" of situations, where a pupil is placed in a context, a group, a situation ... as well as within situations, where the pupil's participation and learning are optimised'. This leads him to raise the question 'Rather than being solely concerned with the formative evaluation practices of teachers, why not conceptualise and observe more widely the process of regulation at work in classroom situations and the classroom organisation that underlies them?' (Perrenoud, 1998: 92). Unless this bigger picture is understood, and pupils treated as individuals who bring different capacities into the classroom, 'the feedback given to pupils in class is like so many bottles thrown out to sea. No one can be sure that the message they contain will one day find a receiver' (Perrenoud, 1998: 87).

We have quoted Perrenoud at length because it struck a chord and Paul has been working on these challenges ever since. In 2015 we find him quoting Perrenoud's comments on feedback:

> This no longer seems to me, however, to be the central issue. It would seem more important to concentrate on theoretical models of learning and its regulation

and their implementation. These constitute the real systems of thought and action, in which feedback is only one element.

(Perrenoud, 1998: 86)

Paul admits, 'I did not take this statement seriously at the time in part because, whilst it seemed then to be the only serious criticism of the review, it was not clear to me how the review could have been altered or supplemented to meet the criticism' (p.164). However, he did not leave it there but went on to grapple with Perrenoud's ideas, especially the theory of 'regulation' and the mechanisms of classroom management, particularly in relation to feedback and classroom dialogue.

Translate into classroom practice

Publishing a 67-page 'best evidence synthesis' in an academic journal is by itself hardly going to change teachers' thinking or classroom practices. Most teachers have very busy professional lives and little spare time, so reading academic publications hardly figures on their to-do list. Paul and Dylan took the decision to provide an accessible version for teachers and produced *Inside the Black Box: Raising Standards through Classroom Assessment*. This twenty-one-page pamphlet was initially an in-house publication from King's College which offered teachers direct ways of improving learning through changes to classroom assessment practices. This was not simply a synopsis of their review; it addressed the questions teachers would ask and provided some practical examples.

It hit the spot – sales were so vigorous for the inexpensive pamphlet that the King's staff could hardly cope with the volume of orders, so it was moved on to a mainstream publisher – but not before it was accessible online and so even more widely circulated internationally. The American *Phi Delta Kappan* journal published *Inside the Black Box* as an article (Black & Wiliam, 1988) and this has been picked up by other websites. Our estimate is that over a quarter of a million copies of the booklet have been sold with probably even more online downloads.

If we are using Paul's work on classroom assessment as a model of good practice, it's worth exploring what was in *The Black Box* (a reference to systems engineering and the complex interactions in the classroom rather than to Paul himself). It was written at a time of considerable activity 'upstream' in terms of national curriculum testing, exam reform and accountability based on league tables of test performance. The pamphlet's aim was to refocus on the importance of assessment in helping pupils learn, rather than meeting test-based performance targets.

Assessment was defined as 'all those activities undertaken by teachers, *and by their students in assessing themselves,* which provide information to be used as feedback to modify the teaching and learning activities in which they are engaged. *Such assessment becomes "formative assessment" when the evidence is actually used to adapt the teaching work to meet the needs*' (Black & Wiliam, 1998a: 2, original italics).

Three questions teachers would ask are then addressed:

1. Is there evidence that improving formative assessment raises standards?
2. Is there evidence that there is room for improvement?
3. Is there evidence about how to improve formative assessment?

No surprise that the answer to each is 'yes', but the evidence drawn upon is the kind that resonates with teachers. After summarizing an earlier review by Fuchs and Fuchs (1986), which showed statistically significant gains in learning from a range of formative assessment practices, the reader is gently introduced to the statistical concept of *effect size*. This could result in a glazed-over 'so what?' from teachers, so the 0.4–0.7 effect size range is speculatively translated into what this would mean to performance in schools if formative assessment was effectively implemented. The claim that met the eye, of politicians and policymakers as well, was 'A gain of effect size 0.4 would improve performances of pupils in GCSE by between one and two grades' and 'a gain of effect size 0.7, if realised in the recent international studies in mathematics … would raise England from the middle of the 41 counties involved to being one of the top five' (Black & Wiliam, 1998b: 4). In a performance culture this kind of claim hits the spot – do this and you'll get that. As we shall see later these speculative claims we treated as facts and have come back to haunt.

It was not difficult to show there was room for improvement and a series of quotations from the Inspectorate and teachers underlined a poverty of practice. This is followed by some of the negative impacts of current assessment practices: the overemphasis on marks and grades; pupil comparisons which make learning competitive; and the use of classroom assessment primarily for management purposes. Teachers in England would have no difficulty recognizing the educational climate which was pushing them into such practices.

These weaknesses in the then formative practice were not about 'teacher blaming', and the role of policymakers in creating these pressures was, and still is, vigorously critiqued. We suspect this critique of policy was animated by the treatment Paul's TGAT report had received at the hands of politicians who systematically shifted the focus of assessment from formative classroom assessment to high-stakes summative testing.

The third question asked how formative assessment can be improved. The answers may seem obvious good practice now – but they were not at the time (which shows how far Paul's work has brought us). So here is some of the advice for improvement:

- Feedback to any pupil should be about particular qualities of his or her work, with advice on what he or she can do to improve, and should avoid comparisons with other pupils. (Black & Wiliam, 1998b: 9)
- For formative assessment to be productive, pupils should be trained in self-assessment so that they can understand the main purposes of their learning and thereby grasp what they need to do to achieve. (Black & Wiliam, 1998b: 11)
- The dialogue between pupils and teacher should be thoughtful, reflective, focused to evoke and explore understanding, and conducted so that all pupils have an opportunity to think and express their ideas. (Black & Wiliam, 1998b: 12)

Disseminate the ideas

Inside the Black Box was launched at a press conference hosted by the Nuffield Trust. Key policymakers as well as senior school inspectors from England, Scotland and Wales were present. The press had been invited – and this led to headlines the next day in most newspapers that showed how radical some journalists had found the ideas. From the *Daily Express* the message was 'Marking is bad for you' (6 February 1998). *The Times* even devoted its main editorial to it:

> Headlined 'TWO OUT OF TEN For educationalists who want the world to be a different place', the editorial went on 'educationalists such as Paul Black ... seem determined to cocoon pupils from reality. Children, he says, should not be given marks out of ten, grades or gold stars, for then they "look for the ways to obtain the best marks rather than the needs of their learning"'.

The editorial writer then let us know that 'learning to look for the ways they can win the best marks is one of the most useful life skills to be gained from school. Much of life is about working a system to its full advantage. Pupils who know how to maximise their test results will be equipped for the world of work'. And a career at *The Times*?

This publicity clearly did not put teachers off and other policymakers who responded to the *Black Box's* claims – leading to an overwhelming demand for the pamphlet.

Road testing the theory

It is one thing to make claims based on other people's academic research, another to go out and try and put the principles into practice in the classroom. And that's exactly what the King's team, by now including Christine Harrison, Clare Lee and Bethan Marshall, did.

Securing funding from the Nuffield Foundation, which proved to be a consistent supporter of formative assessment projects, the King's team worked with local authority advisors from Medway and Oxfordshire (Rose Collinson, Sue Swaffield and Dorothy Kavanagh) to identify state schools willing to take part in implementing these ideas in the classroom. The project became known as the King's-Medway-Oxfordshire Formative Assessment Project, inelegantly known as KMOFAP. Six schools took part, involving thirty-six teachers of English, maths and science in an eighteen-month project. The first six months involved eleven one-day in-service training days combined with introducing formative assessment practices into their classrooms. The emphasis was on teachers developing their own classroom action plans followed by putting them into practice and then discussing the response. The King's team also took part in regular lesson observation and feedback sessions. This continued over two years and produced rich information about the impact on both teachers and pupils. The resulting book, *Assessment for Learning – Putting It into Practice* (Black et al., 2003) and the pamphlet *Working inside the Black Box* (Black et al., 2002), which was based on the project, tell the story and have been a source of ideas for many practitioners. It has also been a source of inspiration as teachers revealed the resistance they met, their own struggles to make changes to their teaching and the professional satisfaction they enjoyed from the changes they made.

The school accountability system in England leads to schools being judged by their examination results. A natural question therefore was whether the KMOFAP project makes any difference to the kind of learning required by tests. The King's team took up this challenge by analysing shifts in classroom test scores – which were positive (Wiliam et al., 2003) – and provided answers to schools and policymakers about the outcomes of assessment for learning.

Working alongside teachers to develop formative assessment led to the classroom practices with which other teachers could themselves experiment – as they subsequently did around the world.

Scaling up nationally – Scotland's Assessment is for Learning project

It is one thing to get individual teachers and schools to adopt assessment for learning, another to convince policymakers to implement it nationally. This was the next step for the King's team, and teachers from KMOFAP, as they went north of the border to help launch a national initiative. This was the Assessment is for Learning (AifL) project. The claims of Black and Wiliam's *Classroom Assessment and Pedagogy* (1998) had a major influence on the national assessment programme in Scotland. While the article may only have been read by enthusiasts, *Inside the Black Box* was a bestseller. Scotland's teachers contributed in numbers to the publication problem in King's College. Even if they had not read the original article, teachers and policymakers knew it was there. It was extensive and rigorous and had been used to inform the shorter, focused *Inside the Black Box* publication. Paul and colleagues sought to communicate, to open up minds to ideas in ways likely to connect with different communities. For policymakers, the quantifiable improvement; for practitioners, the impact on learners and teachers; and, for all involved, a sense of respect that allowed each to understand the importance of their own contribution to the bigger endeavour- to improve learning. The future had to be co-constructed.

The idea of assessment as an integral part of learning had been part of assessment policy in Scotland since 1991 when *Assessment 5–14 (SOED), Improving the Quality of Learning and Teaching* was published. The related policy document *Reporting 5–14* (SOED,1992) invited teachers and schools to offer assessment feedback in terms of identifying strengths, areas for development (growth points or challenges from which every learning might build) and next steps (the identification of future-focused actions with proposals as to how action might be taken forward). However, in addition to the *Assessment* and *Reporting 5–14* policies, there was a third Policy document *Testing 5–14* (SOED, 1991). Scottish government policy was clear; teacher's professional judgement mattered. Limited testing in English and mathematics would be used only to moderate professional judgement and, if the test result differed from professional judgement, professional judgement would prevail. However, seven years on, things had not gone as planned. Although *Assessment* policy had been warmly received by teachers and policymakers, in practice, perhaps predictably, testing had dominated thinking and practice and many teachers found the practical implications of well-intentioned policy, challenging. Teachers reported that although they believed the approaches to assessment advocated in *Assessment 5–14* consistent with their professional values, the language of strengths, areas for development and next steps made the process seem deceptively simple. It was, they argued, far from that.

In an attempt to support teachers in using assessment to inform learning, the Scottish Council for Research in Education Diagnostic Procedures project (1995) developed sets of research-informed processes in English (Hayward & Spencer), mathematics (Pearson) and science (Harlen). Again well received by teachers, the impact of this work was patchy – effective with those teachers and schools who chose to engage but not all teachers did. A National Conversation stimulated by the then Education Minister highlighted assessment to be focused on judgement and accountability and in need of change.

The publication of the Black and Wiliam (1998a) review offered an opportunity for Scotland to try again to generate the kind of national assessment culture originally intended in *Assessment 5–14* but this time premised on a stronger, more responsive, evidence base. This evidence base could re-energize *Assessment* in Scotland. However, previous experience in assessment innovation had demonstrated that having a programme be research-informed was not enough.

What attracted policymakers, practitioners and many researchers to the work of Black and Wiliam (1998a; 1998b) was a sense of their desire to make a difference, as exemplified by the work they had undertaken with Chris Harrison, Bethan Marshall, Jeremy Hodgen and thirty-six teachers in six schools in two education authorities in England (Medway and Oxfordshire) in KMOFAP.

The design of what was to become the national Assessment is Learning (AifL) programme in Scotland set out to be far more ambitious than any of its previous assessment programmes had been. Inspired by the KMOFAP project, AifL shifted from previous models of professional learning that sought to show teachers how to enact formative assessment to one that sought to work with teachers to explore how ideas from research might be put into practice in different schools by teachers working in different circumstances. The process of change itself became national capacity building. The KMOFAP project had set work with schools in the context of local policy. The design of the AifL programme also attempted to join up research, policy and practice but on a larger scale. For any innovation to be sustainable, however complex, it would have to involve all parts of the system. In a small country such as Scotland, that seemed possible.

The AifL project designers set out to identify all those who had to be involved in the project for it to become securely embedded in education in Scotland. This was not a project for the faint hearted. Two main sources of evidence were used to inform AifL design. The first was research evidence on assessment. The work of Paul and Dylan lay at the heart of this assessment evidence. The second evidence strand used to influence the design of AifL came from research on processes of change. Peter Senge and Otto Scharmer had undertaken a research review of public and private organizations who had been successful in sustaining transformational change. Their theory of community action research was used as the framework for the design of AifL. Senge and Scharmer (2001) set out three characteristics of change likely to be sustainable:

1. *'fostering relationships and collaboration among diverse organizations, and among the consultants and researchers working with them';*
    - AifL brought together researchers, policymakers and practitioners from a wide range of educational and social organizations, funding groups in ways that required participants to work collaboratively.
2. *'creating settings for collective reflection that enable people from different organizations to "see themselves in one another"';*
    - The programme created opportunities for collaboration where people across communities would work to tackle an assessment issue in a way that would work best for them.
3. *'leveraging progress in individual organizations through cross-institutional links so as to sustain transformative changes that otherwise would die out'.*
    - AifL funded leads in each local authority to coordinate projects across the authority and to create school networks. It also identified key players in the system where alignment would be essential for change to be sustainable, e.g. school inspectors (HMiE), where it was crucial that when HMiE went into schools, they looked for the approaches to assessment being advocated in AifL.

The AifL programme was an attempt to build formative assessment into policy and practice in Scotland in ways where it would become and remain embedded. It involved national policy communities, all thirty-two local education authorities, schools in each education authority, researchers from every university in Scotland involved in teacher education, school inspectors, national agencies, parents and young people.

The KMOFAP project focused on formative assessment and AifL included a strand of work that mirrored the KMOFAP work. In response to other challenges that had emerged in Scotland, it had a number of other strands, for example, how to manage what was described as assessment bureaucracy, how to engage parents, how to balance formative and summative purposes and how to reconcile assessment for learning and accountability. The formative assessment strand was by far the most successful and influential.

In the early days of AifL, the formative assessment strand had thrown up some interesting challenges. Teachers involved were suspicious of the more open, project-based approach to development. They asked policymakers and researchers when they were going to start telling them what to do and were suspicious when neither policy-makers nor researchers were able to do that, arguing instead that ideas had to come from those who would have to put them into practice. Paul, with colleagues from King's College and teachers from the KMOFAP schools, was invited to join one of the AifL national meetings, where teachers from across Scotland involved in the formative assessment strand came together to plan for action in their schools and classrooms. The session was a turning point. Paul's balance of deep knowledge, careful listening and gentle humility resonated well with the Scottish communities. The respectful, open relationship he had with KMOFAP teachers was clear and served as a model for the relationships that were to develop across research, policy and practice communities in the AifL programme. The teachers involved in AifL in Scotland listened to the KMOFAP teachers and began to believe that there were no predetermined answers and it was OK to engage in informed experimentation where the focus was learning rather than judgement. This was not part of the neoliberal project designed to control; it was a genuine attempt to learn and to use formative approaches to assessment not only to improve learning in schools but to improve the national system: 'a procedure for making … inferences about … learning' (Balck and Wiliam, 2008: 553).

AifL in Scotland was subject to a number of evaluations (Condie et al., 2005; George Street Research, 2007; Hallam et al., 2003), all were constructive and three years later, AifL was described by the then Education Minister as 'a quiet revolution in Scottish Education'. AifL was making a difference.

Twenty years on, assessment for learning is still a recognized concept in schools across Scotland although how well it is enacted is uneven. The collaborative model for change (*Changing with Integrity*, Hayward & Spencer, 2010), innovative at the time, has become the ways things are done in Scotland, although now it has emerged in a range of forms.

Scotland has almost come full circle and there is now a need to revisit assessment. There is new work to do: aspects of the formative process remain under-designed; for example, the approach taken to AifL needs now to be reformed to address issues of progression in learning in Curriculum for Excellence; the tensions between different assessment purposes still interfere with alignment and need to be tackled; and the dependability of teachers' professional judgement remains variable. There remains a long and winding road ahead to align curriculum, pedagogy, assessment and learning but the contribution of the work of Paul to this journey in Scotland will always be recognized and valued.

Keep developing theory as well as practice

Since *Inside the Black Box* tackled the broad matter of improving classroom assessment practice, it raised significant conceptual issues that needed further work and elucidation, some of which were raised by others in the field. Paul has enjoyed the critique and engagement from the field that these matters have generated; he has consistently sought to develop his understanding of the ideas, definitions and theoretical connections and underpinnings of formative assessment. Four issues stood out from the beginning and have continued to form part of Paul's conceptual developments: the distinction between formative and summative assessment, the relationship between assessment and pedagogy, quality issues for teacher assessment and learning theory underpinning formative assessment. In a 2018 article celebrating twenty-five years of the journal *Assessment in Education, Principles, Policy & Practice*, he and Dylan Wiliam advanced thinking on these issues again.

Formative and summative assessments

For decades, the discussion about the distinction between formative and summative assessments raged a debate characterized by protagonists on both sides. In many Western democracies, neoliberal ideologies have resulted in education accountability systems that manage teachers and schools through the quantification generated by summative assessments. Some have referred to this as *governing by numbers* (Grek, 2009). The resulting dominance of summative assessment has meant that formative assessments did not have a clean break from the influence of summative assessments and therefore the distinction and relationship needed to be addressed. Originally, like others, Paul categorized assessments as being formative, summative or diagnostic (Black, 2002). More recently, he has argued that assessments themselves do not have the inherent properties of formative or summative assessments; rather it is how they are used that matters and the decisions for which they provide evidence. They defined educational assessments in general as 'a procedure for making inferences about student learning' (Black & Wiliam, 2018: 553). Utilizing external, summative assessments in a formative way opens up the possibility of transforming the effects of even high-stakes summative assessments. Rather than instruments that narrow the curriculum and produce drilling and rote learning, they could be used to help structure learning progression for pupils.

Assessment and pedagogy

Summative assessment has traditionally been seen as something which occurs outside of the teaching and learning process, usually at the end. Until the 1980s, teaching, learning and the curriculum had much more focus than assessment in educational thinking and literature. Assessment was its own specialized field. Black and Wiliam (2018) made the point that theories of pedagogy that do not encompass a view of assessment are partial because assessment is an important part of pedagogy. Further, they agreed with Bennett (2011) that it was important to distinguish formative assessment as *assessment*, rather than to see it as classroom practice and pedagogy more broadly. Paul has consistently emphasized the role of dialogue in pedagogy; it is integral to formative assessment, with the role of oral questioning and feedback, peer assessment, co-construction of objectives and constructing the way forward for individual students. He has set himself against the narrower notion of instruction because of the de-professionalizing notions that it entails. Training teachers only to instruct leaves them without broader frameworks to fall back on when they need to adapt their teaching to the real-world demands of student learning and classroom experiences.

Pupils' voices in the formative assessment pedagogical dialogue are not given much treatment in Paul's work. In this way his work is traditional. However, he has drawn upon the self-regulated learning literature (e.g. Boekaerts et al., 2005) to explicate how learners can use meta-cognitive strategies to control and direct their own learning (Black & Wiliam, 2009). Nonetheless, his consistent belief in teachers' professional practice has perhaps left a blind spot regarding the way that feedback has been received by learners. Judging what support learners need at any given time is demanding and teachers can get it wrong, giving feedback that cannot be acted upon, at the wrong time, misjudging what students know and so on (Gamlen & Smith, 2013). This is now an active area of research (e.g. van der Kliej, Aidie and Cummings, 2019).

Quality of teacher assessment

In judging the quality of formative assessment, teacher assessment broadly is typically contrasted with the dominant other system – examinations. Criteria of validity, reliability and fairness are brought to bear. Large-scale, high-stakes examination systems have constructed elaborate procedures for ensuring consistency in the scoring and grading of assessments, comparing very favourably with teacher assessments in terms of reliability (Johnson, 2011). However, Paul has consistently argued that teacher assessment is more valid than examinations because of the capacity for teachers to assess a broader range of knowledge and skill than can be captured in the artificial and time-limited setting of an examination. Essentially, the construct of interest is under-represented by examinations but can be assessed in an elaborated manner, using a broader range of techniques, by teachers. He points to the potential for moderation systems to improve the reliability of teacher assessment (Black & Wiliam, 2018) and recognizes the wider benefits of improving teachers' assessment literacy. Still, this problem of unreliability of teacher assessment remains live. Paul argues that more investment in teacher training could have assured the retention of teacher-assessed coursework in the GCSE examinations in England (Black & Wiliam, 2018). But this overlooks the problems of cheating in coursework by pupils, parents and their teachers (Meadows & Black, B., 2018), which are exacerbated by the accountability pressures that teachers are under, access to model answers or bespoke coursework for sale on the internet and the instrumental approach to learning that has been fostered by economic models of education.

Concluding remarks: Theoretical underpinnings for formative assessment

As discussed above, a theoretical model of formative assessment is required to provide a framework for teachers and researchers alike, so that they know how their practices fit within a wider way of thinking. As Perrenoud (1998: 95) put it,

> Without a theoretical model of the mediations through which an interactive situation influences cognition, and in particular the learning process, we can observe thousands of situations without being able to draw any conclusions.

The practice of formative assessment was initially characterized as aligned with socio-cognitive models of learning, but in later years, Black and Wiliam have turned towards sociocultural models. The socio-cognitive approach emphasized learners' sense-making of the learning objectives, as opposed to previous behaviourist traditions in which learners were simply the recipients of information. In sociocultural views of assessment, it is seen as a cultural activity with its own practices and norms. Learning, in this model, is a negotiated activity with knowledge being co-constructed by the teacher and learner. Thus, it is influenced by the cultural, social and political norms of the educational situation in which it is conducted. Still, some argue that consideration of the social norms has not gone far enough in Paul's work and that in many ways his writing situates learning as something that happens in the head, rather than seeing it as part of cultural practice (Elwood, 2006).

These academic debates continue, from which Paul has never shied away. He has also always been engaged with policymakers, politicians and educationalists. His quiet and respectful style has impressed all those he has worked with and the thousands he has spoken to. The dilemma now is how to reinvigorate these debates and integrate them with post-Covid policies on 'differential learning', 'learning loss' and 'catch-up'.

This is a story in which we've learned from every chapter. As educationalists who have been profoundly influenced by Paul's work and example, we say, 'Thank you, Paul.'

References

Bennett, R. E. (2011). 'Formative assessment: A critical review'. *Assessment in Education: Principles, Policy and Practice*, 18(1): 5–25.

Black, P. (1997). *Testing: Friend or Foe? Theory and Practice of Assessment and Testing*. London: Routledge.

Black, P. & D. Wiliam (1998a). 'Assessment and classroom learning'. *Assessment in Education, Principles, Policy and Practice*, 5(1): 7–71.

Black, P. & D. Wiliam (1998b). *Inside the Black Box: Raising Standards through Classroom Assessment*. London: Kings College.

Black, P. & D. Wiliam (1998c). 'Inside the black box: Raising standards through classroom assessment'. *Phi Delta Kappan*, 80(2): 139–48.

Black, P., C. Harrison, C. Lee, B. Marshall & D. Wiliam (2002). *Working inside the Black Box*. London: Department of Education and Professional Studies, King's College London.

Black, P. & D. Wiliam (2003). 'In praise of educational research': Formative assessment'. *British Educational Research Journal*, 29(5): 623–37.

Black, P., C. Harrison, C. Lee, B. Marshall & D. Wiliam (2003). *Assessment for Learning: Putting It into Practice*. Maidenhead: Open University Press.

Black, P. & D. Wiliam (2009). 'Developing the theory of formative assessment'. *Educational Assessment, Evaluation and Accountability*, 21(1): 5–31. https://doi.org/10.1007/s11092-008-9068-5

Black, P. & D. Wiliam (2018). 'Classroom assessment and pedagogy'. *Assessment in Education: Principles, Policy & Practice*, 25(6): 551–75. DOI: 10.1080/0969594X.2018.1441807

Boekaerts, M., S. Maes & P. Karoly (2005). 'Self-regulation across domains of applied psychology: Is there an emerging consensus?' *Applied Psychology*, 54(2): 149–54.

Condie, R., K. Livingston & L. Seagraves (2005). *The Assessment Is for Learning Programme: An Evaluation*. Edinburgh: Scottish Executive Education Department, 9 June 2014. http://www.scotland.gov.uk/Publications/2005/12/0792641/26439

Crooks, T. J. (1988). 'The impact of classroom evaluation practices on students'. *Review of Educational Research*, 58(4): 438–81.

Elwood, J. (2006). 'Gender issues in testing and assessment'. In C. Skelton, B. Francis & L. Smulyan (Eds.), *The SAGE Handbook on Gender and Education*, 262–78. London: Sage.

Fuchs, L. S. & D. Fuchs (1986). 'Effects of systematic formative evaluation: A meta-analysis'. *Exceptional Children*, 53: 199–208.

Gamlem, S. V. & K. Smith (2013). 'Student perceptions of classroom feedback'. *Assessment in Education: Principles, Policy & Practice*, 20(2): 150–69. DOI: 10.1080/0969594X.2012.749212

George Street Research (2007). *Assessment of Learning Evaluation. Final Report for Learning and Teaching Scotland*, 5 July 2012. http://wayback.archiveit.org/1961/20100730140426/http://www.ltscotland.org.uk/publications/e/publication_tcm4509473.asp?strReferringChannel=assess

Grek, S. (2009). 'Governing by numbers: The PISA "effect" in Europe'. *Journal of Education Policy*, 24(1): 23–37. DOI: 10.1080/02680930802412669

Hallam, S., A. Kirton, J. Pfeffers, P. Robertson & G. Stobart (2003). *Interim Report of the Evaluation of Programme 1 of the Assessment Is for Learning Development Programme: Support for Professional Practice in Formative Assessment*. London: Institute of Education, University of London, 9 June 2014. http://www.scotland.gov.uk/Publications/2004/10/19947/42989

Hayward, L. & E. Spencer (2010). 'The complexities of change: Formative assessment in Scotland'. *Curriculum Journal*, 21: 161–77.

Johnson, S. (2011). *A Focus on Teacher Assessment Reliability in GCSE and GCE*. Coventry: Office of Qualifications and Examination Regulation (OFQUAL).

Martinez, J. G. R. & N. C. Martinez (1992). 'Re-examining repeated testing and teacher effects in a remedial mathematics course'. *British Journal of Educational Psychology*, 62: 356–63.

Meadows, M. & B. Black (2018). 'Teachers' experience of and attitudes toward activities to maximise qualification results in England'. *Oxford Review of Education*, 44(5): 563–80. DOI: 10.1080/03054985.2018.1500355

Natriello, G. (1987). 'The impact of evaluation processes on students'. *Educational Psychologist*, 22: 155–75.

Perrenoud, P. (1998). 'From formative evaluation to a controlled regulation of learning processes: Towards a conceptual field'. *Assessment in Education: Principles, Policy & Practice*, 5(1): 85–102. DOI: 10.1080/0969595980050105

Sadler, R. (1989). 'Formative assessment and the design of instructional systems'. *Instructional Science*, 18: 119–14.

Scottish Council for Research in Education (1995). *Taking a Closer Look: Key Ideas in Diagnostic Assessment*. Edinburgh: Scottish Council for Research in Education.

Senge, P. & O. Scharmer (2001). 'Community action research: Learning as a community of practitioners'. In P. Reason & H. Bradbury (Eds.), *Handbook of Action Research: Participative Inquiry and Practice*, 238–49. London: Sage.

Slavin, R. E. (1991). 'Synthesis of research on cooperative learning'. *Educational Leadership*, 48(5): 71–82.

SOED (1991). *National Guidelines: 5–14 Assessment: Improving the Quality of Learning and Teaching*. Edinburgh: HMSO.

SOED (1992). *National Guidelines: Reporting 5–14*. Edinburgh: HMSO.

Tittle, C. K. (1994). 'Toward an educational-psychology of assessment for teaching and learning – theories, contexts, and validation arguments'. *Educational Psychologist*, 29: 149–62.

Van der Kleij, F., L. A. Adie & J. J. Cumming (2019). 'A meta-review of the student role in feedback'. *International Journal of Educational Research*, 98: 303–23.

Wiliam, D., C. Lee, C. Harrison & P. Black (2004). 'Teachers developing assessment for learning: Impact on student achievement'. *Assessment in Education: Principles, Policy and Practice*, 11(1): 49–66.

5

Unifying the Purposes of Teacher Assessment

Wynne Harlen

Introduction

The theory and practice of formative assessment owe much to the work of Paul Black and his colleagues over the past forty or so years. Several aspects of this work are discussed in this chapter, beginning with the possible origin of the use of the term 'formative assessment' and some recent definitions. Definitions, however, only identify the actions involved in the process, that is, the features that make an assessment event formative. We need to go further than this to begin to understand how the process of formative assessment brings about improvement in learning, which is its declared purpose. For this, we consider the component parts of the process and how they are combined in attempts to produce a theory, or model, of the process that can begin to tackle questions such as how can assessment help learning? How do the components of formative assessment, identified in research projects and reviews, come together in synergy to improve learners' achievement? The development of theory that can answer these questions is still ongoing, spurred by the ambition to combine the features of formative assessment with those of established good pedagogical practice into an overall model of assessment, pedagogy and curriculum content.

The possible relationship between formative and summative assessment is a major focus of later sections. Since all assessment in education is a process of collecting, interpreting and using evidence of learning outcomes for some purpose, formative assessment and summative assessment are terms used for the same process carried out for different purposes. Consideration of similarities and differences between assessment used for these different purposes suggests that there is an asymmetrical relationship between them; while evidence gathered for formative use can be accumulated and, with important conditions, used for summative reporting, evidence intended for summative use is insufficiently detailed to be used formatively. However, it is argued that these purposes of assessment are not entirely distinct from each other. Rather, they are at opposite ends of a continuum from being mainly formative to being mainly summative with a certain assessment event falling somewhere along this continuum. What this implies is that there can be a formative element in any assessment in education and so, to some degree, all assessment has the potential to improve learning.

Development of the concept of formative assessment

The formative use of assessment is one of the key features of good practice in twenty-first-century education, but its practice is by no means of recent origin. It was implied in the work of Dewey, Froebel, Rousseau and Pestalozzi and in the concept of 'matching' learning activities to children's existing ideas, as spelled out in the influential Plowden report in England (CACE, 1976: para 533). These sources, in different ways, advocated a number of features of what has become known as formative assessment: finding out (by observing, listening, questioning) about the ideas and understanding students already have; what this means in terms of where students have reached in the progress towards the goals of their learning and feeding back this information into decisions about how to help students take the next steps in their learning. The key point here is the use by teachers and students of assessment data for making decisions about how to help further progress.

How this process came to be given the label 'formative assessment' is sometimes thought (e.g. Dolin et al., 2018) to be connected to the explosion in curriculum development in the mid-twentieth century. In the post–Second World War years, the need to review and update what students were taught was realized most acutely in relation to mathematics and science, in what Atkin and Black (2003: 27) describe as the 'post-Sputnik reform'. It soon spread to other subject disciplines, opening up the new academic fields of curriculum development, evaluation and assessment. The relatively large sums that were then being invested in the creation of new teaching and learning materials – and controversy about some of the innovative approaches being advocated – prompted calls for information about the impact and results of using the new resources. The evaluation of curriculum innovations became a growing area of activity among educational researchers. While evidence of impact on students' learning was expected and sought, it was also important to be sure that the new materials were in fact providing opportunities for students to achieve the intended learning outcomes. Two different purposes for collecting data from trials of the new materials were thus identified: to provide information about the use and content of the materials to improve its quality and to report on the effect on students' learning. The first of these was described as 'formative evaluation', leaving the term 'summative evaluation' to refer to judging the effect of the final product. Such a distinction between formative and summative is relevant to other kinds of data and it was readily transferred to different purposes of collecting and using data about students' performance and achievement.

Possibly the most significant use of the term 'formative' in the context of student assessment was in the report of the Task Group on Assessment and Testing (TGAT), set up by the Department of Education and Science and the Welsh Office in 1988 to advise on the assessment and testing within the national curriculum. The Task Group, which was chaired by Paul Black, stated in its report:

> [T]he results (of national assessment) should provide a basis for decisions about pupil learning needs: they should be formative.
>
> (DES/WO, 1988: para 5)

Definitions

It is convenient for some purposes to make a distinction between assessment and evaluation; using the term 'assessment' to refer to judgements of learners' achievements and 'evaluation' for judgements about teachers, teaching, educational materials and policies, etc., as suggested in OECD reports (for example Nusche et al., 2012: 24). However, in many countries, especially the United States, the terms are used interchangeably. Furthermore, some languages use the same words for assessment and evaluation, and the context has to be used to makes clear which is meant.

To underline its role in developing learning, formative assessment is also known as assessment for learning (AfL), with summative assessment alternatively named as assessment of learning (AoL). Various definitions confirm that formative assessment and AfL refer to similar concepts, simply placing slightly different emphasis on key features of the construct. For example, the definition offered by the Assessment Reform Group (ARG) in 2002 lays emphasis on use by learners and teachers and on having learning intentions in mind:

> Formative assessment is the process of seeking and interpreting evidence for use by learners and their teachers to decide where the learners are in their learning, where they need to go and how best to get there.
>
> (ARG, 2002)

In their definition Black and Wiliam (2009) emphasize that what makes an assessment formative is how it is used, not what form it takes, and so any assessment designed to promote learning can be formative:

> Assessment for learning is any assessment for which the first priority in its design and practice is to serve the purpose of promoting pupils' learning. It is thus different from assessment designed primarily to serve the purposes of accountability, or of ranking, or certifying competences.
>
> (Black & Wiliam, 2009: 9)

And:

> Practice in a classroom is formative to the extent that evidence about student achievement is elicited, interpreted, and used by teachers, learners, or their peers, to make decisions about the next steps in instruction that are likely to be better, or better founded, than the decisions they would have taken in the absence of the evidence that was elicited.
>
> (Black & Wiliam, 2009)

Modelling formative assessment

Statements such as those above identify the purpose of formative assessment but not how the parts of the process combine to make changes in the learning environment that improve learning opportunities. What these events are, and the connections between them, is better conveyed diagrammatically than in prose. Figure 5.1 depicts the process as a repeating cycle of connected events. An early version of this (Harlen, 2006: 87) has been adapted in various publications since (e.g. Harlen & Qualter, 2018). It was extended in Dolin et al. (2018: 57) to indicate how assessment data can be used for both formative and summative purposes.

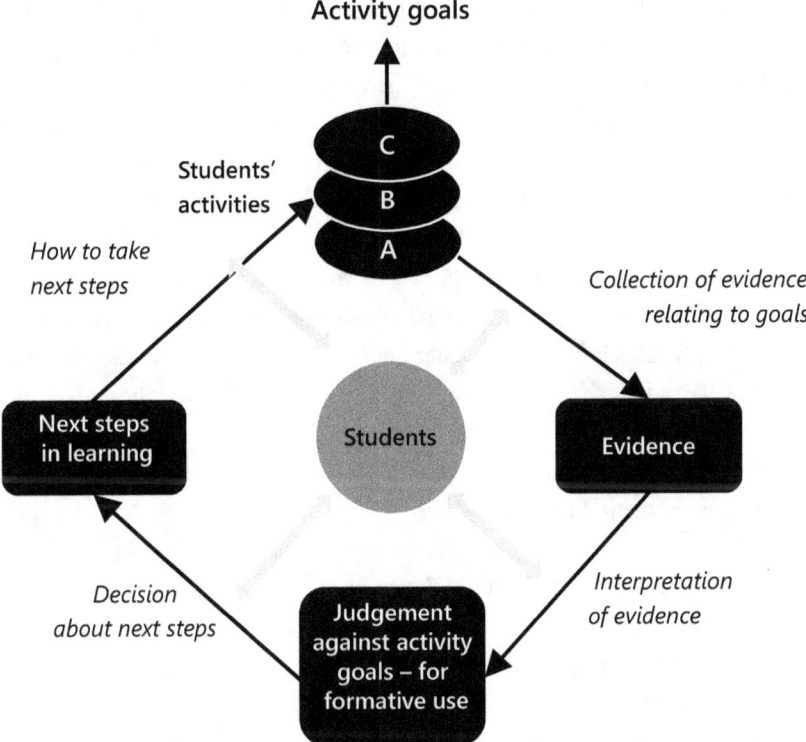

Figure 5.1 Formative assessment as a cycle of events.

Figure 5.1 represents a continuing cyclic process in a clockwise direction that involves teachers and students in

1. establishing the goals of students' activities (represented by A, B and C) and what will count as evidence of working towards them;
2. collecting evidence relating to the goals of an activity (say, A) while students are engaged in it;
3. interpreting the evidence by judging to what extent there is progress towards the learning goals of this activity;
4. using the judgement of progress, and other relevant factors such as effort and interest, to decide what next steps are appropriate;
5. making decisions about what is needed to help the student to take the next steps, leading to activity B, which may be a new experience or further development of activity A that the evidence shows is needed before moving on.

The elements in this process are not stages to be worked through, as in the stages of a lesson, but features of the actions that together move students forward in their learning. Placing the students at the centre underlines that it is students who do the learning and conveys the message that they need to be involved in all parts of the process. As the two headed arrows indicate, students are both sources of evidence about their learning and receivers of feedback that helps them take their next steps. To understand how to improve, students need to know the learning goals of their work and the standards of quality expected; with this knowledge, they can take part in assessing their progress. Positive and constructive feedback from the teacher helps them to decide and take their next steps, but if students are dependent only on their teacher for these decisions, they will not become independent learners. Actions that teachers can take to involve students in decisions about their learning, consistent with the model of formative assessment, include:

1. Helping students to understand the goals of their work.
2. Providing opportunity for students to discuss and recognize the standards they should be aiming for (what it means to do something well rather than just doing it).
3. Exploring students' current ideas, through questioning and observation.
4. Using this information to adjust teaching.
5. Giving focused feedback to illustrate how to make decisions about next steps.
6. Demonstrating confidence that all students can learn.

Empirical evidence for the power of these actions to raise levels of achievement has been uncovered in various reviews of research into classroom assessment. In addition to the seminal review by Black and Wiliam published in 1998, there have been at least fifteen substantial reviews including those by Natriello (1987), Kulik and Kulik (1989), Crooks (1988), Brookhart (2007), Hattie & Timperley (2007) and Wiliam (2009).

Similar points appear again in the activities identified by Black and Wiliam when developing a theory that brings together teaching, learning and assessment. Theory development is valuable because a theory not only identifies the parts of a system but suggests how they interact, offers explanations, and enables predictions of what may happen when changes are made (Hawking, 1988). In several publications Black and Wiliam (2006, 2009, 2012) Black and Wiliam sought to describe a theory that would bring together research evidence of the classroom assessment practices found to promote learning, as listed above, and aspects of established effective classroom practice. These practices include starting from students' existing ideas, encouraging talk, reflection and dialogue (Alexander, 2020), and scaffolding learning to enable students to take a step ahead (Vygotsky, 1978).

In 2006 Black and Wiliam used activity theory to model a classroom system having three main components: teachers, learners and the subject discipline; the teacher's role in the regulation of learning, feedback and student-teacher interaction; and the student's role. But in 2012 they wrote:

> A typical activity theory representation … contains six main elements and 15 possible interactions between them, which serves to illustrate the potential complexity and range of the issues that a broader theory would have to investigate. However, not all of the components and interactions which we now see as central fit comfortably into this scheme. We have since attempted a new approach in a more detailed discussion of some of the issues.
> (Black & Wiliam, 2012: 226/7)

One of the main aims of the 'new approach', published in Black and Wiliam (2006) and revisited in 2012, was 'to incorporate ideas about formative assessment into a comprehensive theory of pedagogy' (Black & Wiliam, 2012: 227). In pursuing this aim Black and Wiliam identified three key processes in learning and teaching:

1. Establishing where the learners are in their learning
2. Establishing where they are going
3. Establishing what needs to be done to get them there.

Consideration of the role of teacher, learner and peers in these processes led Black and Wiliam to identify a model of learning and teaching, derived from a framework proposed by Wiliam and Thompson (2007), which sets out five key aspects of formative assessment in action:

1. Clarifying and sharing learning intentions and criteria for success
2. Engineering effective classroom discussions and other learning tasks that elicit evidence of student understanding
3. Providing feedback that moves learners forward
4. Activating students as instructional resources for one another
5. Activating students as the owners of their own learning.

The practice of formative assessment, as summarized in the above five points, finds support in findings of empirical research and in theoretical arguments based on how people learn.

In relation to research, most studies have investigated one or two aspects of formative assessment rather than the impact of the whole set together. For example, a study by Fontana and Fernandes (1994) investigated the effect of involving students in regular and frequent self-assessment. Since self-assessment necessarily requires recognizing learning goals and using criteria for assessing work in relation to these goals, this study involved more than using procedures for judging progress, but it did not go as far as being able to report on a more complete range of actions related to formative assessment. Several of the studies included in the Black and Wiliam review (1998a) related to the use of mastery learning, a popular concept of the 1960s (Bloom, 1971). Those by Whiting et al. (1995) and Martinez and Martinez (1992) involved frequent testing and feedback. The results showed greater gains for groups tested more frequently but also showed that the effect was dependent on the experience of the teacher. In another example, the provision of different forms of feedback was explored in a controlled experimental study. In this frequently quoted – and sometimes challenged – study, Butler (1987) compared groups given feedback in different ways on different types of task. A study by Schunk (1996) concerned students being given goals expressed in different ways – some as learning outcomes and some as performance goals, with and without self-assessment in terms of these goals. The results suggested that the effect of self-evaluation overpowered the difference in expression of goals.

The point is that these studies, and others reviewed by Black and Wiliam (1998a), generally involved making changes in one feature of formative assessment at a time while attempting to control for other factors, raising the question of whether such studies are validly evaluating the practice of formative assessment as a whole. That is, can you claim to be practising formative assessment if you are only adopting, say, different forms of feedback, or asking students to assess their work, or ensuring that students know the goals of their work, or ... ? Does it require all the component parts of the formative assessment cycle to be in operation in order to study the impact of formative assessment?

Just posing these questions reflects an instrumental view of formative assessment – as a particular collection of separate actions or tools – as opposed to a process view. In a process view, each of the actions in the formative assessment cycle is regarded as being imbued with a shared view of learning and values which can have an impact on students' achievement. Thus any or all of the component actions can improve learning and findings of studies such as those just mentioned can be taken as due to the impact of formative assessment. Attempts have been made to estimate the extent of this impact by Black and Wiliam (1998b) and by Leahy and Wiliam (2012) who concluded:

> The general finding is that a range of different school subjects, in different countries, and for learners of different ages, the use of formative assessment appears to be associated with considerable improvements in the rate of learning. Estimating how big these gains might be is difficult ... but it seems reasonable to conclude that use of formative assessment can increase the rate of student learning by some 50 to 100%.
> (Leahy & Wiliam, 2012: 19)

Theoretical arguments in support of formative assessment follow from the view of learning embedded in its practice. This is consistent with the widely held social constructivist view that emphasizes the role of learners constructing their understanding through working with others rather than individually. In a collaborative group, an individual learner takes from a shared experience what is needed to help his or her understanding and communicates the result as an input into the group discussion. There is a constant to-ing and fro-ing from individual to group as knowledge is constructed together through social interaction and dialogue. Physical resources and language also have important roles in this process (James & Lewis, 2012: 192/3). Regarding learning as a social and collaborative activity recognizes the value of talk. But this is not the only way in which we learn from others; in classrooms, the interaction between students and between students and teacher is mostly face to face, but learning from, and with, others can be through the written word as well. Feedback in writing (marking) can be an effective channel for dialogue between teacher and student, providing that the comments take learning forward. Reading what others have written in books or blogs or other media may bring to a learner information or ideas that change or expand their own ideas.

Relationships between formative and summative assessment

The Black and Wiliam model of formative assessment was developed, as noted earlier, to provide a rationale for the activities involved in formative assessment consistent with features of existing pedagogical strategies considered to be effective in advancing learning. The model provides a rationale for the components of formative assessment and can be used to suggest how the process and its practice can be improved. But it is primarily concerned with the internal structure of formative assessment, not with the relationship of formative assessment with assessment for other purposes. For this, we return to the cyclic model in Figure 5.1. But before discussing how assessment for these purposes might be brought together – variously described as being combined, connected, coordinated, unified, linked or interrelated in some way – it is worth considering why this is desirable or necessary.

There is no doubt that formative and summative assessment both have a role in effective classroom practice. Both are needed on account of their different purposes and timing. This was made clear in the TGAT report (DES/WO, 1988: para 23) where two of the five purposes of national assessment were described as:

- formative, so that the positive achievements of a student may be recognized and discussed and the appropriate next steps taken;
- summative, for the recording of the overall achievement of a student in a systematic way.

At that time, however, there was no substantial evidence of assessment serving two distinct purposes in practice. Research (e.g. Broadfoot et al., 1992) showed that, in the immediate years after the introduction of national assessment, there was very little difference between formative and summative assessment; or rather, there was very little formative assessment. What happened, and still happens to a substantial extent, was that the better-known procedures of summative assessment overwhelmed attempts to use assessment formatively. Given the considerable efforts needed to develop practice in formative assessment – reflected, for instance, in the work described in Black et al. (2003) and Gardner et al. (2010) – it is hardly surprising that a simple statement in a formal document failed to result in what is now seen as a considerable change in pedagogy. Further, the statement in TGAT:

> It is possible to build up a comprehensive picture of the overall achievements of a pupil by aggregating, in a structured way, the separate results of a set of assessment designed to serve formative purposes
>
> (TGAT, 1988: para 25)

appeared to support the notion that formative assessment is a series of mini-summative assessments. This was reinforced by the assumption that because formative assessment is always carried out by teachers, then all teacher assessment is formative. This fails to acknowledge the different criteria for judgement that apply when evidence is used for formative and summative purposes. So there is a need to protect the practice of formative assessment from such misunderstandings and to look in more detail at the similarities as well as the differences between summative and formative assessment.

The key features of both formative and summative assessment relate to having clear goals, collecting evidence of learning, using criteria to make judgements and making some use of the result. These four features take different forms in formative and summative assessment:

1. In formative assessment, the goals are short term and specific to activities or lessons. In summative assessment, they are medium-term goals, such as stated in a school's curriculum plan for a period of time such as a semester or year, and which are achieved only through a range of experiences rather than specific lessons.
2. In formative assessment, the evidence collected and used relates to the detailed lesson goals. In summative assessment, it relates to the broader medium-term goals.
3. In formative assessment, the judgement of progress is both criterion-referenced to the lesson goals and student-referenced so that the help given is tailored to the needs of individual students. In summative assessment, in the interests of a fair result, the judgement should be strictly criterion-referenced.
4. In formative assessment, the result is used in feedback to guide students in their next steps and to adjust the teaching challenges to individual students and there may not be a need for a tangible report. In summative assessment, there is generally a record of some kind that can be shared with students, parents and teachers.

It follows from these differences that there is an unequal relationship between assessment for formative and summative purposes. The results of summative assessment lack the detail to be used formatively. In contrast, the more detailed evidence from day-to-day activities, extracted from the 'evidence' box in Figure 5.1, can be accumulated from lesson to lesson and brought together for reporting achievement over a period of time. But this process is not a matter of simple aggregation. It must take account of the different criteria used in making judgements. It means that, if evidence collected from ongoing activities and used formatively to help learning is also to be used for summative reporting, it must be *reinterpreted* in the same way for all students against the medium-term goals of achievement.

Basing summative assessment on evidence collected over time by teachers recognizes that regular class activities that enable learners to develop understanding and competencies are at the same time opportunities for collecting evidence about progress in their learning. The whole curriculum, if it can be taught, can in theory be assessed without the narrowing effect of focusing on what can be tested. Teachers can use evidence from a wider range of activities and observations than can readily be covered by a test. Further, students are not subject to the anxiety that accompanies tests and can be given some role in the process. These properties increase the validity of the result, meaning the accuracy of the inferences that can be made about students' capabilities (Messick, 1989).

At the same time, summative judgements need to be reliable, that is, as accurate as possible, and repeatable. This is where there is a further difference between formative and summative assessments, as noted by Dolin et al. (2018):

> In the case of formative assessment, reliability is often lower, and it matters less than for summative assessment. This is because the notion of making a repeatable judgement and treating all students in the same way is not equally relevant when the purpose is to support well founded decisions about next steps for students who may be at different stages in their learning.
>
> (Dolin, 2018:64)

The emphasis on using evidence in this discussion is important. As noted above and in the earlier discussion of Figure 5.1, page 67, formative assessment judgements may not be strictly criterion-referenced but take account of the circumstances that affect individuals or groups of students. It is entirely appropriate for this to be the case in formative assessment since it means that students have the tailored support they need to take them from where they are towards the activity goals. But evidence used to report on learning for summative purposes must be judged against the same criteria for all students, not influenced by factors which apply only to certain students or by how individual teachers interpret the criteria. That is, assessment for summative purposes needs high reliability as well as high validity. Hence it is important that procedures for summative assessment by teachers include some measures for ensuring optimum reliability.

There are several ways in which the reliability of teachers' summative judgements can be increased, common ones being the use of exemplars of student' work and some form of group moderation. The most useful exemplars take the form of a collection of examples of students' work and observations of their actions, annotated to highlight aspects which indicate the extent of agreement with the relevant learning goals or criteria. This enables teachers to apply similar standards of judgement to the work of their own students. Since teachers will be basing their judgements on a range of each student's work, it is most useful if exemplars include several pieces from the same student, illustrating what it means to apply criteria holistically across different activities.

Group moderation involves meetings of teachers and others involved in making summative judgements to share examples of their assessment of their students' work and discuss their interpretations of learning goals and outcomes. Group moderation of teachers' summative judgements of learners at the end of year six and year nine involving clusters of primary and secondary schools has been practised in Wales since 2006 when externally marked tests at these ages were discontinued. Research (Estyn, 2016) shows that group moderation has benefits beyond the reliability of the assessment results, particularly for professional development in understanding the assessment process.

Although described as formative or summative according to the purpose it serves, an assessment event often has some element of both, lying somewhere along a continuum of purposes from mainly formative to mainly summative (Harlen, 2012: 98). Just where it fits depends on the actual use of the result. For formative assessment there is one main use, to help learning. Indeed, by definition, if the information is not used in this way, the assessment can hardly be called formative. By contrast, the result of summative assessment can be used in several ways: some relating to individual students, such as reporting to parents, tracking progress, selection, certification and accreditation; others relating to the performance of groups of students, for school evaluation and national monitoring (Newton, 2007).

In some circumstances, the use of the result of summative assessment can be moved along the dimension of purposes towards the formative end. Black et al. (2003) provide examples of techniques for doing this that were devised by teachers in response to the advice to focus on formative and 'steer clear of summative assessment because of the negative influence of summative assessment on formation practice' (Black et al., 2003: 53). Teachers, faced with the reality of the established role of tests classroom, could not accept this advice. Instead, they found various ways in which the preparation for tests and review and reflection on results added to the learning process.

Conclusion: Several routes, a single purpose?

To go further and suggest that all summative assessment and testing can serve some formative purpose may seem to be stretching a point. What about, for example, national or international surveys of achievement, where there is no possibility of immediate feedback to the students or teachers? But even there in the long term such survey results can and should be used to improve the learning conditions and opportunities of students in the future. Otherwise, why would governments provide the considerable funding that such surveys require?

These arguments lead to the proposition of a principle that the results of any assessment have the potential of having some formative purpose and that

> assessment of any kind should ultimately improve learning.
>
> (Harlen, 2010: 31)

This does not mean that the distinction between formative and summative assessment is not necessary. Knowing whether the purpose of an assessment event is mainly formative or mainly summative is important for teachers and students and can influence the behaviour of both (Dolin et al., 2018: 71). Further, awareness of the different characteristics of formative and summative assessment events is necessary to ensure that the opportunities for formative use are recognized and seized and that assessment can indeed be used to help learning.

References

Alexander, R. (2020). *A Dialogic Teaching Companion.* London: Routledge.

Assessment Reform Group (ARG) (1999). *Assessment for Learning. Beyond the Black Box.* Cambridge: Cambridge School of Education.

Assessment Reform Group (ARG) (2002). *Assessment for Learning 10 Principles.* https://www.researchgate.net/publication/271849158_Assessment_for_Learning_10_Principles_Research-based_principles_to_guide_classroom_practice_Assessment_for_Learning

Atkin, J. M. & P. Black (2003), *Inside Science Education Reform.* Buckingham: Open University Press.

Black, P. (1993), 'Formative and summative assessment by teachers'. *Studies in Science Education*, 21: 49–97.

Black, P. & D. Wiliam (1998a). 'Assessment and classroom learning'. *Assessment in Education*, 5(1): 7–74.

Black, P. & D. Wiliam (1998b). *Inside the Black Box.* London: King's College London School of Education.

Black, P., C. Harrison, C. Lee, B. Marshall & D. Wiliam (2003). *Assessment for Learning Putting It into Practice*. Maidenhead: Open University Press.

Black, P., R. McCormick, M. James & D. Peddar (2006). 'Learning how to learn and assessment for learning: A theoretical inquiry'. *Research Papers in Education*, 21(2): 119–32.

Black, P. & D. Wiliam (2006). 'Developing a theory of formative assessment'. In J. Gardner (Ed.), *Assessment and Learning*, 81–100. London: Sage.

Black, P. & D. Wiliam (2009). 'Developing the theory of formative assessment'. *Educational Assessment Evaluation and Accountability*, 21(1): 5–31.

Black, P. & D. Wiliam (2012). 'Developing a theory of formative assessment'. In J. Gardner (Ed.), *Assessment and Learning*, 2nd edn, 206–30. London: Sage.

Bloom, B.S. (1971). 'Mastery learning'. In J. H. Block (Ed.), *Mastery Learning, Theory and Practice*. New York: Holt, Rinehart and Winston.

Broadfoot, P., B. Dockrell, C. Gipps, W. Harlen & D. Nuttall, Eds. (1992). *Policy Issues in National Assessment*. Clevedon: Multilingual Matters.

Brookhart, S. M. (2007). 'Expanding views about formative classroom assessment: A review of the literature'. In J. H. McMillan (Ed.), *Formative Classroom Assessment: Theory into Practice*, 43–62. New York: Teachers College Press.

Butler, R. (1987). 'Task-involving and ego-involving properties of evaluation: Effects of different feedback conditions on motivational perceptions, interest and performance'. *Journal of Educational Psychology*, 79: 474–82.

CACE (Central Advisory Council for Education) (1976). *Children and Their Primary Schools* (Plowden Report). London: HMSO.

Crooks, T. J. (1988), 'The impact of classroom evaluation practices on students'. *Review of Educational Research*, 58: 438–81.

Department of Education and Science and Welsh Office (1988), *Task Group on Assessment and Testing. A Report*. London: DES.

Dolin, J., P. Black, W. Harlen & A. Tiberghien (2018). 'Exploring relations between formative and summative assessment'. In J. Dolin & R. Evans (Eds.), *Transforming Assessment*. Switzerland: Springer.

Estyn (2016). *Moderation of Teacher Assessment at KS2 and KS3: A Review of Accuracy and Consistency*. Cardiff: Estyn.

Fontana, D. & M. Fernandes (1994). 'Improvements in mathematics performance as a consequence of self-assessment in Portuguese primary school pupils'. *British Journal of Educational Psychology*, 64: 407–17.

Gardner, J., W. Harlen, L. Hayward, G. Stobart with M. Montgomery (2010). *Developing Teacher Assessment*. Maidenhead: McGraw-Hill.

Harlen, W. (2006). *Teaching, Learning and Assessing Science 5–12*. London: Sage.

Harlen, W. (2007). *Assessment of Learning*. London: Sage.

Harlen, W. (2010). 'Professional learning to support teacher assessment'. In J. Gardner, W. Harlen, L. Hayward, G. Stobart with M. Montgomery *Developing Teacher Assessment*, 100–29. Maidenhead: McGraw-Hill Education.

Harlen, W. & J. Gardner (2010). 'Assessment to support learning'. In J. Gardner, W. Harlen, L. Hayward, G. Stobart with M. Montgomery, *Developing Teacher Assessment*, 15–28. Maidenhead: McGraw-Hill Education.

Harlen, W. (2012). 'On the relationship between assessment for formative and summative purposes'. In J. Gardner (Ed.), *Assessment and Learning*, 2nd edn, 87–102. London: Sage.

Harlen, W. & A. Qualter (2018), *The Teaching of Science in Primary Schools* 7th edn, Abingdon: Routledge.

Hattie, J. & H. Timperley (2007). 'The power of feedback'. *Review of Educational Research*, 77: 81–112.

Hawking, S. W. (1988). *A Brief History of Time*. London: Bantam Books.

James, M. & J. Lewis (2012). 'Assessment in harmony with our understanding of learning: Problems and possibilities'. In J. Gardner (Ed.), *Assessment and Learning*, 2nd edn, 186–206. London: Sage.

Kulik, C. L. & J. A. Kulik (1989). 'Mastery testing and student learning: A meta-analysis'. *Journal of Educational Technology Systems*, 15: 325–45.

Leahy, S. & D. Wiliam (2012). 'From teachers to schools: Scaling up professional development for formative assessment'. In J. Gardner (Ed.), *Assessment for Learning*, 2nd edn, 48–72. London: Sage.

Martinez, J. G. R. & N. C. Martinez (1992). 'Re-examining repeated testing and teacher effects in a remedial mathematics course'. *British Journal of Educational Psychology*, 62: 356–63.

Messick, S. (1989), 'Validity'. In R. L. Linn (Ed.), *Educational Measurement*, 3rd edn, 12–103. London: Collier MacMillan.

Natriello, G. (1987). 'The impact of evaluation processes on students'. *Educational Psychologist*, 22(2): 155–75.

Newton, P. E. (2007). 'Clarifying the purposes of educational assessment'. *Assessment in Education*, 14(2): 149–70.

Nusche, D., D. Laveault, J. MacBeath & P. Santiago (2012). *Reviews of Evaluation and Assessment: New Zealand 2011*. Paris: OECD.

Schunk, D. H. (1996). 'Goal and self-evaluative influences during children's cognitive skill learning'. *American Educational Research Journal*, 33: 359–82.

Vygotsky, L. S. (1978). 'Interaction between learning and development'. In L. S. Vygotsky, *Mind in Society*, 79–91. Cambridge, MA: Harvard University Press.

Whiting, B., J. W. Van Burgh & G. F. Render (1995). 'Mastery learning in the classroom', paper presented at the Annual Meeting of the AERA San Francisco 1995.

Wiliam, D. (2009). 'An integrative summary of the research literature and implications for a new theory of formative assessment'. In H. L. Andrade & G. J. Cizek (Eds.), *Handbook of Formative Assessment*. New York: Taylor and Francis. Chapter 2.

Wiliam, D. & M. Thompson (2007), 'Integrating assessment with instruction: What will it take to make it work?' In C. A Dwyer (Ed.), *The Future of Assessment: Shaping Teaching and Learning*, 53–82. NJ: Lawrence Erlbaum Associates.

6

The Revolutionary International Transformation of Educational Assessment

Rick Stiggins

Introduction

This volume provides a wide variety of testimonials to Paul Black's contributions to our collective understanding of the meaning of sound assessment practice. Chapter authors detail his impacts on research, scholarship and leadership in assessment; learning and cognition; teacher development; and educational policy as all of those contributions have spanned the globe. But the story I wish to tell goes in a very different direction. I intend to illustrate the impact of Black's work on the actual learning lives of students and teachers as they use classroom assessment in pursuit of academic success in their very real classrooms.

This part of the story is important because it reveals the profound classroom-level effect of the groundbreaking classroom assessment work of Paul Black, Dylan Wiliam and others. I hope the telling and retelling of the tale of their leadership and the classroom stories I share herein will encourage practising educators at all levels from the boardroom to the classroom to invest in, learn about, embrace and implement a new vision of excellence in assessment: a vision that transforms assessment from being merely a measure of learning into being one of the *causes* of that learning; a vision of excellence in assessment that offers educators an opportunity for direct and positive impact on student learning success and their sense of academic well-being.

The UK researchers shifted the assessment focus from school improvement via large-scale standardized summative testing to the promise of greater student learning success via improved formative classroom assessments FOR learning. Both foci are important, but only one has proven its ability actually to increase student achievement. Perhaps most importantly, Paul's work has changed our sense of the student's role in assessment from the student as the object (victim) of assessment to student as an important user of assessment results as they learn to take charge of their own learning success.

A journey of discovery

My knowledge to this body of work began at the annual meeting of the American Educational Research Association in 1999. In conversation with a colleague about the assessment literacy focus of our new Assessment Training Institute (ATI), I mentioned our very exploratory work in what we were calling 'student-centered classroom assessment'. My colleague immediately suggested that I examine Paul Black's work at King's College, London, on 'assessment for learning'. I confessed to knowing nothing about that research but that I loved their label and promised to dig right into it.

Upon returning home, I studied Paul's work with Dylan Wiliam in their groundbreaking synthesis of research on the impact on student learning success of involving students in monitoring their own achievement while they are learning (Black & Wiliam, 1998a & 1998b). To our delight, we found that our tentative exploration of student-involved assessment based only on common sense is backed as it turned out by a strong international body of research. We began to rethink our professional learning programmes. Our original mission was to help practitioners become assessment literate defined as maximizing the quality of their classroom assessments (Stiggins, 1991). But now our definition of assessment literacy needed to be expanded, we thought, to help teachers learn to use the assessment process and results as an instructional tool to cause student learning.

We identified the classroom assessment practices that the UK team's research had revealed the ability to enhance student learning and we began to weaving those ideas into our learning experiences. This was a watershed time for ATI; the research conducted by Paul and his associates changed everything for us. I describe our new vision briefly in the next section.

Then from there, I will go directly into the classroom and share three illustrations that reveal what teachers do with these classroom assessment ideas once they gain access to them. Considered together, these stories reveal the transformation of classroom assessment environments from (a) an accountability cultures where assessment is merely the source of anxiety and evidence for grading to (b) learning culture where assessment provides the pathway to confidence, motivation and learning success for all students and to greater professional fulfilment for their teachers. In these classrooms, Paul's contributions come alive.

A vision of excellence in classroom assessment

Assessment is the process of gathering information to inform educational decisions. Sound instructional decisions depend on the quality of the information upon which they are based. To be truly effective, the assessor must do the following in order:

- Begin the assessment process with a *clear sense of purpose*; that is, with a clear understanding of who will use the results to inform what decisions. The assessment must be capable of providing that specific information.
- Begin the process with a clear vision and understanding of the *learning target*(s) to be assessed. The assessment exercises and scoring schemes must reflect those targets dependably.
- Once the assessment context is defined in terms of purpose and target, then the assessor must develop or select a *high-quality assessment* capable of providing the needed information. The dependability of the evidence rests on the quality of the assessment.
- Once the assessment is conducted, the results must be *effectively communicated* to the intended user in a timely and understandable manner. Dependable evidence miscommunicated is wasted.

Each of these standards can be broken down into more specific practices within them that are required to achieve excellence in assessment. These standards and their sub-practices must be met by all assessment users in all contexts. *This includes teachers as they develop and use classroom assessments.*

But what is crucial about the work of Paul Black and his associates is that they have added another dimension to the definition of good practice that is unique to teachers. They have charged teachers with professional responsibility for using assessments effectively in a variety of different ways.

Some classroom decision contexts require *summative* judgements about the sufficiency of student learning in relation to expectations. The report card grading process represents the clearest example of this. But other far more frequent classroom assessment contexts require that teacher make *formative decisions* that use assessment results to adjust instruction on the fly (while students are learning) in ways that lead to greater student learning success.

In formative assessment contexts, teachers can invite students to partner with them in pursuit of students learning success. In effect, when teachers use assessment in this manner, they use assessment FOR learning; that is, to bring students into this process as active data-based instructional decision-makers capable of co-managing their own learning.

The addition of students to the formative assessment team opens the doors to their involvement in all aspects of quality assessment listed and described above:

- When articulating *assessment purpose*, teachers need to add their students to the list of decision-makers and anticipate how assessment can serve their information needs. If presented properly, this information can help students decide what comes next in their learning and what to do about it.
- When *clarifying learning targets*, teachers can provide students with student-friendly versions of important targets from the very beginning of instruction. This understanding can help students see the pathway to their own success and track their own progress as they travel. This is a confidence builder.
- When *building formative assessments* that provide dependable evidence of student achievement status, one must attend, as always, to standards of quality. But beyond this, students can become partners in creating and using practice assessments like those for which they will be held accountable later on. This involvement can help them but see the target and track their own progress.
- When it comes to *effective communication*, students can be made partners with their teacher in telling the story of their own growth in, for example, student-led parent/teacher conferences. If they build growth portfolios over time, they can show their parents concrete evidence of how their work has improved over time.

Taking advantage of the positive dynamics of being assessed

To help us understand the emotional dynamics of student-involved assessment, Paul and his team directed the assessment community to the work of Sadler (1989) who advised that student learning is enhanced when students are kept continuously aware of their unique answers to three driving questions: Where am I going in my learning? Where am I now in relation to those expectations? How can I close the gap between the two?

My colleague, Jan Chappuis, has articulated specific strategies teachers can rely on to keep their students informed. To help them know where they're headed, begin instruction with a student-friendly version of the targets along with samples of strong and weak work. To stay in touch with where they are now, provide continuous access to descriptive feedback and help students learn the skills of self-assessment and goal setting. And to help them manage the narrowing of the gap, plan teaching around visible gaps in student learning, design focused instruction, and engage students in tracking, reflecting on and communication with others about their own progress (Chappuis, 2015).

If we educators are to fulfil our assigned mission of 'leaving no child behind' – of promoting much higher levels of academic success for all students – *we can no longer have any students giving up in hopelessness*. Hopelessness is the enemy of learning and it arises when the feedback students receive leads them to the conclusion that learning success is beyond reach for them – it's too late, I'm too far behind, why try? Obviously, this is a crucial emotional dynamic from the student's point of view. It robs them of a sense of control of their own learning success and increases their anxiety, another enemy of learning.

Historically, educators have operated on the belief that assessment is an act that teachers carry out on students. Teachers and administrators gather the assessment results, we have believed, and then act on them in the student's best interest. While this certainly should be (indeed, must be) a prominent part of teaching, it overlooks the reality that students interpret their own results too and make important data-based instructional decisions. The key is to understand that students get to interpret their own results and make their instructional decisions first. Students decide whether success is within reach, worth the effort required to succeed, or worth the risk of more public failure. If they come down on the wrong side of these choices, which struggling learners often do, it doesn't matter what we adults decide; the learning stops and perhaps for a very long time.

We help students build and maintain a strong sense of academic self-efficacy (control over their own chances of success) when we help them understand that they have a two-part role in day-to-day classroom assessment:

- Strive to understand what success looks like from the beginning of the learning and get help when that is not clear;
- Analyse each formative assessment for evidence of or keys to their own improvement over time.

The teacher's support role is to be sure students gain access to the evidence they need from each formative assessment to determine how they can do better the next time. The teacher's goal is to help every student get on a winning streak and know it and then help them stay there.

Illustrations of excellence in the classroom

Let me share three stories from the classroom that have been shared with me over the decades illustrating what assessment FOR learning classrooms as defined by Paul and his associates can look like. These are stories that encourage practitioners to want to learn more about quality assessment and assessment FOR learning. Each one connects to the keys to sound practice described above but especially on the new assessment role of students. Names have been altered.

A story from high school English

By way of background, Melissa, an Oregon 11th grade (students aged 15–16) English teacher, wanted to take her students through a major writing assignment built around their analysis of literature. She wanted them to learn to write literary analysis paper by actually doing it. Students were to read two pieces of literature by the same author and either (1) develop a literary question from the literature selected and answer it with evidence from the selected readings or (2) comment on the author and defend their comment with it based on the literature.

To set the context for my story, now, students have selected and read the literature and now her goal is to guide them into the writing of their theme paper.

She begins by giving them a copy of a theme paper to examine, informing them in advance that it is poorly written. Their homework assignment is to return to class the next day ready to discuss what makes this paper as bad as it is. What's wrong? What's missing? What's done poorly? Be specific.

The next day they analyse, evaluate and identify the various problems with this first example as Melissa lists them on a white board.

Next, she gives them copies of a paper that is of outstanding quality with a similar homework challenge. What makes it good? What are the keys to its effectiveness as writing?

The next day they brainstorm the strengths of the second paper. Again, the teacher serves as recorder collecting a list of positive features next to yesterday's list of problems. Then she inquires: Are there things listed as positives in one and as negatives in the other? This discussion yields a list factors that seem important in both cases, like sentence quality, punctuation, ideas expressed, word choice, organization of ideas etc.

The following day, she leads them through what she calls a 'boiling down' the long list for features into a manageable number by combining things closely related to one another. Ultimately, they agree on five key relatively independent elements that cover the truly important things, including sentence structure, organization, voice, expression etc.

On the surface, Melissa appears to be turning the definition of the learning targets over to her students. But, in fact, she deeply understands the keys to success and is bringing her students to the same level of understanding she possesses through discussion and inference. Then having done this, as things proceed, she helps them fill in details about each of the agreed-upon ingredients of quality work. Here's how:

She divides the class into five teams of five and assigns each team one of the keys with a two-part assignment: (1) rely on appropriate resources to develop a definition of their key and then (2) draft a scale or continuum of quality for their key: What does their assigned key to effective writing look like when it's done very well, when it's done poorly, and how would you describe mid-range performance? Their next assignment due by the end of the week is to be ready to present the results of their team's work (definition and evaluation scale) to the rest of class for discussion and refinement.

Next week, teams take turns sharing their definitions and levels of quality, debating and refining the keys. In effect, they are both finalizing and learning (hopefully mastering) **in advance** *the standards of quality that will guide and determine the quality of their theme papers. The result is five clear and agreed-upon definitions and performance continuums for the features of writing that (1) can guide their evaluation and revision of their work as they write, and (2) will guide Ms Ridley's evaluations of their work when it's done. Every student receives a copy of those standards.*

Please note that this multi-step brainstorming discussion is carried out under the knowing leadership of an experienced and competent writer, Ms Ridley. She is guiding her students to a clear understanding of the definition of their own success. Finally, note we're a few days into this project and no one has written a word of their paper yet! But now everyone is really ready.

Now Melissa releases students to write. They go to work identifying their theme or assertion, tapping the literature for supportive references as needed, and composing their papers. As they go, Melissa keeps reminding them to tune into the keys to their success. Further, she informs them that in-class and homework time can be spend sharing their evolving work with classmates and giving each other feedback on how to improve the work. They even are invited to ask for clarification of keys or evaluation of some element of their drafts from their teacher if they wish. This sharply focused interactive work went on until the papers were done and submitted to Ms Ridley for evaluation and grading. And throughout the process, Melissa continuously encouraged students to notice and communicate with each other about changes in the quality of their work and in their confidence as a writer.

It is interesting to speculate on the individual and collective quality of the resulting papers. That quality probably was pretty good and the students knew this when they submitted them. And from Melissa's point of view, this was a product-based performance assessment carried out according to standards of good assessment practice. Therefore, clearly defensible grades can be assigned to each paper based on the agreed-upon evaluation scales.

But, in a deeper sense, the benefits that result from this student/teacher collaboration extend far beyond the successful completion of one theme paper assignment. These students developed the ability to evaluate and produce good writing – a critical lifelong learner skill. And in the process, *they gained confidence in themselves as managers of their own academic well-being.*

A story of effective communication of assessment results

This story came to me from Anne Davies of British Columbia, Canada, a devout student of Paul Black's work and one of my earliest teachers in the realm of assessment FOR learning.

To set the stage, Ms Murphy has decided to engage her students as partners in telling the story of their own growth by replacing traditional parent-teacher conferences with student-led conferences. She has prepared her students for success in telling their own stories by doing the following:

- Basing her instruction on very clear learning targets, which she shared with students from the outset of instruction
- Developing high-quality assessments of those targets
- Engaging students in ongoing self-assessment as they learned helping them not only to understand the learning targets but also to develop the vocabulary needed to tell the story of their growth
- Having each student build a growth portfolio full of examples of her or his work as it changed over time to present to and discuss with parents

- Giving students class time to practise their conference presentations with one another; this not only helped them improve their presentation skills but also set them to be ready to think long term about their learning gains.

Here, then is what happened:
The student-led conferences are scheduled for the late afternoon and staggered so that there were three or four families in meetings in the classroom at a time. Students welcome their family members as they arrived, introduce them to Ms Murphy, retrieve their growth portfolios from the file and usher their family to a designated table. Ms Murphy circulates among the tables as students give their presentation, sharing their work, describing problems with their early work and how much it improves in later samples, discussing the reasons for their progress with their families. She contributes to the discussions as needed.

As they are leaving, Ms Murphy meets them at the door and thanks them for coming. Last to leave is Grandma, who simply clasps Ms Murphy's hand with a tear in her eye and says 'thank you' in English. When they are gone, Ms Murphy comments to her student on his use of Spanish and asks him how the conference had gone. The student replies that it went really well and it was fun! He adds that, when his family talks about really important things and Grandma is involved, they speak in Spanish to include and honour her. Ms Murphy could see how proud his family was of him.

This, I submit, is truly effective communication of assessment results. Everyone involved understood or came to understand the meaning of academic success. It was OK for students not to be good at particular tasks at the beginning of instruction because they were just getting started. Ms Murphy helped them understand the learning targets they needed to hit. Collaboration ruled here. Teacher and student were partners in the accumulation and evaluation of evidence showing changes in student performance over time. The student came to his conference with both an understanding of the targets and the vocabulary needed to talk about them with their families. But the real pride for the student came from knowing he had grown and was able to prove it to all concerned. He knew he was strong and confident.

A story of assessment FOR learning in action beyond the classroom

We share this story frequently to kick off ATI assessment FOR learning professional development programmes (Chappuis & Stiggins, 2020; Stiggins & Chappuis, 2017). The story was shared with me by a writing assessment consultant.

To set the stage in this case, visualize yourself at a particularly important meeting of the board of directors for the local schools. This is the once-a-year meeting at which the local school leaders present the annual report of standardized test scores to the board, community and local media.

What attendees this evening can't realize as the meeting begins is that, this year, they are in for a big surprise with respect to both the achievement information to be presented and the manner of the presentation. The audience includes a young woman named Emily, a junior at the high school, sitting in the back of the room with her parents. She knows she will be a big part of the surprise. She's only a little nervous. She understands how important her role is.

The school leaders begin the meeting by reminding that the standardized tests sample broad domains of achievement with just a few multiple-choice test items. They turn to carefully prepared charts depicting student scores in each important achievement category tested. Results are summarized by grade and school, concluding with a clear description of how district results had changed from the year before and from previous years. Board members ask questions and receive clarification. Some scores are down slightly; some are up. Participants discuss possible reasons. This is a routine annual presentation that proceeds as expected.

Next comes the break from routine. The presenters explain how the schools have gathered some new information about an important student skill not covered in the annual multiple-choice tests. The faculty have implemented a new writing programme to address what they know to be the weak writing skills of their students. The English faculty completed a training programme on assessing writing proficiency by evaluating actual samples of student writing and integrating such a performance rating/evaluation process into the teaching and learning.

For the next part of the evening's discussion of assessment results, the high school English department faculty shares the results of their evaluation of the new writing programme. The English chair, Ms Weatherby distributes a sample of student writing to the board members (with Emily's name removed), asking them to read and judge the quality of this writing. They do so, expressing their dismay aloud. They're indignant in their commentary on this sample of student work. The new writing programme is not working. This is weak performance. Emily's mom puts her arm around her daughter's shoulder and hugs her.

She distributes another sample of student writing, asking the board to read and evaluate it. Ah, this, they report, is more like it! This work is much better! But be specific, the chair demands. What do you like about this work? They list positive aspects: good choice of words, sound sentence structure, clever ideas and so on. Emily is ready to burst!

The reason she's so full of pride at this moment is that this has been a special year for her and her classmates. For the first time ever, they became partners with their English teacher (Ms Weathersby by the way) in watching and managing their own improvement as writers. Early in the year, Ms W (to the students) made it crystal clear to Emily that she was, in fact, not a very good writer and that just trying hard to get better was not going to be enough. She expected Emily to be better – nothing else would suffice.

Ms W started the year by helping students set high writing standards for word choice, sentence structure, organization, voice and so on. She defined each of this in student-friendly terms with examples of good- and poor-quality writing. When Emily and her teacher evaluated her first few pieces of writing using these standards, she received very low ratings that she understood and wanted to change.

But Emily also began to study samples of good writing and slowly she began to understand why they were good. The differences between these and her work started to become clear. Ms W shared strategies that would help her writing improve one step at a time. As time passed, Emily and her classmates kept samples of their old writing to compare to their new writing, and they began to build growth portfolios. Her writing skills were improving before her very eyes.

Now, having set the board up by having them analyse, evaluate and compare these two samples of student work, Ms W springs the surprise: The two pieces of writing they had just evaluated, one of less sophistication and one of outstanding quality, were produced by the same writer at the beginning and at the end of the school year! This, she reports, is evidence of the kind of impact the new writing programme is having on student writing proficiency.

Needless to say, all are impressed. However, one board member wonders aloud, 'Have all your students improved in this way?' Having anticipated the question, the rest of the English faculty joins the presentation and produces carefully prepared charts depicting dramatic changes in typical student performance over time.

Further, Ms W informs the board that the student whose improvement has been so dramatically illustrated in the samples they have just analysed is present at this board meet, along with her parents. This student is ready to talk with the board about the nature of her learning experience. Emily, you're on!

Interest among the board members runs high. Emily talks about how she has come to understand the truly important differences between good and bad writing. She refers to differences she had not understood before, how she has learned to assess her own writing and to fix it when it doesn't 'work well,' and how she and her classmates have learned to talk with her teacher and each other about what it means to write well. Ms W talks about the improved focus of writing instruction, increase in student motivation and important positive changes in the very nature of the student-teacher relationship.

A board member asks Emily if she likes to write. She reports, 'I do now!' This board member turns to Emily's parents and asks their impression of all of this. They report with pride that they had never seen so much evidence before of Emily's achievement and most of it came from Emily herself. Emily had never been called on to lead the parent-teacher conference before. They had no idea she was so articulate – her portfolio of work collected over time really showed marked improvement. They loved it. Their daughter's pride in and accountability for achievement had skyrocketed in the past year.

A journey of transformation

Emily and her classmates were fortunate to learn from teachers who had been given the opportunity to develop their assessment literacy in a new era of thinking about a new role for students as key players in sound classroom assessment practice. It is impossible to overstate the significance of this transition into this new era of student-involved assessment over the past two decades. I believe it was triggered and has been supported by the work of Paul Black and his associates in the UK beginning at the turn of the century.

Perhaps the most compelling effect of the last twenty years of classroom assessment research and development arising from Paul's work is that we stopped seeing assessment as a source of intimidation and anxiety and have begun seeing it as wellspring of encouragement to be used to increase student confidence, motivation, productive effort and, ultimately, greater learning success. In this same spirit, our thinking has shifted from seeing assessment as a sorting tool to benefit a few winners to a learning tool that can benefit all learners: from assessment as a source of scores and data to assessment as a rich source of useful information supporting student success.

The research on sound practices guided by Paul has provided the impetus for the creation of professional learning programmes pointed in dynamic new directions. It has had the effect of opening channels for professional learning for teachers and school leaders around the world, as they gain access to and master important new (and long-neglected) assessment competencies. This promises an assessment future in which students team up with their teachers to become lifelong learners, assessing their own needs and managing their own growth.

References

Black, P. & D. Wiliam (1998a). 'Assessment and classroom learning'. *Assessment in Education*, 5(1): 7–74.

Black, P. & D. Wiliam (1998b). 'Inside the black box: Raising standards through classroom assessment'. *Phi Delta Kappan*, 80(2): 139–48.

Chappuis, J. (2015). *Seven Strategies of Assessment FOR Learning*, 2nd edn. Boston: Pearson Education.

Chappuis, J. & R. Stiggins (2020). *Classroom Assessment FOR Student Learning: Doing It Right-Using It Well*, 3rd edn. Boston: Pearson Education.

Sadler, D. R. (1989). 'Formative assessment and the design of instructional systems'. *Instructional Science*, 18: 119–44.

Stiggins, R. J. (1991). 'Assessment literacy'. *Phi Delta Kappan*, March 1991: 534–9.

Stiggins, R. J. and J. Chappuis (2017). *An Introduction to Student-Involved Assessment FOR Learning*, 7th edn. Boston: Pearson Education.

The Impact of Two Key Themes from Paul Black's Work on U.S. K-12 Policy and Practice

Margaret Heritage and Caroline Wylie

Introduction

We are deeply honoured to make this contribution to Paul Black's Festschrift. We are both British transplants to the United States (U.S.) who have taken leadership roles in the areas of research, development and implementation of formative assessment across the nation's classrooms. As we describe in the chapter, the adoption and development of formative assessment have not been an easy road, and we, our colleagues and others have encountered many bumps along the way. Paul's vision for formative assessment has been the north star for both scholars and educators as they travelled this uncertain terrain, always providing a source of reaffirmation and renewal. It would be fair to say that in very many jurisdictions in the U.S. there has been an uptake of formative assessment, which is now widely regarded as central to good teaching and learning as Paul's research has consistently shown.

We knew of Paul's work before we arrived in the U.S. Margaret was a county inspector of schools in England when the National Curriculum and National Assessment System were introduced in the 1980s. Both reforms were a great departure for English schools and caused a significant amount of consternation among educators. The guidance in the report from Task Group on Assessment and Testing (TGAT) (Department of Education and Science [DES], 1988) led by Paul, seemed eminently sensible to educators. The report valued teacher judgement, the formative uses of assessment and recommended systems to be put in place to support shared understanding of standards and expectations. Paul's wisdom shone through this report and has since been a mainstay for her of how to think about external summative assessment and classroom assessment.

A section of Caroline's graduate school dissertation focused on the role of teacher-driven standard setting procedures applied to short, classroom-administered tests that each targeted a single National Curriculum level. The purpose of the procedures was to support teachers in operationalizing each level of the National Curriculum by helping them to calibrate and moderate their assessments of students. The TGAT report elevated the role of teacher assessment combined with moderation processes, which influenced her work on assisting teachers to reconcile classroom judgements about students with the results of external assessments both in the U.K. and U.S. (Morrison, Healy & Wylie, 1995; Wylie, 2017).

Paul's work first came to the attention of U.S. educators when the review of assessment during the learning process, co-authored with Dylan Wiliam, was published (Black & Wiliam, 1998a). The U.S. dissemination of Black and Wiliam's review was greatly assisted by the publication of its key messages in *Phi Delta Kappan* (Black & Wiliam, 1998b), a journal commonly read by practitioners. Their groundbreaking review made formative assessment a specific domain of practice for U.S. educators and set the foundation for decades of research and scholarship on and about formative assessment. However, we recognize that Paul's vision of formative assessment predates this review by at least five years (cf. Black, 1993). In the succeeding years, he has maintained the core ideas of his vision and elaborated and expanded on them in ways that have made sense to educators and invigorated the thinking and investigations of numerous researchers.

In this chapter, we explore two themes of Paul work and how they have played out in the last twenty years or so in the U.S.: (1) complexity and coexistence of assessment for summative and formative purposes and (2) formative assessment in support of teaching and learning. For over a decade, we have had the privilege of leading the Council of Chief State School Officers (CCSSO), a multi-state collaborative group focused on how leaders in state departments of education could support and influence the work of formative assessment at a national and local level. This group is widely regarded as having had a major impact within the U.S. in terms of state policies and practices for formative assessment, and we draw considerably from its work in our exploration of the two themes.

Complexity and coexistence of assessment for summative and formative purposes

In 1983, a U.S. government report, *A Nation at Risk* (National Commission on Excellence in Education, 1983), sounded alarm bells about the state of American education. In response, the eighties and nineties saw the rise of the standards-based reform movement and the beginning of state-wide testing in some subjects and grades (USDOE, NCES, 2003). As Paul Black noted at the time, 'the extensive reforms in the USA seem to be directed to improving the external assessments and there appears to be little discussion at state level of new practices in formative assessment' (Black, 1993: 83).

This observation was further borne out in two significant acts of federal legislation, the No Child Left Behind Act of 2001 (NCLB; Public Law No. 107-110, §115, Stat. 1425, 2002) and its successor, the Every Students Succeeds Act of 2015 (ESSA; Public Law No. 114-95, §114 Stat. 1177, 2015). Both acts considerably ratcheted up the accountability pressure on schools across the nation. Under the requirements of NCLB, external summative assessments were administered to all students annually from third grade (students aged 8–9) on, and failure to meet established achievement targets resulted in increasingly harsh sanctions, including closing schools. ESSA reduced some of the sanctions of NCLB but kept external summative assessment as an accountability requirement.

NCLB made no reference to formative assessment, and in the almost 400 pages of ESSA regulations it is only addressed three times and these references are at odds with one another. There is no attention in both acts to the student role in formative assessment, either through self-assessment, self-regulated learning processes, or in support of peer learning. In the words of Paul and colleagues, 'These current dominant forms [of accountability] have undermined what should be the normal and healthy relationship between formative and summative assessment' (Black, Wilson & Yao, 2011: 72).

Long before accountability testing had reached its peak in the U.S., Paul wrote, 'High-stakes testing can dominate classroom work and so distort teaching that the conditions for good formative assessment do not exist' (Black, 1993: 52). This is what happened in the U.S. While there were some modest benefits to classroom teaching and learning as a result of the external testing programme in place under NCLB (Braun, 2004; Cizek, 2001; Hanushek & Raymond, 2005), there were also significant distortions to teaching. These included reducing or eliminating time spent on subjects that were not part of the accountability testing programme, which essentially meant everything except mathematics and English language arts (ELA), increasing time for test preparation and teaching to the test, and focusing on students who were close to attaining proficiency to the detriment of those who were further from meeting proficiency levels (Nichols & Berliner, 2008).

By 1993, prior to such distortions being documented, Paul had raised consequential validity concerns about the impact of assessment on teaching, observing that 'if an assessment could be judged to reinforce styles of teaching which are inappropriate for the aims of science education, its validity could be prejudiced on these grounds alone' (Black, 1993: 62). In later work, co-authored with scholars from the University of California, Berkeley, he continued to articulate consequential validity concerns with respect to the use of summative assessment data, suggesting that by overshadowing formative assessment, summative assessment had taken a central role in guiding instructional practices, thus inhibiting effective pedagogy. To mitigate this situation, he and his co-authors advocated for systems that brought the two forms of assessment into synergistic coexistence to benefit students' educational progress (Black, Wilson & Yao, 2011).

One way that Paul envisaged synergy between formative and summative purposes in an assessment system was through teacher moderation. Harkening back to the 1988 proposals from the TGAT report (DES 1988) and its elevation of the role of teachers in assessment, he recommended 'that external testing be used mainly as a moderation instrument, with teachers responsible, after group moderation, for final decisions about individual pupils' (Black, 1993: 83). Moderation, or social moderation as it is sometimes called, is not commonly used in the U.S. In this structured process, groups of teachers discuss samples of student work at different levels of quality in conjunction with associated standards and rubrics. The process is intended to develop consistency of interpretation of each level of the rubric across teachers (e.g. Connolly, Klenowski & Wyatt-Smith, 2012; Wyatt-Smith, Klenowski & Gunn, 2010). The TGAT recommendation was that standardized annual assessments be used in moderation processes to help develop uniformity of expectations across teachers for their own classroom assessment. At the same time, Paul recognized that the unmet need for significant investment in training, standardization and moderation procedures to ensure public confidence in the process would likely mean that this vision could not become reality.

The potential for Paul's vision for complementary roles of summative and formative assessment received a potential boost with the introduction of Common Core State Standards for mathematics and ELA (CCSS) (National Governors Association Center for Best Practices, CCSSO, 2010). The CCSS, along with the Next Generation Science Standards (NGSS) (NGSS, Lead States, 2013), defined grade-level expectations for students to be college and career ready at the end of grade 12 (age 17–18). Just as the report, *A Nation at Risk*, had spurred earlier reforms, the CCSS were intended to raise and clarify achievement expectations in the U.S. to respond to students' poor performance on international tests, among others. Subsequently, states developed their own standards, which were, in the main, closely aligned with the CCSS and the NGSS.

Alongside the introduction of the CCSS, two federally funded assessment consortia were established to improve external assessments in mathematics and ELA and promote the use of common summative assessments by each state to measure students' achievement of the newly adopted standards. The consortia assessments were an improvement on prior state-level standardized assessments in terms of quality indicators such as the use of a broader set of item types and greater depth of knowledge assessed (McClellan, Joe & Bassett, 2015).

Paul's observation in the early 1990s that '[m]ost of the investment in assessment and testing ... has been devoted to the certification and accountability functions, to the neglect of the formative function' (Black, 1993: 50) appears prescient, given how the funding for these new assessments was spent. While one consortium created interim assessment options and a digital library with formative resources, the bulk of the government funding for both consortia was spent on developing end-of-year summative assessments.

Despite ideas of teacher moderation being an important part of several international assessment systems, the U.S. did not take the opportunity to expand the teacher role in this overhaul of the nation's assessment programmes. Moreover, a fatal blow to the possibility of including teacher moderation was the use of student assessment results as part of a teacher's performance evaluation, the inevitable consequence of which was to heighten the stakes for these external assessments even more.

Throughout his career, Paul has held out the need for clarity of assessment for summative purposes and the importance of formative assessment for supporting student learning (e.g. Black, 2015). The members of the CCSSO formative assessment group advocated for the value of formative assessment within their state policy requirements. While a few states were successful in bringing attention to formative assessment through assessment policies that included formative assessment and provided professional learning for its implementation, regrettably, Paul's broader vision for a healthy relationship between summative and formative assessment purposes with teacher moderation as an integral component of the assessment system has not materialized in the U.S. Nonetheless, his ideas for educators and policymakers still stand and, perhaps someday, they may realize the worth of those ideas to student learning.

Formative assessment in support of teaching and learning

While the more expansive vision of how formative and summative assessment can cohabitate successfully together has not been fully realized in the U.S., Paul Black's view of formative assessment being 'intimately connected with the process of teaching and learning' (Black, 1993: 15) has taken hold in many parts of the country, albeit slowly. Deep-seated approaches to teaching and assessment characterized by a transmission model of teaching and learning with assessment as the means to determine if students 'got it' or 'didn't get it' have persisted in American classrooms. According to Erickson (2007) many cultural and organizational factors account for this prevailing view of teaching and assessment. Erickson noted the dominance of summative testing as a tool of evaluation and the associated disprivileging of teachers' discretionary authority relative to psychometrics. Together with cultural assumptions about the basic nature and content of teaching and learning, the emphasis on psychometrics resulted in a distrust and deskilling of teachers' professional judgements about teaching and learning on which the effective practice of formative assessment depends.

As we noted in the introduction, the publication of Paul's landmark paper with Dylan Wiliam (Black & Wiliam, 1998a) generated interest among U.S. educators (and also commercial test publishers) in formative assessment as a means to improve student learning. However, in accord with the transmission view of teaching and learning, formative assessment was typically viewed as more frequent testing. Perie, Marion and Gong (2009) pointed out that many so-called formative assessments were actually interim or benchmark assessments, administered several times each year. Dylan Wiliam (2005) suggested these assessments are better thought of as 'early warning' summative assessments (cited in Shepard, 2005). Even efforts to redress the long-time emphasis on external summative assessment, such as calls for 'balanced assessment systems' that incorporated 'formative as well as summative measures' (Darling-Hammond, 2010: 1), sustained the predominant paradigm for formative assessment as one of measurement. Formative assessment was squarely construed within the measurement community as a test rather than within a learning paradigm (Heritage, 2010), which Paul has advocated for so long.

However, guided by Paul's work, many scholars and educators steadfastly chipped away at the conception of formative assessment as a specific test, and several members of the CCSSO formative assessment group introduced professional learning programmes state-wide to support teachers who wished to incorporate formative assessment into their classroom practice. They received assistance when teachers started to implement the CCSS and the NGSS described earlier. These standards provide well-defined aims 'in relation to constructs which are useful conceptualisations of pupils' learning' (Black, 1993: 57). The conceptualizations of learning inherent in the CCSS and the NGSS are consistent with three major ideas in Paul's work: the importance of classroom dialogue, the role of students in formative assessment and progressions or roadmaps for learning. Below, we discuss these three ideas, in turn.

Classroom dialogue

The aim of classroom dialogue is to promote the participation of all students in exploring and developing their understanding in discussion with the teacher and with each other (Black, Wilson & Yao, 2011). In classrooms where peer dialogue is frequent, students alternate between whole class activity and small group discussions (Black et al., 2003). In both instances, teachers develop strategies to strengthen classroom talk in order to prompt students to be active participants in discussion and to probe their thinking to provide evidence about their learning (Harrison & Heritage, 2019). A further benefit of dialogue in groups and/or at the whole-class level is to 'empower learners to make their own decisions in well-informed and thoughtful ways, thereby serving the overall aim of preparing them to meet the complex tasks they will encounter beyond school' (Black, 2018: 149).

Prior to the introduction of the CCSS and the NGSS, most U.S. classrooms were dominated by teacher talk; student talk was generally in response to teachers asking known-answer questions, which the teacher then evaluated as either correct or incorrect (cf. Mehan, 1979). Paul Black and his research colleagues found a similar situation in U.K. classrooms at the beginning of King's-Medway-Oxfordshire Formative Assessment Project (Black et al., 2003). Achieving the expectations of CCSS and NGSS requires a much greater emphasis on students' dialogue with their teacher and with one another. For example, in mathematics, students must communicate their reasoning about concepts, construct viable arguments and critique the reasoning of others (CCSS.MATH.PRACTICE.MP3 2010). In ELA, students must 'prepare for and participate effectively in a range of conversations and collaborations with diverse partners, building on others' ideas and expressing their own clearly and persuasively' (CCSS.ELA-LITERACY.SL.1 2010, 48). One of the NGSS practices is 'engaging in argument from evidence', and many of the related performance expectations require students to construct or use arguments (NGSS Lead States, 2013).

Meeting the expectations of these standards cannot be accomplished in a classroom characterized by primarily teacher talk and the dissemination of information from the expert (teacher) to novices (students). Consequently, many teachers have had to make significant changes to their approaches to teaching and learning in the direction that Paul Black has long promoted, adopting inquiry- and discourse-based strategies (Shepard, Penuel & Pellegrino, 2018; Wylie & Heritage, 2020). Interaction is increasingly becoming the 'heart of pedagogy' (Black & Wiliam, 1998a: 16) with a focus on students' thinking and their engagement in purposeful discussion driven by their own ideas (Black et al., 2003). Correspondingly, opportunities for formative assessment are more easily designed into the ongoing flow of interaction in the classroom, providing teachers with evidence of how student thinking is developing while students are in the process of learning (Heritage and Harrison, 2020).

Such transformations in pedagogy are not easy for teachers because they require a re-appraisal of their roles (Black & William, 2009). This re-appraisal is exemplified by one U.S. teacher who, after acknowledging that changing her practice left her sometimes 'out of my comfort zone in a productive struggle sort of way', went on to say:

> My planning has changed a lot. Instead of being focused on the activity and what I am going to say, I'm focusing on what are the students learning and what are they doing with the learning, and then me thinking through what they might not understand and how could I question in a way to help push them towards understanding, as opposed to me presenting information and students passively consuming it.
>
> (Heritage & Harrison, 2019: 69)

Noticeable in this teacher's comment is how her students have changed from being passive consumers of information to being actively involved in their own learning. This changing role for students is a hallmark of formative assessment.

The role of students

Central to Sadler's theoretical position on formative assessment is that its core activity lies in the sequence of two actions. The first is the perception by the learner of the gap between a desired goal and his or her current learning status. The second is the action taken by the learner to close the gap (Sadler, 1989). In line with Sadler's position on the active involvement of students in the learning assessment process, Paul added, 'The learner needs to understand the gap if she is to cross it; the teacher can help the learner but cannot actually cross it for her' (Black, 1998: 130). An ongoing thread throughout his work is the importance of self- and peer assessment for enhancing metacognition and self-direction so that students have the means to both understand and cross the gap.

In a 1993 paper, although recognizing that the research on student self-assessment was still in its infancy, Paul identified it as a 'potentially powerful source for the improvement of learning' (Black, 1993: 82). His 1998 paper with Dylan Wiliam went further, arguing for the inevitability of the link between self-assessment and formative assessment and advancing the view that far from being a luxury students' own assessment was essential to the practice of formative assessment (Black & Wiliam, 1998b). His work also revealed a corollary between self-assessment and peer assessment, for instance, 'Our work with [foreign language] teachers has shown that peer assessment helps pupils develop their self-assessment skills' (Black & Jones, 2006: 8).

When formative assessment began to gain traction in the U.S., there was little initial uptake to include students as active participants in the assessment process. Assessment was seen as within the purview of teachers, and expanding teachers' assessment practices to include students was not on the table. For example, several subgroup members of the assessment consortium mentioned earlier, who were tasked with developing a framework for formative assessment, regarded formative assessment as a teacher-only practice. The idea that 'learners need to exercise a degree of autonomy from the teacher as the assessor and judge of quality' (Black et al., 2006: 128) was yet at some distance from U.S. educators' views and practice.

Paul flagged the fragility of students' mindset for self-assessment as a result of students' experience with summative assessment. Students viewed summative assessment as producing information for other people, having no meaning or value to them, and resulting only in pressure. To counteract these attitudes, he stressed the need for teachers to help students understand why self-assessment was important for their learning and to provide support for learning how to engage in the process of self-assessment (Black, 1998).

At the onset of explicit formative assessment implementation in U.S. classrooms, teachers were open to communicating clear learning goals to students in language they understand. However, it took longer for many teachers to grasp the idea that these goals could be drivers of students' own assessment by being couched at a 'level of detail that helps them relate directly to their learning efforts' (Black, 1998: 130). When teaching practices began to change in the U.S. to be less teacher-centric, as we have discussed, educators took small steps to include students in a more active role in learning and assessment. Their greater involvement was supported by the CCSSO group's definition of formative assessment, which called out self- and peer assessment as core practices (CCSSO, 2008). A subsequent revision to the definition bolstered formative assessment as instrumental in student self-direction capabilities (CCSSO, 2018).

In the last few years, some state departments of education in the U.S. have begun to issue policy guidance on priorities for K-12 education that include student self-direction skills as a key outcome. Such policies, combined with the benefits teachers attribute to student learning from their active involvement in formative assessment, have provided further impetus to expanding their role in learning and assessment.

Progressions or roadmaps for learning

Paul has stressed the value of progressions or roadmaps to both learning and assessment. For example, in his co-authored paper with Dylan Wiliam, they pointed to the need for 'a sound model of students' progression in the learning of the subject matter' so that teachers could interpret and respond to evidence in a formative way (Black & Wiliam, 1998a: 37). Similarly, he and colleagues noted that when teachers are orchestrating classroom discussions and responding to student ideas, particularly when the ideas are unanticipated, they need to have in mind an underlying scheme of progression of the topic in order to advance student thinking in productive ways (Black, Wilson & Yao, 2011). It is also noteworthy that in the same paper, the authors suggested that a 'healthy relationship' between formative and summative assessment could be established if they were based on a common roadmap or backbone for a learning progression, whereby both types of assessment would be supportive of the roadmap (Black, Wilson & Yao, 2011).

The idea of learning progressions – descriptions of how student thinking about a concept typically evolves over time – has recently gained ground in the U.S. as a way to provide more detailed and nuanced descriptions of learning in support of instruction and assessment, particularly in mathematics and science, and some in ELA (Deane & Sparks, 2019; Heritage & Wylie, 2020). Currently, there are too few research-based progressions to be useful for a wide range of classroom work. However, while the CCSS and NGSS cannot be construed as learning progressions per se (e.g. Corcoran, Mosher & Rogat, 2009; Heritage, 2008), they offer a better progression in learning than prior standards with benefits accruing to teaching, learning and formative assessment.

Standards describe learning expectations at the end of a grade level or a set of grade levels rather than identifying the intra-grade development of underlying knowledge, concepts and skills necessary for meeting these expectations. For example, foundational skills such as knowledge of text structures are presupposed by standards that require students to identify and summarize main ideas. For the purpose of topic and lesson planning and formative assessment, teachers can take advantage of the standards inherent in progression and articulate an intra-grade-level pathway of development at a smaller grain size (Bailey & Heritage, 2014). When teachers create these quasi-progressions there are several other pay-offs for formative assessment.

First, rather than the long-standing tendency to create discrete learning objectives that generally begin 'students will be able to ...' as guides for their teaching, a progression helps teachers plan a sequence of lessons that are coherent and build on one another, resulting in a deeper learning experience for students in relation to the concepts, skills and analytic practices called for in the standards (Heritage, 2008). Students can see the big picture of learning – the standards – while having a grasp of the smaller, connected learning goals derived from the standards, as well as what accomplishing them entails. Student involvement in the assessment process is supported through such an orientation to goals. Specifically, when students are clear about the goals and the associated criteria that need to be met, they are positioned to engage in constructive self-assessment day by day (Deane & Sparks, 2019). With a reference level – the goal and criteria – students can make judgements about where they think they are in their learning and what they might need to do to move forward (Clark, 2012).

Second, if teachers are to effectively respond to evidence elicited during the lesson, they benefit from having an underlying scheme of progression in mind. By way of illustration, a second-grade (students aged 7–8) teacher had been working with her students on a series of lessons focused on 'decomposing' and 'composing' two- and three-digit numbers (breaking down and regrouping numbers into units, tens and hundreds). The teacher created a problem for the students to work on and they were asked to select one of three number pairs ((28, 4), (292, 4) or (568, 4)) to use in their version of the problem so that they could work with numbers that they felt most confident with. Aided by her knowledge of the typical development of student understanding in relation to the learning goal, the teacher was able to interpret the evidence obtained from the students' responses to the task and from their discussions. Her insights informed the differential supports she made, in the moment, to advance each student's learning beyond its current status. These ranged from supporting students who had less sophisticated understanding and were using concrete materials to solve the problem, to those who had progressed to drawing diagrams to depict the problem, to students who had the deepest understanding and had begun to write number sentences that represented the problem (Heritage & Wylie, 2020).

Third, a progression of incremental steps en route to meeting the standards can provide a sound foundation for improvement-oriented feedback (Black, Wilson & Yao, 2011). The mathematics teacher from the previous paragraph could have equally used her progression knowledge to remind students of what they had already achieved and then provide feedback about their task performance that gave them clear aims for improvement, but not a solution to the task. Using this kind of teacher feedback engages student thinking and supports their learning autonomy and self-efficacy by encouraging them to make decisions about how they will respond to the feedback (Black & Wiliam, 1998a).

As we noted earlier, the introduction of the CCSS and the NGSS gave a boost to formative assessment in U.S. classrooms. They promoted a move away from discrete learning objectives and assessments with atomistic items to a focus on deeper learning over a more extended period of time, paving the way for teachers to think more in terms of a progression. The state departments of education represented in the CCSSO formative assessment group took advantage of the opportunities provided by CCSS and NGSS, changing their guidance to include the importance of clarifying learning goals within a broader progression of learning. To date, although it cannot be said that all teachers have embraced the notion of progressions, there is a growing understanding of their value to formative assessment and student learning (Alonzo, 2018; Gotwals, 2018).

Conclusion

When formative assessment came to the attention of U.S. policymakers and educators some twenty years ago, consistent with the long-time predominance of psychometrics, there was a rush by many school districts and testing companies to produce formative assessments, which were akin to more frequent summative tests. Paul Black has led the way to an understanding in the U.S. that successful implementation of formative assessment depends on teachers incorporating a set of practices into their everyday teaching and by finding ways to do this in their own patterns of classroom work (Black et al., 2003). This is not to suggest a sink or swim approach. Rather, teachers need to be supported by an investment in teacher professional learning (Black, 1993), a view promoted by the CCSSO formative assessment group for many years, and which is now widely accepted in the U.S. However, there is still work to be done to understand how best to engage teachers in disciplinary-based professional learning that supports formative assessment implementation.

Paul's respect for teachers and the work they do shines through all his writing, as does his deep knowledge of teaching and learning. It is still rare to find a researcher who firmly situates assessment so centrally to the promotion of learning as Paul does.

He has surely done more than anyone to connect teaching, learning and assessment; teachers and students in the U.S. are undoubtedly better off because of his work.

References

Alonzo, A. C. (2018), 'An argument for formative assessment with science learning progressions'. *Applied Measurement in Education*, 31(2): 104–12.

Bailey, A. L. & M. Heritage (2014). 'The role of language learning progressions in improved instruction and assessment of English language learners'. *Tesol Quarterly*, 48(3): 480–506.

Black, P. (1993). 'Formative and summative assessment by teachers'. *Studies in Science Education*, 21(1): 49–97. https://doi.org/10.1080/03057269308560014

Black, P. (1998). *Testing, Friend or Foe?: The Theory and Practice of Assessment and Testing*. Milton Park, U.K.: Psychology Press.

Black, P. & D. Wiliam (1998a). 'Assessment and classroom learning'. *Assessment in Education: Principles Policy and Practice*, 5: 7–73.

Black, P. & D. Wiliam (1998b). 'Inside the black box: Raising standards through classroom assessment'. *Phi Delta Kappan*, 92(1): 81–90.

Black, P., C. Harrison, C. Lee, B. Marshall & D. Wiliam (2003). *Assessment for Learning: Putting It into Practice*. Maidenhead, U.K.: Open University Press.

Black, P. & J. Jones (2006). 'Formative assessment and the learning and teaching of MFL: Sharing the language learning road map with the learners'. *Language Learning Journal*, 34(1): 4–9.

Black, P., R. McCormick, M. James & D. Pedder (2006). 'Learning how to learn and assessment for learning: A theoretical inquiry'. *Research Papers in Education*, 21(02): 119–32.

Black, P. (2015). 'Formative assessment – an optimistic but incomplete vision'. *Assessment in Education: Principles, Policy and Practice*, 22(1): 161–77.

Black, P., M. Wilson & S. Y. Yao (2011). 'Road maps for learning: A guide to the navigation of learning progressions'. *Measurement: Interdisciplinary Research and Perspective*, 9(2–3): 71–123.

Black, P. & D. Wiliam (2018). 'Classroom assessment and pedagogy'. *Assessment in Education: Principles, Policy and Practice*, 25(6): 551–75.

Black, P. & D. Wiliam (2009). 'Developing the theory of formative assessment'. *Educational Assessment, Evaluation and Accountability*, 21(1): 5.

Braun, H. (2004). 'Reconsidering the impact of high-stakes testing'. *Education Policy Analysis Archives*, 12(1): 1–43.

Cizek, G. J. (2001). 'More unintended consequences of high-stakes testing'. *Educational Measurement: Issues and practice*, 20(4): 19–27.

Clark, I. (2012). 'Formative assessment: Assessment is for self-regulated learning'. *Educational Psychology Review*, 24(2): 205–49.

Connolly, S., V. Klenowski & C. M. Wyatt-Smith (2012). 'Moderation and consistency of teacher judgement: Teachers' views'. *British Educational Research Journal*, 38(4): 593–614.

Corcoran, T. B., F. A. Mosher & A. Rogat (2009). 'Learning progressions in science: An evidence-based approach to reform'. *Consortium for Policy Research in Education Research* Report # R-63, May. https://repository.upenn.edu/cpre_researchreports/53/

Council of Chief State School Officers (CCSSO) (2008). 'Attributes of effective formative assessment'. In *A Work Product Coordinated by Sarah McManus, NC Department of Public Instruction, for the Formative Assessment for Students and Teachers (FAST) Collaborative*. Washington, DC: Author.

Council of Chief State School Officers (CCSSO) (2018). *Revising the Definition of Formative Assessment*. Washington, DC: Author.

Darling-Hammond, L. (2010). *Performance Counts: Assessment Systems that Support High-Quality Learning*. Washington, DC: Council of Chief State School Officers.

Deane, P. & J. R. Sparks (2019). 'Scenario-based formative assessment of key practices in the English language arts'. In H. L. Andrade, R. E. Bennett & G. J. Cizek (Eds.), *Handbook of Formative Assessment in the Disciplines*, 68–96. New York: Routledge.

Department of Education and Science (1998). *National Curriculum: Task Group on Assessment and Testing*. London: Author.

Department of Education and Science / Welsh Office (1988). *National Curriculum Task Group on Assessment and Testing: A Report*. London: DES/WO.

Erickson, F. (2007). 'Some thoughts on "proximal" formative assessment of student learning'. *Yearbook of the National Society for the Study of Education*, 106: 186–216.

Gotwals, A. W. (2018). 'Where are we now? Learning progressions and formative assessment'. *Applied Measurement in Education*, 31(2): 157–64.

Hanushek, E. A. & M. E. Raymond (2005). 'Does school accountability lead to improved student performance?'. *Journal of Policy Analysis and Management*, 24(2): 297–327.

Harrison, C. A., & Heritage, M. (2019). *The Power of Assessment for Learning: Twenty years of Research and Practice in UK and US Schools*. Sage Publications.

Heritage, M. (2008). *Learning Progressions: Supporting Instruction and Formative Assessment*. Washington, DC: Council of Chief State School Officers.

Heritage, M. (2010). *Formative Assessment and Next-Generation Assessment Systems: Are We Losing an Opportunity?*. Washington, DC: Council of Chief State School Officers.

Heritage, M. & C. Harrison (2019). *The Power of Assessment for Learning: Twenty Years of Impact in UK and US Classrooms*. Thousand Oaks, CA: Corwin.

Heritage, M. & E. C. Wylie (2020). *Formative Assessment in the Disciplines: Framing a Continuum of Professional Learning*. Cambridge, MA: Harvard Education Press.

Hurst, D., A. Tan, A. Meek, J. Sellers & E. McArthur (2003). 'Overview and inventory of state education reforms: 1990 to 2000, NCES 2003–020'. In *U.S. Department of Education, National Center for Education Statistics*. Washington, DC.

Mehan, H. (1979). *Learning Lessons: Social Organization in the Classroom*. Cambridge: Harvard University Press.

McClellan, C., J. Joe & K. Bassett (2015). 'The right trajectory: State teachers of the year compare former and new state assessments'. *National Network of State Teachers of the Year*. http://www.nnstoy.org/wp-content/uploads/2015/11/Right-Trajectory-FINAL.pdf (accessed 1 December 2019).

Morrison, H., J. Healy & E. C. Wylie (1995). 'Teacher knows best: A solution to the marks-to-levels problem in National Curriculum testing'. *British Educational Research Journal*, 21(2): 175–82.

National Commission on Excellence in Education (1983). *A Nation at risk: The Imperative for Educational Reform*. Washington, DC: U.S. Department of Education.

National Governors Association Center for Best Practices, Council of Chief State School Officers (2010). *Common Core State Standards for English Language Arts and Literacy in History/Social Studies, Science, and Technical Subjects*. Washington, DC: Author.

National Governors Association Center for Best Practices, Council of Chief State School Officers (2010). *Standards for Mathematical Practices*. http://www.corestandards.org/Math/Practice/ (accessed 10 March 2021).

NGSS Lead States (2013). *Next Generation Sciences: For States, by States*. Washington, DC: The National Academies Press.

Nichols, S. L. & D. C. Berliner (2008). 'Testing the joy out of learning'. *Educational Leadership*, 65(6): 14–18.

Perie, M., S. Marion & B. Gong (2009). 'Moving toward a comprehensive assessment system: A framework for considering interim assessments'. *Educational Measurement: Issues and Practice*, 28(3): 5–13.

Sadler, D. R. (1989). 'Formative assessment and the design of instructional systems'. *Instructional Science*, 18(2): 119–44.

Shepard, L. A. (2005). 'Caveat emptor'. Presented at *ETS Invitational Conference, The Future of Assessment: Shaping Teaching and Learning*, New York, 10–11 October 2005.

Shepard, L. A., W. R. Penuel & J. W. Pellegrino (2018). 'Using learning and motivation theories to coherently link formative assessment, grading practices, and large-scale assessment'. *Educational Measurement: Issues and Practice*, 37(1): 21–34.

Shepard, L. A. (2019). 'Classroom assessment to support teaching and learning'. In A. Berman, M. J. Feuer & J. W. Pellegrino (Eds.), *The ANNALS of the American Academy of Political and Social Science*, 183–200. Thousand Oaks, CA: Sage.

U.S. Department of Education, National Center for Education Statistics (2003). *Overview and Inventory of State Education Reforms: 1990 to 2000, NCES 2003-020*, by David Hurst, Alexandra Tan, Anne Meek, and Jason Sellers. Washington, DC.

Wiliam, D. (2005). 'Personal Communication Cited'. In Shepard, L. A. (2005). *Formative Assessment: Caveat Emptor*. Paper presented at the ETS Invitational Conference, The Future of Assessment: Shaping Teaching and Learning, New York, NY.

Wyatt-Smith, C., V. Klenowski & S. Gunn (2010). 'The centrality of teachers' judgement practice in assessment: A study of standards in moderation'. *Assessment in Education: Principles, Policy and Practice*, 17(1): 59–75.

Wylie, E. C. (2017). 'Winsight™ Assessment System: Preliminary Theory of Action'. In *ETS Research Report Series Research Report No. RR-17-26*. Princeton, NJ: Educational Testing Service. DOI: 10.1002/ets2.12155

Wylie, E. C. & M. Heritage (2020). 'Supporting equity through formative assessment in the era of Covid-19'. *Teachers College Record*. https://www.tcrecord.org/Content.asp?ContentId=23330 (accessed 19 June 2020).

8

The Role of Teachers in Making and Moderating Assessment Judgements: Opening the Black Box to Challenge Paradigms in Australia

Claire Wyatt-Smith and Lenore Adie

Introduction

The field of assessment is widely recognized to be a contested space, with various paradigms competing for dominance. This is not a recent development. There is, for example, the paradigm of assessment as measurement, typically geared to tests and students working alone and unaided, in controlled conditions. There is also the paradigm promoting assessment as learning focused and responsive to individual and group differences, to name but one other. While such differences have long been recognized, the contestation surrounding assessment has undoubtedly increased in an era of intense social change and uncertainty about schooling and its fitness for purpose to prepare young people for unchartered futures (Wyatt-Smith et al., forthcoming). Some of the most complex questions about schooling concern the relationship between assessment and learning, the distinction between purposes of assessment (i.e. formative and summative), and the use of standards, evidence and teachers' professional judgement. Paul Black has advocated quality assessment tasks, effective feedback, alignment of assessment and pedagogy, and the use of assessment information to inform pedagogy. Over the past four decades, he has wrestled with these heavy-weight issues to make significant knowledge contributions that have informed policy, practice and research, working with colleagues in the UK and internationally.

In beginning this chapter, the authors were mindful of the significant corpus of new knowledge that Black's work has generated, with its reach into so many countries, including Australia. This weighty realization became all the more pressing within the limitations of a single chapter. In this chapter, our aim is to offer research-informed reflections on some of the key insights from Black's work and discuss implications of these in Australian assessment research and practice. The discussion extends to consider the influence of his writing on how the authors have built on his work in addressing teacher judgements and decision-making, evaluative expertise and moderation. Black's insights have fuelled the challenges taken up in the authors' work regarding the suitability of historic assessment paradigms as they have opened spaces for learner-focused ideas, working at scale with teachers, students and researcher colleagues. As an illustrative example, we introduce the current application of Black's writing in our work of developing and implementing an internationally distinctive approach to a new Australian assessment of graduate competence on entry to the teaching workforce. In this, we draw on Black's writing on assessment, along with thinkers in the fields of data analytics, digital design and systems thinking. Our aim is to profile Black's intellectual contributions to the field of assessment and their broader application.

Exploring the concept of the black box

The term 'black box' landed in the field of educational assessment in 1998, undoubtedly achieving demonstrable impact since that time (Black & Wiliam, 1998b). Evidence for this includes the large body of writing that engages with the metaphor of the black box (e.g. Baird, 2011; Hargreaves, 2005; Harrison & Howard, 2009; Hattie, 2009; Ravet, 2013; Stobart, 2008). Black has been a leading thinker opening the black box of assessment in the interests of teachers, students and the wider community. To begin, we take up the foundational question: What does the term 'black box' mean? We then explore how Black has used the term as a metaphor, inviting teachers and policymakers to go inside the black box of assessment to improve teacher practice and student learning.

What does the term 'black box' mean?

The term 'black box' has been defined variously, dependent on the domain in which it has been applied. A common definition relates to something that is hidden, mysterious, not easily accessible or is yet to be worked out. For example, black box is defined in the Merriam Webster dictionary as 'a usually complicated electronic device whose internal mechanism is usually hidden from or mysterious to the user; anything that has mysterious or unknown internal functions or mechanisms'. The term has also been applied in diverse fields including philosophy, politics, medicine and engineering. Broadly speaking, the term has been associated with efforts to describe phenomena or 'things that can only be accurately defined by looking at their inner workings' (Bradley, n.d., n.p.). The primary interest with the black boxes lies in 'the function of the thing coupled with an understanding of how its exterior correlates within its interior' (Bradley, n.d., n.p.). For example, Bradley describes a view adopted in the field of politics that political systems can only be truly known by 'opening or exposing the box' (n.p.). To successfully see into the interior of the black box – lift the lid – some argue that it is necessary to be part of the system and have first-hand experience of its inner workings. As applied to politics, 'you have to be either an insider or must seek to break through the superficial appearances' (Bradley, n.d., n.p.).

What is the black box of educational assessment?

In canvassing the corpus of writing by Paul Black, the centrepiece is the critical link between assessment and learning. With Wiliam, Black used the metaphor of the black box to capture how assessment practice is complex, multifaceted and may not be readily accessible to novices or beginning teachers, those with limited study of assessment in their teacher preparation, and the wider public who may typically think of the most-valued assessment as examinations. Black and Wiliam (1998b) related this metaphor to classroom assessment practices and questioned the relationship between the policy inputs into classroom practice and the expected outputs. They proposed that is it necessary to understand what is happening in the black box of classroom practice to ascertain this relationship. In particular, their focus was on formative assessment practice which they asserted was 'at the heart of effective teaching' (p. 140):

> [P]resent policies in the U.S. and in many other countries seem to treat the classroom as a black box. Certain inputs from the outside – pupils, teachers, other resources, management rules and requirements, parental anxieties, standards, tests with high stakes, and so on – are fed into the box. Some outputs are supposed to follow: pupils who are more knowledgeable and competent, better test results, teachers who are reasonably satisfied, and so on. But what is happening inside the box? How can anyone be sure that a particular set of new inputs will produce better outputs if we don't at least study what happens inside?
>
> (Black & Wiliam, 1998b:140)

Black's work constantly reminds us that assessment is inherently social practice; while policies can invest in a succession of inputs, bringing these from 'the outside' to be fed into the classroom, there is a key role for studying 'what happens inside' classrooms to show the efficacy of the inputs, as indicated below:

> Learning is driven by what teachers and pupils do in classrooms. Teachers have to manage complicated and demanding situations, channelling the personal, emotional, and social pressures of a group of 30 or more youngsters in order to help them learn immediately and become better learners in the future. Standards can be raised only if teachers can tackle this task more effectively.
>
> (Black & Wiliam, 1998b:140)

Here the authors highlight the complexities of teaching; the social and cognitive mix of pressures that impact on classroom teaching. Black has actively promoted as essential the focused professional learning for teachers in contexts of changing assessment practices in both policy and practice (Black et al., 2011).

To elaborate, Black brought to assessment policy, practice and research:

1. Key strategies in teacher formative assessment including clarifying learning intentions and criteria for success (Black, 2015; Black & Wiliam, 2018);
2. New understandings about teacher learning and discussion to develop shared understanding of criteria and standards (Black et al., 2004; Black & Wiliam, 2006; Black et al., 2006; Dolin et al., 2018);
3. Teacher strategies to support students to self-assess (Black & Wiliam, 2018);
4. Sustained advocacy for the formative use of summative assessments (Black, 2014; Black et al., 2003, 2004; Black et al., 2011);
5. Issues of evidence and purpose, showing how they are central to improving learning; and
6. New insights into designing quality assessments that would 'evoke evidence of the attainment it was designed to test' (Black et al., 2011: 455).

Black's work is characterized by a strong authenticity of tone, particularly notable in his in-field research. When writing on the King's Oxfordshire Summative Assessment Project (KOSAP), he reflected how 'the extent of the collaborative development, between ourselves and the teachers, that was needed was such that we could not get beyond the development, with the teachers and schools, of the skills and practices needed' to improve the quality of the teachers' summative assessments (Black et al., 2011: 464). These types of observations fuelled his interest in teachers' collaborative conversations as they think through their assessment practices and learn to implement new valid and reliable assessment practices.

Teachers' professional judgement, standards and moderation

To begin, we declare a position on teacher judgement that is far broader than arriving at a grade. In the course of a lesson and a teaching day, teachers routinely make a myriad of professional judgements. These can range from deciding the intentions for a lesson; deciding mid-lesson whether the intentions, as initially selected, are being met; and deciding how these may need to be modified based on first-hand observations of student learning. Teachers' professional judgement is at the core of their teaching and assessment practice and involves evaluative expertise (Wyatt-Smith & Adie, 2019) and connoisseurship (Sadler, 1989).

Here we turn to the thinking and practices of moderation and reflect on Black's contribution and its influence in Australia. Moderation is 'a form of quality assurance for delivering comparability in evidence-based judgments of student achievement' (Maxwell, 2007: 2). It can occur in different contexts, both internal (within and across schools) and external (administered at system level), and take different forms, the two most widely recognized being social and statistical moderation.

Statistical moderation is widely used in many examination systems. Social moderation tends to occur within schools at and across year levels and across schools within a sector. Social moderation is practised in a range of countries (e.g. Republic of Ireland, Scotland, Canada, New Zealand and Australia) and involves teacher collaboration to review, discuss and judge samples of student work against stated expectations or characteristics of quality. This can be undertaken for formative purposes, as well as for summative purposes to inform school reporting. Each of these forms of moderation relies on particular judgement practices.

Human judgement has been regarded historically in many fields as subjective, open to bias, inconsistency and whimsy. In opening the black box to look into what happens in the classroom, Black recognized the critical role of teachers' talk 'to re-think their own understandings of criteria and standards, and to be more confident about the validity and consistency of their judgments' (Black et al., 2011: 459). The theme of judgement was powerfully evident in the writing of Black and Wiliam (2006) in highlighting how the dependability (validity and reliability) of teachers' summative judgements requires a shared understanding of criteria and standards. This opened the space to consider the benefits for teachers and learners when assessment-as-judgement is made explicit through teacher talk as part of professional dialogue, taken up again in a later section of this chapter.

Classroom assessment, learning and moderation: Illustrations from Australia

To this point we have highlighted several main lines of inquiry in Black's work. In the following section, we focus on two that have had direct impact on policy, research and practice in Australia. These are (1) the synergies between assessment and classroom learning (Black, 1995; Black et al., 2003, 2004) and (2) raising standards through classroom assessment (Black & Wiliam, 1998b), with the related focus on reliability and improving consistency in teachers' professional judgements (Black, 2016; Black et al., 2010; Black & Wiliam, 1998a), including in the context of moderation. Using illustrative examples from Australia, we describe how Black's work has contributed to assessment and moderation practices in Australia.

Assessment and learning synergies

Education Services Australia (ESA; https://www.esa.edu.au/) is an illustrative instance of the influence and impact of Black's work. ESA is a national not-for-profit company owned by the state, territory and Australian government education ministers that provides technology-based services for education. The site includes the research findings of Paul Black and Dylan Wiliam with particular reference to *Inside the Black Box* (Black & Wiliam, 1998b). The site provides a summary of the findings of their review of formative assessment and its role in improving student achievement (ESA, n.d.). These insights have been included in resources for teachers to inform their teaching practice. The resources include the five practices related to developing learning intentions and success criteria, asking questions that guide student learning, providing feedback that progresses learning, supporting students to self-assess and using information from summative assessments for formative purposes. These practices direct teacher attention to features or characteristics of quality in student work as a basis for improving teaching and student learning.

In addition to the use of teacher judgement and feedback for formative purposes, also of interest is the under-researched link between teachers' formative and summative uses of assessments. Broadfoot and Black (2004) suggested that one way to overcome the limitations of high-stakes external testing is 'to use teachers' own knowledge of their students as a source of data for the purposes of certification and accountability' (p.15). The resources teachers bring and the actions they take for formative assessment overlap and add to the resources and actions required for summative assessment. Classroom-based assessment for formative and summative purposes is a strong feature of teachers' routine work in Australia. To work in this system, teachers need to be skilled in developing programmes and related assessments that ensure alignment between curriculum, assessment and pedagogy, and continually apply their knowledge of students as a source of data to connect assessment, achievement and learning.

Standards, reliability and consistency

In the second sustained line of inquiry, Black's writing brings student learning to the centre and, with it, the complexity of classroom teaching (Black & Wiliam, 1998b). The focus on what will 'produce better outputs' (Black & Wiliam, 1998b:140), frequently referred to as 'what works', is strongly evident in Australian curriculum, policy and related guidelines relating to formative assessment, feedback and the use of standards in moderation.

To turn to Queensland, Australia, in December 1970 the junior (year 10) public examination was held for the last time, and the first fully school-based assessment system was introduced in 1971. In the next five decades, the state became recognized internationally for its approach to school-based assessment, most notably in senior schooling (years 11 and 12). The student assessment approach was argued to have merit but to be sufficiently distinctive from the most fully and developed existing varieties of standards-referenced assessment to merit independent investigation (Sadler,1992).

Guided by Black's writing and others (e.g. Sadler, 1992; Board of Secondary School Studies, Assessment Unit Discussion Papers;[1] Maxwell & Cumming, 2011), the authors and colleagues took up the challenge to look inside the black box of teacher judgement in the context of standards-referenced moderation in Queensland, working with teachers. Black and colleagues (2011) had revealed the importance of teachers' discussions of their judgements and their engagement with judgement differences. Teachers' professional conversations about quality were valued recognizing that teachers needed to be supported to 're-think their own understandings of criteria and standards, and to be more confident about the validity and consistency of their judgments, in ways that would have a positive impact on the achievements of their students' (Black et al., 2011:459).

Informed by these insights, the authors and other writers turned to moderation and teachers' professional dialogue about criteria and standards. Of relevance to this chapter is a large-scale three-year commencing 2006 that was undertaken over a three-year period in an industry partnership with the Queensland Studies Authority.[2] The study generated empirical data showing the practices teachers relied on in their reading and assessment of student work. The ARC project generated new knowledge about how teachers use stated and unstated criteria and standards in moderation for promoting judgement consistency. Key findings included how

1. Teachers opened up their judgements as they talked about their expectations of quality and their perceptions of the features that they saw in, or missing from, student work (Wyatt-Smith et al., 2010);
2. Teachers connected understandings about the assessment task, the quality of the work, official statements of criteria, and other features that they felt were relevant, even when these were missing from the official criteria (Wyatt-Smith et al., 2010);
3. Teachers took risks to reveal the basis of their judgements, bringing to the surface the qualities that they valued which typically had remained unarticulated (Wyatt-Smith & Klenowski, 2010);
4. Moderation was shown to be a forum for dialogic enquiry into the basis for judgements and decisions about the standard of the work. In this forum, teachers' knowledge about criteria and standards, and their confidence in applying them were shown to be enhanced (Wyatt-Smith & Klenowski, 2008);
5. Involvement in moderation supports teachers to clarify their understanding of criteria and standards and how these are exemplified in actual work samples (Adie et al., 2012);
6. Customized decision aids can support the development of teachers' evaluative expertise. The aids included statements of criteria and standards and accompanying illustrative exemplars of student work intended to demonstrate the expected features of quality (Wyatt-Smith et al., 2010);
7. Teachers' professionalism was enhanced when they participated in moderation conversations where they engaged with colleagues' assessments and where differences in judgements occurred (Klenowski & Wyatt-Smith, 2010);

8. Moderation was identified as not only an end-of-teaching activity but rather as a deliberate inclusion in planning, during teaching as teachers discuss their developing understandings of quality, and at the end of teaching as they apply those understandings to promote consistency of judgements (Adie et al., 2012; Wyatt-Smith & Adie, 2019).

Looking inside the black box of social moderation to understand what is going on and whether these practices lead to consistency of judgement in high-stakes assessment was the focus of another large-scale study of moderation across subjects in the Queensland senior assessment system (Wyatt-Smith & Colbert, 2014). Prior to this study, moderation in senior schooling had not been the study of cross-curriculum, large-scale research to inform teacher practice. Key findings from the study were the following:

1. While moderation is expected to build confidence and trust in an assessment system, moderation, of itself, does not produce high reliability. A more comprehensive approach to building judgement reliability and comparability should have at its centrepiece calibration training and other systematic quality assurance mechanisms relating to assessment integrity and fidelity of implementation;
2. 'Participation in moderation panels substantially contributes to teachers' knowledge and skills in assessment design, syllabus understanding and application of standards in judgement of student work' (p. 30);
3. Teachers with experience of moderation typically focused their talk on matching the properties of the work with the stated expectations of quality (criteria);
4. Teachers' domain knowledge and curriculum knowledge as well as their prior evaluative experiences were heavily drawn on in moderation conversations;
5. Formulation of official statements of criteria and standards had a significant influence on how teachers understood their role as judges: what was permitted, and not permitted, as legitimate influences on judgement;
6. Teachers actively referred to their prior experiences with assessing student work and their recollections of classroom interactions which carried forward in their judgements, albeit, tacitly;
7. Teachers combined the official stated criteria and standards with a range of other unstated standards frameworks (e.g. letter grades, numeric scores, grade cut-offs). These diverted attention away from the properties

of the work to the teachers' perception of how the work related to other frameworks with which they were most familiar;
8. Specified standards and accompanying criteria do not automatically deliver transparency of judgement and, in turn, what is valued in assessment;
9. Sustained professional learning of the teaching workforce and investment in moderation are essential for maintaining public confidence in the reliability and fairness of the assessment system.

Following the Queensland government review of the senior assessment system (Matters & Masters, 2014), significant changes were made with the intent to strengthen quality assurance mechanisms, especially as these related to comparability of assessment demands and to maintain public confidence in the system. The discussion of these changes is beyond the scope of this chapter.[3] It is worth mentioning here, however, that across the five decades since external examinations were abolished in the state, there were several iterations of moderation approaches. In its final form, moderation was enacted as 'external' (as distinct from moderation done within a school), 'social' (involving teachers across the state meeting in person and in panels) and 'standard-referenced'. The dual purposes of moderation were to contribute to system processes and practices for quality assuring student results on course completion and to build teacher capability in using standards.

These insights into judgement and moderation are currently stimulating innovative approaches to the use of digital technologies, data analytics and methodologies for examining the inner workings of professional judgement in schooling and teacher education. In the following section we overview two of the authors' current relevant studies that are illustrative of how digital technologies can be used to support moderation and the collection and use of evidence for formative purposes and summative purposes, as long advocated by Black (Black, 2014; Black et al., 2003, 2004; Black et al., 2011; Dolin et al., 2018). The studies, discussed next, have in common an interest in data analytics, and digital technologies opening a reconceptualization of moderation in the digital age.

What is the digital black box of assessment?

In the twenty-first century, systems have an insatiable appetite for data needed to investigate performance in schools and universities within nations and internationally. Of relevance in this chapter is the potential contribution of moving moderation online and supporting judgement consistency through new approaches to data analytics and the formative use of summative data, as advocated by Black.

Study 1: The application of online moderation in middle schooling

Consistency of teacher judgement is an ongoing concern, even among school systems that incorporate social moderation. As Black (2015) identified, there is scant large-scale empirical evidence regarding teachers' use of standards to assess student learning for formative (improvement) purposes and summative (reporting) purposes. The ARC Linkage Project (LP180100046: *Improving teacher assessment capability using scaled annotated exemplars of achievement standards in online moderation*) aims to address the consistency of teacher judgements through the potential of scaled student classroom assessment samples that exemplify A-E standards within a new online moderation method. The project utilizes the psychometric scaling method of pairwise comparison (Heldsinger & Humphry, 2010) combined with *cognitive commentaries* of teacher judgements (Smith, 1989, 1995;[4] Wyatt-Smith & Bridges, 2007) to connect standards and judgement practice. Pairwise comparison involves raters judging which of two performances is considered the better performance against criteria. Multiple ratings and statistical processes enable a hierarchical scale of the level of achievement evident in performances to be established. In this project, pairwise comparison is also used in the comparison of a subset of scaled performances and descriptors of quality to establish stable representations of samples illustrating A-E standards.

The term 'cognitive commentary' refers to the product of a teacher's or assessor's articulation of how they judged a sample of student work, that is, the features of the work that were brought to bear in their overall judgement decision. This includes how they combined both the explicit or stated criteria and any latent or unstated criteria, offsetting stronger and weaker aspects of the work in their judgement (Sadler, 1989; Wyatt-Smith & Klenowski, 2013). The commentaries capture teachers' thinking and decision-making in the process of judgement making. The combination of pairwise comparison of work samples and then against standard descriptors with cognitive commentaries addresses a recognized missing link in improving teacher assessment practice – in particular, the comparability of standards to improve judgement dependability and teacher confidence in their judgement practices.

The establishment of an online repository with the scaled samples and corresponding cognitive commentaries will provide a resource for teachers to use, regardless of location, to moderate their ongoing student work. This study, funded by the Australian government, is contributing to rethinking the moderation practice through the use of statistical measures in the development of the scale, and cognitive and social measures in the development of the commentaries alongside verified and established achievement standards.

Study 2: The application of online cross-institutional moderation and data analytics in teacher education

In 2016, the Australian government called for the introduction of a competence assessment – teaching performance assessment (TPA) – in teacher education. While there was a history of such assessments in the United States, there was no precedent in Australia. The expectation was that preservice teachers complete a TPA as a mandatory high-stakes summative assessment in their final year of preparation with an overall pass required for licensure. A function of the TPA was to establish graduate preparedness for entry to the classroom.[5]

When the requirement for the new summative assessment was introduced, Australia lacked a national evidence base to show the quality of graduates from the country's teacher education programmes. While a national approach to professional standards, which informed programme development and accreditation, had been in place for some time, these tended to serve as inputs and there was no approach to cross-institutional moderation in teacher education within and across states. It was also a time when there was mounting concern about the quality of graduates entering the teaching workforce: large-scale workforce studies in teacher education were in their infancy.

The authors' response to this concern was to develop and implement a multi-pronged approach. The first prong included the development of a TPA, known as the Graduate Teacher Performance Assessment (GTPA˙),[6] which was subject to a large-scale trial, validation and standard-setting process. The second prong was to develop and implement online scoring methodologies for supporting online moderation as well as innovative data analytics, designed as fit for formative and summative purposes. This could only be achieved by collaborating at scale across universities and with a multidisciplinary team of assessment researchers, digital architects, statisticians, teacher educators and regulatory authorities.

Bringing this together required the development of digital infrastructure to enable online moderation conducted at scale. Online cross-institutional moderation was at the heart of generating data for analyses at scale that could provide evidence of consistency of judgement in real time, patterns of performance against specified criteria, interrater reliability in the application of the established standard and rater severity measures. Through these approaches the assessment is serving systemic credentialing purposes and confidential reporting purposes to participating universities. Additionally, the data analyses and related reports are being taken up for formative purposes, including programme review and curriculum renewal, as internationally distinctive features of the GTPA. As part of this multi-pronged approach, the *Evidence for Quality in Initial Teacher Education* (EQuITE) system was developed to enable data entry by universities, data storage, cross-institutional moderation, and the generation and distribution of reports. The system includes five critical components:

1. A web portal for online *submission of selected GTPA performance samples*;
2. A web portal for online *cross-institution scoring of samples against the established standard*;
3. The GTPA app for online *collation and storage of data on initial teacher education performance* for cohorts of preservice teachers;
4. *Data analysis and automated report generation* to provide confidential evidence to universities from their own data; and
5. *Access to a repository of de-identified longitudinal data* on consistency of judgement, application of the standard and patterns of initial teacher education (ITE) programme cohort scores.[7]

Components 1–3 enable the collection and collation of de-identified samples for blind review and scoring by teacher educators, and the annual submission of results for analysis. Components 4–5 support analysis for summative purposes and generate data for formative purposes used to inform teacher educator decisions in curriculum review and programme renewal.

Conclusion

This chapter has shown the profound influence of Black's thinking about the power of feedback for engagement and improvement, the formative use of summative assessment and the value of collaborative interrogation of measures of quality. Through the affordances of digital technologies, we are aiming to conceptualize the relationships among assessment purposes and judgement practices in moderation, working at-scale and online. At the deepest levels Black's work has been foundational to these endeavours including reviewing the black box in the contemporary era of social change and digital disruption.

Notes

1. https://www.qcaa.qld.edu.au/downloads/publications/research_qbssss_rosba_11.pdf
2. The Queensland Studies Authority is now known as the Queensland Curriculum and Assessment Authority (https://www.qcaa.qld.edu.au/).
3. The new Queensland Senior Assessment officially was introduced in 2019. Notable changes included (1) required endorsement of assessment tasks for summative purposes; 'QCAA assessors (endorsers) evaluate each [summative] assessment instrument and decide whether it provides evidence of the endorsement criteria. Endorsement decisions are based on the demonstration of two of the attributes of quality assessment – validity and accessibility' (Queensland Curriculum and Assessment Authority [QCAA], 2020c); (2) confirmation of judgements as a quality-assurance process intended to check 'the accuracy and consistency of the judgments made by teachers' (QCAA, 2020b); and (3) the introduction of a common assessment (an externally set examination) to be untaken by all students (QCAA, 2020a).
4. Now writing as Claire M. Wyatt-Smith.
5. Readers interested in background to this policy reform are referred to the Teacher Education Ministerial Advisory Group (TEMAG) report titled *Action Now: Classroom Ready Teachers* (Craven et al., 2014) and the accompanying *Australian Government Response to Action Now: Classroom Ready Teachers Report* (Department of Education and Training, 2015).
6. Acknowledgment: The Graduate Teacher Performance Assessment' Project (GTPA) was created by the Institute for Learning Sciences and Teacher Education, Australian Catholic University, and has been implemented in a Collective of Higher Education Institutions in Australia (graduatetpa.com).
7. Readers interested in further information about EQuITE are referred to Wyatt-Smith et al. (2022).

References

Adie, L. E., V. Klenowski & C. Wyatt-Smith (2012). 'Towards an understanding of teacher judgement in the context of social moderation'. *Educational Review*, 64(2): 223–40. https://doi.org/10.1080/00131911.2011.598919

Baird, J. (2011). 'Does the learning happen inside the black box?'. *Assessment in Education: Principles, Policy & Practice*, 18(4): 343–5. http://dx.doi.org/10.1080/0969594X.2011.614857

"Black box." *Merriam-Webster.com Dictionary*, Merriam-Webster. https://www.merriam-webster.com/dictionary/black%20box

Black, P. (1995). 'Curriculum and assessment in science education: The policy interface'. *International Journal of Science Education*, 17(4): 453–69. https://doi-org.ezproxy1.acu.edu.au/10.1080/0950069950170405

Black, P. (2014). 'Assessment and the aims of the curriculum: An explorer's journey'. *Prospects*, 44(4): 487–501. https://doi.org/10.1007/s11125-014-9329-7

Black, P. (2015). 'Formative assessment: An optimistic but incomplete vision'. *Assessment in Education: Principles, Policy & Practice*, 22: 37–41. https://doi-org.ezproxy1.acu.edu.au/10.1080/0969594X.2014.999643

Black, P. (2016). 'The role of assessment in pedagogy – and why validity matters'. In D. Wyse, L. Hayward, J. Pandya & P. Black. (Eds.), *The SAGE Handbook of Curriculum, Pedagogy and Assessment*, 725–38. London: SAGE Publications Ltd. https://doi.org/10.4135/9781473921405.n45

Black, P., C. Harrison, J. Hodgen, B. Marshall & N. Serret (2010). 'Validity in teachers' summative assessments'. *Assessment in Education: Principles, Policy and Practice*, 17(2): 215–32. https://doi.org/10.1080/09695941003696016

Black, P., C. Harrison, J. Hodgen, B. Marshall & N. Serret (2011). 'Can teachers' summative assessments produce dependable results and also enhance classroom learning?' *Assessment in Education: Principles, Policy & Practice*, 18(4): 451–69. https://doi.org/10.1080/0969594X.2011.557020

Black, P., C. Harrison, C. Lee, B. Marshall & D. Wiliam (2003). *Assessment for Learning: Putting it into practice*. Maidenhead, UK.: Open University Press.

Black, P., C. Harrison, C. Lee, B. Marshall & D. Wiliam (2004). 'Working inside the black box: Assessment for learning in the classroom'. *Phi Delta Kappan*, 86(1): 9–21. https://doi-org.ezproxy1.acu.edu.au/10.1177/003172170408600105

Black, P., R. McCormick, M. James & D. Pedder (2006). 'Learning how to learn and assessment for learning: A theoretical inquiry'. *Research Papers in Education*, 21(02): 119–32. https://doi.org/10.1080/02671520600615612

Black, P. & D. Wiliam (1998a). 'Assessment and classroom learning'. *Assessment in Education: Principles, Policy & Practice*, 5(1): 7–74. https://doi.org/10.1080/0969595980050102

Black, P. & D. Wiliam (1998b). 'Inside the black box: Raising standards through classroom assessment'. *Phi Delta Kappan*, 80(2): 139–48. http://www.jstor.org/stable/20439383

Black, P. and D. Wiliam (2006). 'The reliability of assessments'. In J. Gardner (Ed.), *Assessment and learning*, 119–31. London: Sage.

Black, P. & D. Wiliam (2018). 'Classroom assessment and pedagogy'. *Assessment in Education: Principles, Policy & Practice,* 25(6): 551–75. https://doi.org/10.1080/0969 594X.2018.1441807

Bradley, J. (n.d.). 'Black box theory of politics'. https://classroom.synonym.com/black-box-theory-politics-6095.html

Broadfoot, P. & P. Black (2004). 'Redefining assessment? The first ten years of Assessment in Education'. *Assessment in Education: Principles, Policy & Practice,* 11(1): 8–27. https://doi.org/10.1080/0969594042000208976

Craven, G., Beswick, K., Fleming, J., Fletcher, T., Green, M., Jensen, B., Leinonen, E., & Rickards, F. (2014a). *Action now: Classroom ready teachers.* Teacher Education Ministerial Advisory Group, TEMAG. Department of Education, Australia.

Dolin, J., P. Black, W. Harlen & A. Tiberghien (2018). 'Exploring relations between formative and summative assessment'. In J. Dolin & R. Evans (Eds.), *Transforming Assessment: Through an Interplay between Practice, Research and Policy,* 54–80. Cham, Switzerland: Springer International Publishing.

Education Services Australia (ESA) (n.d.). *Assessment for Learning.* https://www.assessmentforlearning.edu.au/research_background/research_background_landing.html

Hargreaves, E. (2005). 'Assessment for learning? Thinking outside the (black) box'. *Cambridge Journal of Education,* 35(2): 213–24. https://doi.org/10.1080/03057640500146880

Harrison, C. & S. Howard (2009). *Inside the Primary Black Box: Assessment for Learning in Primary and Early Years Classrooms.* London: GL Assessment.

Hattie, J. (2009). 'The black box of tertiary assessment: An impending revolution'. In L. H. Meyer, S. Davidson, H. Anderson, R. Fletcher, P. M. Johnston & M. Rees (Eds.), *Tertiary Assessment and Higher Education Student Outcomes: Policy, Practice and Research,* 259–75. Ako Aotearoa: Victoria University of Wellington.

Heldsinger, S. & S. Humphry (2010). 'Using the method of pairwise comparison to obtain reliable teacher assessments'. *Australian Educational Researcher,* 37(2): 1–19.

Klenowski, V. & C. Wyatt-Smith (2010). 'Standards-driven reform years 1–10: Moderation an optional extra?' *Australian Educational Researcher,* 37(2): 21–39. https://doi.org/10.1007/BF03216920

Matters, G. & G. N. Masters (2014). *Redesigning the Secondary–Tertiary Interface, Queensland Review of Senior Assessment and Tertiary Entrance.* Brisbane: Australian Council for Educational Research. https://research.acer.edu.au/qld_review/1/

Maxwell, G. (2007). 'Implications for moderation of proposed changes to senior secondary school syllabuses'. Paper commissioned by the Queensland Studies Authority. Brisbane: Queensland Studies Authority.

Maxwell, G. S. & J. J. Cumming (2011). 'Managing without public examinations: Successful and sustained curriculum and assessment reform in Queensland'. In L. Yates, C. Collins & K. O'Connor (Eds.), *Australia's Curriculum Dilemmas: State Perspectives and Changing Times,* 202–22. Melbourne: Melbourne University Press.

Queensland Curriculum and Assessment Authority (2020a). 'About external assessment'. https://www.qcaa.qld.edu.au/senior/assessment/external-assessment/about

Queensland Curriculum and Assessment Authority (2020b). Confirmation. https://www.qcaa.qld.edu.au/senior/assessment/quality-assurance/confirmation

Queensland Curriculum and Assessment Authority (2020c). Endorsement. https://www.qcaa.qld.edu.au/senior/assessment/quality-assurance/endorsement

Ravet, J. (2013). 'Delving deeper into the black box: Formative assessment, inclusion and learners on the autism spectrum'. *International Journal of Inclusive Education,* 17(9): 948–64. https://doi.org/10.1080/13603116.2012.719552

Sadler, D. R. (1989). 'Formative assessment and the design of instructional systems'. *Instructional Science,* 18(2): 119–44. https://doi.org/10.1007/BF00117714

Sadler, D. R. (1992). 'Expert review and educational reform: The case of student assessment in Queensland secondary schools'. *Australian Journal of Education,* 36(3): 301–17.

Smith, C. M. (1989). *A Study of Standards Specifications in English.* Unpublished Master of Education thesis. University of Queensland.

Smith, C. M. (1995). *Teachers' Reading Practices in the Secondary School Writing Classroom: A Reappraisal of the Nature and Function of Pre-specified Assessment Criteria.* Unpublished Doctor of Philosophy thesis. University of Queensland.

Stobart, G. (2008). *Testing Times: The Uses and Abuses of Assessment.* Routledge.

Wyatt-Smith, C. & S. Bridges (2007). *Meeting in the Middle: Assessment, Pedagogy, Learning and Students at Educational Disadvantage.* Final Evaluation Report for the Department of Education, Science and Training on Literacy and Numeracy in the Middle Years of Schooling.

Wyatt-Smith, C. M. & V. Klenowski (2008). 'Examining how moderation is enacted within an assessment policy reform initiative: You just have to learn how to see'. *International Association for Educational Assessment,* 7–12 September.

Wyatt-Smith, C. M. & V. Klenowski (2010). 'The role and purpose of standards in the context of national curriculum and assessment reform for accountability, improvement and equity in student learning'. *Curriculum Perspectives,* 30(3): 37–47.

Wyatt-Smith, C., V. Klenowski & S. Gunn (2010). 'The centrality of teachers' judgement practice in assessment: A study of standards in moderation'. *Assessment in Education: Principles, Policy and Practice,* 17(1): 59–75. https://doi.org/10.1080/09695940903565610

Wyatt-Smith, C. & V. Klenowski (2013). 'Explicit, latent and meta-criteria: Types of criteria at play in professional judgement practice'. *Assessment in Education: Principles, Policy and Practice,* 20(1): 35–52. https://doi.org/10.1080/0969594X.2012.725030

Wyatt-Smith, C. M. & P. J. Colbert (2014). 'An account of the inner workings of standards, judgement and moderation: A previously untold evidence-based narrative. Informing paper for the Review of Queensland Senior Assessment and School Reporting and Tertiary Entrance Processes undertaken by Australian Council for Educational Research (ACER). Brisbane, Australia: Learning Sciences Institute Australia, Australian Catholic University'. https://research.acer.edu.au/cgi/viewcontent.cgi?article=1006&context=qld_review

Wyatt-Smith, C. & L. Adie (2019). 'The development of students' evaluative expertise: Enabling conditions for integrating criteria into pedagogic practice'. *Journal of Curriculum Studies*. https://doi.org/10.1080/00220272.2019.1624831

Wyatt-Smith, C., L. Adie & J. Nuttall, Eds. (2022). *Achieving Accountability through Collaboration in Initial Teacher Education: Another Pathway for Teaching Performance Assessments*. Springer Series: Teacher Education, Learning Innovation and Accountability.

Wyatt-Smith, C., B. Lingard & E. Heck, Eds. (forthcoming 2021). *Digital Disruption in Teaching and Testing: Assessments, Big Data, and the Transformation of Schooling*. London, England: Routledge.

Wyatt-Smith, C., Adie, L., Haynes, M, & Day, C. (2022). *Professionalizing Teacher Education: Performance Assessment, Standards, Moderation, and Evidence*. New York: Routledge.

Student Involvement in Assessment: Queensland Teacher Repertoires of Practice

Valentina Klenowski and Jill Willis

Introduction

Paul Black's academic contribution and extensive intellectual exploration of educational assessment have inspired many in the research of student involvement in assessment processes and their relationships with learning. The helpful guidance and advice for practical action from Paul's research, writing and teaching, motivated our research pursuits in classroom assessment to discover and understand the processes and practices for teaching and learning.

In this chapter we draw on the wide-ranging research and publications of Paul and his colleagues to illustrate the impactful outcomes at the various levels of educational systems, assessment and learning theories, and classroom teaching practices. We demonstrate the significance of Paul's far-reaching contributions with reference to curriculum and assessment change in Australia and through our own educational research and experiences. In particular, we refer to how insights gained from our study of Paul's practical research and assessment theorizing, impacted on our own explorations of how assessment can help students develop as effective and responsible learners. This has included studies of teacher practice of classroom assessment in the context of achieving fairness and equity through co-regulation, classroom co-regulation with students and teacher peers, and co-regulation through technology use in facilitating assessment practice.

Background

In 1998 in his classic text 'Testing: Friend or foe? Theory and practice of assessment and testing', Paul Black argued why learners' involvement in their own assessment was essential. In particular, he maintained that self-assessment was intrinsic to learning. His insights involved a more profound understanding of how changes in the role of the student and in the relationship with their teachers occur because of their active involvement in assessment. However, to fully understand student involvement in assessment and the impact on learning, further research was needed. Paul identified the following areas for further research and development. He was aware that students perceived assessment results as indicators of their success yet were unaware of the way in which feedback could help improve their learning and the way in which students themselves work. He was also aware that students did not understand the learning aims and did not know of the learning criteria by which to assess their own progress. He argued that self-assessment required 'reflective judgement of one's own work' (1998: 136) and that the capacity to make judgements was an essential and intrinsic feature of effective learning. Paul drew attention to how students quickly learn to label themselves as good or helpless learners, with the latter becoming demotivated and believing that there is no point in making efforts to learn. He concluded that good formative assessment needed to be ipsative, that is assessed according to the individual student's previous results rather than normative, which involves assessment based on other students' results or a set of static criteria. Ipsative assessment was considered to be devoted to building self-esteem and a belief in oneself (1998: 136). He heightened awareness of the negative impact of traditional summative assessment practices on students' efforts to improve and their will to learn. Formative self-assessment he saw as an opportunity to develop such capacities and with this awareness further important areas for research were identified.

It was also in 1998 that Paul worked with Dylan Wiliam on their world-renowned analysis of classroom assessment and learning. An evaluation of the literature on assessment and learning was considered essential by the British Educational Research Association Assessment Group, which subsequently became the important Assessment Reform Group. The final review (Black & Wiliam, 1998a) was published in the *Assessment in Education: Principles, Policy and Practice* journal and researchers were invited to write commentaries such as those by contributors: Perrenoud (1998), Sadler (1998) and Biggs (1998). As summed up by Hopfenbeck (2018: 545) the importance of this particular issue of the journal was that it 'pushed the research field of assessment forward'. Research on feedback, self-assessment and formative assessment processes began and has continued to the present day.

The review (Black & Wiliam, 1998a) of the research provided Paul and his colleagues (Black et al., 2003) with both quantitative and qualitative evidence that demonstrated innovations in formative assessment could lead to improvement in student learning. However, the findings were also significant for they revealed that formative assessment practices were underdeveloped. More specifically, the limitations in the quality of classroom assessment practice were identified. These included teacher use of tests that encouraged rote and superficial learning, a tendency for some primary teachers to acknowledge quantity and presentation of work rather than the quality of the learning, and the negative consequences of giving marks and grades to be used solely for comparative purposes. Feedback was also found to be used by teachers for social or managerial purposes instead of to support learning. Consequently, Black, Harrison, Lee, Marshall and Wiliam (2003) in their book *Assessment for Learning*, took up the messages from the review to explore teacher change, students' perspectives and the concept of feedback. The programme of development on which the research was based involved teachers changing their practices. It was evident from the research evidence that what was needed were

> examples of implementation, by teachers with whom they can identify and from whom they can derive conviction and confidence that they can do better, and see concrete examples of what doing better means in practice.
> (Black & Wiliam, 1998b:15–16)

Teacher change to classroom practice is central, and as found by Black and Wiliam (1998b), improvement of formative assessment could not be 'a simple matter':

> [I]f the substantial rewards of which the evidence holds out promise are to be secured, this will only come about if each teacher finds his or her own patterns of classroom work. This can only happen relatively slowly, and through sustained programmes of professional development and support.
> (Black & Wiliam, 1998b:15)

It was also emphasized that teachers would not engage in ideas and general principles unless based on extensive research. Everyday work of the teacher is too demanding and challenging to adapt 'attractive sounding ideas' and principles into their classroom practice without researched assistance. A significant finding for sustainable change from Black et al.'s (2003) study was to get the pupils to do more of the thinking ... to make the learning process more transparent to the pupils. ... spend ... time looking for ways to get pupils to take responsibility for their learning at the same time making the learning more collaborative.

(2003: 94–5)

Black and Wiliam (2009) in *developing the theory of formative assessment* explored formative interactions within theories of pedagogy. They were responding to Perrenoud's (1998: 86) observation that feedback was no longer the most important issue: 'It would seem more important to concentrate on the theoretical models of learning and its regulation and their implementation. ... feedback is only one element.'

The earlier work of Black and Wiliam (1998a; 1998b) was not grounded in a theoretical framework rather they had synthesized a wide range of research findings related to formative assessment (Black & Wiliam, 2009). Perrenoud's recommendation was for

a theoretical model of the mediations through which an interactive situation influences cognition, and in particular the learning process.
(Perrenoud, 1998, cited by Black & Wiliam, 2009:11)

Black and Wiliam (2009:31) examined closely the concept of regulation at the two levels suggested by Perrenoud. The first involved 'the management of situations which favour the interactive regulation of the learning processes' and the second level of interactive regulation which 'takes place through didactic situations' (Perrenoud cited by Black and Wiliam, 2009). The first is a key feature of pedagogy according to Black and Wiliam, and the second involves formative interaction. Black and Wiliam (2009) argued that despite the model of learning whether it be, for example, the self-regulated learning models or the cognitive acceleration programmes, all included a formative approach. The difference was in the underpinning model of pedagogy of the design, within which formative assessment is to a greater or lesser extent implemented. They concluded that 'all involve the teacher in the difficult task of feedback for learning but in different ways'. Drawing on their findings they offered five key strategies of the following:

a. Clarifying and sharing learning intentions and criteria for success.
b. Engineering effective classroom discussions and other learning tasks that elicit evidence of student understanding.
c. Providing feedback that moves learners forward.

d. Activating students as instructional resources for one another and
e. Activating students as the owners of their own learning. (Black & Wiliam, 2009)

In our empirical research, we drew on the extensive findings and salient, helpful, practical studies of Paul and colleagues in the design and conduct of our studies of teaching and learning programmes carried out in Queensland, Australia.

Context: Queensland, Australia

Queensland is a northern state of Australia with a distinctive history in assessment practices. The Queensland Department of Education has operated a school-based assessment system, even at high-stakes level since the 1970s. Teachers design assessment in alignment with the curriculum, integrate formative evaluation with students in their daily practice and grade, review and report on student results. Even with the introduction of a Senior External Examination (SEE) in 2020 after a major review (Matters & Masters, 2014) teachers remain responsible for designing assessment and conducting the peer-review quality assurance processes. There have been regular changes in curriculum and assessment policies that have led to renewal and refinement of assessment practices in Queensland, with our own research studies often situated in these changing assessment reform contexts. Often the changes have involved teachers reconciling competing state and national assessment requirements.

In Australia it is the Australian Curriculum and Assessment Authority (ACARA), co-owned by federal, state and territory governments, that has responsibility for the development of the national curriculum and the administration of the National Assessment Program – Literacy and Numeracy (NAPLAN). Curriculum implementation and student assessment outside the national tests in literacy and numeracy remain a state responsibility (Gleeson, Klenowski & Looney, 2020). At the same time there has been an important shift away from prescriptive specifications of knowledge content to the inclusion of a broader range of skills and attributes for success in the twenty-first century with the introduction of the Australian Curriculum (AC) in 2008. The AC was developed for all students from ages 4–16, with each state then adapting the curriculum and assessment practices.

In our overview of the agentic assessment work of teachers (Willis & Klenowski, 2018), we outline how Queensland teachers are continually making sense of new agendas and how pedagogic frameworks based on the work of Paul Black and Dylan William have been an important source of professional learning for Queensland teachers in their assessment development. Questions about the role of assessment and concerns with student outcomes, and the centrality of the learner have prompted teachers to question some of their long-held assumptions (Klenowski & Willis, 2011). Much of our research over the years has focused on researching with teachers to understand the importance of teaching, learning and assessment practices designed to enhance students' development of attributes and capabilities as well as content knowledge, understanding and skills.

In what follows we draw on our collaborative and individual studies in Queensland that align with the helpful research findings of Black and his colleagues. First and foremost our work has investigated the contexts of teacher and student interactions to understand how assessment can be utilized to develop students as effective and responsible learners. Our studies of teacher assessment practices in their classroom contexts explore patterns of practices that exemplify the management of assessment for learning interactions. In addition, they make connections from practices to theoretical principles that can support teachers as they develop students' reflective judgement through assessment.

Equity and co-regulation

The Queensland school-based assessment system and a valuing of teacher professional knowledge and standards as developed by the Australian Institute for Teaching and School Leadership (https://www.aitsl.edu.au/teach/standards) have contextualized our research and theorizing in assessment. In some of our research on assessment for learning we have utilized a sociocultural view of learning and a critical inquiry approach to pedagogy and assessment. The mediations that we have explored, from this view and using a sociocultural approach, stem from the work of Black and his colleagues and include teacher practice of formative assessment, feedback (Willis & Klenowski, 2018) and student self-assessment (Klenowski, 2002). The understandings gained from Paul Black's research provided opportunities for us to study formative interactions that led us to develop insights into the theories and models of teaching, assessment and learning.

One such study focused on the issue of equity and fairness in assessment, at a time of escalating student diversity and increasing accountability in Australia (Klenowski, 2009). The Australian student population continues to grow increasingly diverse: culturally, ethnically, socially and linguistically, which implies the need for alternative, supportive pedagogic practices with a variety of classroom assessment practices. Quality, alternative assessment practices which result in a more holistic view of the learner and more equitable outcomes for all students are needed in this context of increasing diversity.

In the pursuit of fairness and equity in assessment it is considered important for all students to be given the opportunity to demonstrate learning using a form of assessment which does not prevail over the knowledge to be assessed. Students from different ethnic backgrounds, social circumstances or cultures will have different qualities and experiences that they bring to the classroom learning situation. A significant finding from research of formative assessment approaches to the teaching and learning of Indigenous students (Klenowski, 2014) was that the majority of the teachers interviewed stated that they aimed to 'treat all students the same'. Ironically, by treating all students the way dominant groups have been treated, these teachers regarded this as fair. Such a view exposes a limited understanding of the concept of fairness and of validity in assessment.

We discovered that there was limited evidence of innovation or the building of teacher expertise in classroom assessment (such as task-based assessment or high-quality assessment). Teachers did not find the dominant practices of streaming and ability grouping as problematic in relation to achieving equity and fairness in assessment. Only a few teachers, of the many involved in this study, were aware of Assessment for Learning models, and while many were critical of testing, very few had attempted to modify assessment practice to accommodate or engage with the knowledges and cultures of the Indigenous students in their classes.

Proficiency in assessment practice and/or innovation with classroom-based assessment and the use of models of authentic assessment, assessment for learning or task-based assessment, were found to be valid and fundamental in the teachers' development of concepts of equity and fairness. One such approach to learning and assessment which aligned with the findings of Black et al. (2003) and which appeared to achieve some success was the use of personal learning plans. The process of interacting and providing feedback, engaging actively and acknowledging agency of the student and their parents and carers in this process was considered to be more responsive to student resources and capacities, and the cultural contexts of learning. This approach to learning involved working with each student, partnership with students, parents and carers, to develop a plan of the student's goals, current capabilities and specific learning targets. In the next section we continue with the ways in which teachers and students can develop assessment literacy through classroom co-regulation.

Classroom co-regulation with students and teacher peers

An assessment system that relies on teacher professional judgement, that has as its goal to advance student equity in learning and that is continually undergoing change, depends on teachers having a deeply rooted understanding of assessment principles and practices, and the capacity to be adaptable. This has several implications for teacher assessment literacy when student learning is highlighted as the teacher's central assessment concern:

> In developing teachers' assessment capacity there is a need to attend to assessment literacy so that one sees beyond the raw scores and understands the related equity issues. Classroom assessments that directly contribute to learning need to be maintained, and teachers' theories of learning need to be developed as the basis for a principled understanding of learning and assessment. With attention to these qualities, teacher assessment can itself become a source of dependable results, provided there is adequate moderation practice.
>
> (Klenowski, 2012: 174)

As Paul Black and Dylan William highlighted, teachers need to find their 'own patterns of work'. Our work with teachers highlighted that in developing classroom assessment capacity, teachers draw on multiple assessment literacies. We drew on case studies of assessment with Queensland teachers (Willis, Adie & Klenowski, 2013) that were responses to assessment changes occurring at much the same time in Queensland. Alongside culture-inclusive assessment for Indigenous students (Klenowski, Connolly & Funnell, 2012), schools were introducing Assessment for Learning (Willis, 2011) and teacher social moderation (Adie, 2010). These cases made it clear that teachers worked closely with students, peers, community elders and researchers to negotiate new assessment practices. By negotiation we mean that teachers had to weigh up their curriculum knowledge, their current practices, knowledge about students and what seemed possible within their contexts. To highlight this ongoing, active process of assessment learning for teachers, we proposed a definition of assessment literacy:

> Assessment literacy is a dynamic context dependent social practice that involves teachers articulating and negotiating classroom and cultural knowledges with one another and with learners, in the initiation, development and practice of assessment to achieve the learning goals of students.
>
> (Willis, Adie & Klenowski, 2013: 232)

This definition brought the interactivity of classroom assessment practice to the fore and contributed to sociocultural theories of assessment for learning. It also highlighted the importance of teachers learning *with* and *from* students.

Students are agents in assessment as they make choices and take actions during assessment (Adie, Willis & Van der Kleij, 2018). As Black (1998) highlighted, student capacity to reflect and self-evaluate, and develop self-belief through their judgement-making is an essential feature of effective learning. In all of our projects we have observed teachers designing classroom assessment opportunities for students to reflect on work with peers, leading to the students generating new insights for teachers. Sometimes these practices have helped to reinforce and reproduce disciplinary expectations, as students have learned to use exemplars, criteria and standards as provided by their teachers (Adie & Willis, 2016). We have also observed how classroom routines shifted as students ask more informed questions and use more peer-to-peer talk as students translated teacher expectations to peers using the criteria checklists (Willis, 2011). At other times, students responded in unexpected ways that challenged teacher assumptions. Students who were regarded as 'low achievers' responded to the 'insider knowledge' of what was expected by producing work that surprised teachers (Willis, McGraw & Graham, 2019). Students advocated more assessment for learning practices from other teachers in the school and questioned the mixed messages being given about peer assessment (Willis & Klenowski, 2018). New assessment practices can be confronting to teachers as they can alter established power structures in classrooms, which is why support from teaching peers and researchers has been essential for the sustainability of assessment learning.

Like Black and Wiliam (1998b), we have found that teachers having access to support from researchers helps the teachers to consider new assessment approaches within the complexity of their day-to-day practice. As assessment researchers we provide access to new ideas, new forms of data, facilitate group discussions, and ask questions that challenge assumptions or open up reflections. Also as teachers try out new assessment practices, they raise important questions for researchers to consider. For example in a study with teachers about new national assessment standards (Willis & Adie, 2013) we learned that prior to teachers sharing success criteria with students, teachers needed opportunities for conversations about what the standards looked like in practice with their teaching colleagues to inform their curriculum planning. When facilitated by the research team, these conversations enabled some of the school systems that were taken for granted to be reconsidered. Also when these conversations with colleagues were grounded in samples of student work, and documented as annotations, teachers were able to 'dig in' to their tacit expectations and through the discussion make some of these assumptions more explicit. Teachers found that they were able to share success criteria with students through examples and a deep knowledge of the expected qualities of performance, so students could regulate their own performance. The teachers were often surprised by the quality of the students' results (Willis & Adie, 2014). Importantly as researchers we were able to understand from teacher questions and comments that annotating samples of student work might look similar to giving feedback to students; however, they have important differences in timing, audience and purpose. Annotations of student work samples could not be 'added in' to a teacher's repertoire without accompanying professional learning and support for collegial planning and consideration of the school's marking and reporting systems. Co-regulation with students and teacher peers has implications for how assessment is co-regulated in recording, reporting and data analysis systems across and beyond the school. Increasingly this co-regulation is mediated by technology.

Co-regulation through technology

At the same time that Australia's assessment expectations were changing with the national curriculum, testing and professional standards, there was a simultaneous investment in computing technology across Australian schools. The Rudd/Gillard Australian governments responded to the 2008 financial crisis with a 'Digital Education Revolution' funding package that enabled every Australian school to receive broadband connection and digital infrastructure, secondary school students to receive laptops, and teachers to receive professional development in information and computing technologies and resources (Brown, 2020). Together the national technological, curriculum and assessment policies enabled large-scale accountability systems to be established with schools steered and governed from a distance through data (Brown, 2020). Co-regulation of learning through assessment was occurring beyond the context of the classroom or school across districts, systems, states and nations.

This era of technology and test-based accountability, performance assessments and audits in Australia has threatened school leaders' agency and teachers' pedagogy. From our research (Klenowski & Ehrich, 2016) we have been made aware of how policy expectations have shifted so that teachers and school leaders now need to collect and interpret school and student achievement data as part of their efforts to improve school achievement. We adopted a participatory inquiry paradigm with teachers and the school leader in understanding the demands of the curriculum and assessment policy or practice to consider assessment from a democratic ethic (Klenowski & Woods, 2013). Transitioning towards ethical leadership involves educators at all levels collaborating with communities to ensure all students' educational interests are met in the long term. However, in a context of increasing accountability, tension arises when the focus shifts to the improvement of test results with attention diverted away from issues of equity and inclusion. The framework we adopted in our study drew on three interrelated ethics of care, justice and critique (Starratt, 1996, 2004, 2014). We define ethical leaders to be those who are successful in achieving equity reform through developing an inclusive organizational culture where staff, students and parents are valued and treated with care and respect. We worked with teachers and leaders to purposively ask critical questions about current practices which included those related to assessment and the ethical importance of equity. Ongoing and systematic inquiries about student learning occurred to address equity-related issues and involved leadership support that was guided by ethical principles and practices.

An increasing focus on assessment data and inquiry has also led to a greater emphasis on classroom assessment and teacher professional learning. Assessment for Learning was not a high priority in Australia prior to national assessment (Willis, 2011). With national data sets and easy-to-use technology, leaders have since been able to generate comparative reports that enable teachers to see a students' assessment results within the context of larger trends and temporal patterns. This has led to school leaders and school systems investing in more teacher professional development that elevates formative assessment practices like learning intentions, success criteria and feedback, as highlighted by John Hattie, Robert Marzarno and Lyn Sharratt (Willis & Klenowski, 2018). Technology has also enabled students to access learning and resources in new ways and to engage in peer feedback in online discussion forums where they can see multiple peer examples, teacher feedback, and trace their development over time at home or at school (Willis et al., 2019). However, not all students have equitable access to digital resources or the language and abilities to process complex assessment information (Graham et al., 2018; Willis & Klenowski, 2018).

More assessment research is also needed in collaboration with technology developers as learning analytics are providing new types of assessment interactions and information. Rapid development is occurring in computer-generated feedback and adaptive learning where the computer makes formative decisions for the students about what question or activity is offered next based on the students' responses. Simultaneously the learning analytics are gathered computationally and presented as patterns of data which can be accessed in real time by decision-makers like teachers and administrators and policymakers. Big data has potential to generate alternative ipsative assessment as digital traces of a student's decisions and activities can point to learning in real time (Cope & Kalantzis, 2016). Computational power can lead to faster and scalable visualizations of assessment data, yet sociocultural insights from teachers and learners are also needed to make meaningful assessment and learning connections (Willis et al., 2020). Where teachers have engaged in digitally mediated reflections, we have found that they not only find benefits in reflecting, but the computational reflective writing analytics have enabled new patterns of their own professional learning to be evident over time and at scale (Willis et al., 2017; Willis & Gibson, 2020). Teachers have been able to gain faster, 'capillary level' feedback about their learners at scale so they could engage in dialogic feedback loops and adapt their teaching (Willis et al., 2020). Interestingly where student reflections initiated a feedback loop, the characteristics of feedback also changed, from being focused towards performances on specific assessment tasks, to being focused on the processes of learning directly informing student self-regulation and teacher responsiveness.

The development of assessment technology not only changes the assessment activity but it also raises complex ethical issues. Stakeholder interests and access to data need to be considered at the early design stage rather than well after the algorithmic choices are 'baked into' the software. In developing digitally mediated feedback over a number of projects we recognize several persistent principles of educationally and technologically co-designed digital feedback: interactivity, pragmatic design, respect and trust (Gibson & Willis, 2020). For technology design decisions to focus on what is meaningful for students and teachers, research development cycles that include sociocultural sensitive development and analysis with educators and students are absolutely necessary. This sensitivity to the context and development of practices alongside students and teachers is a researcher stance that has been exemplified by Paul Black's work.

Conclusion

Paul Black's work has been highly influential in Australian classrooms, policy and research. Most teachers in Queensland would be familiar with Paul's recommended five formative assessment practices (Black & Wiliam, 2009). Yet we see that his contribution extends far beyond *which* assessment practices are enacted in classrooms to consider *how* assessment is related to learning and how student involvement in assessment changes learning relationships. His recognition that classroom assessment is a complex activity has informed our research approach, where we have worked alongside teachers in collaborative assessment inquiries to the benefit of the teachers' and our own learning.

Importantly Paul's insistence on the students' involvement in their own assessment has informed our work. While our research has often been prompted by assessment policy changes that were beyond the control of the classroom teacher, when teachers have been supported to engage in ethical inquiry *with* students about new assessment practices, both teachers and students have been able to retain or gain agency in assessment. Paul understood that when students become actively involved in their own assessment, it not only enables students to be self-regulating learners but co-regulates the classroom relationships.

In this chapter we have identified three themes of co-regulation that we see have grown from Paul's work and offer potential for future enquiry. Fairness and equity in assessment can only be achieved as we understand more about the student and teacher relationships in assessment. As teachers and students engage in peer conversations about assessment, challenging questions and ideas that don't 'fit' within current systems are raised. These questions invite practical action and further research. As we ask teachers to engage with uncomfortable or new practices through collaborative inquiry, so too we need to prepare ourselves as researchers to explore collaborations with computer scientists, learning designers and digital developers. The co-regulation of learning through assessment is a persistent principle even when assessment learning is always a project under development. Paul's own long-standing career is an example of this persistence of principle and openness to new practices that we gratefully acknowledge.

References

Adie, L. E. (2010). 'Developing consistency in teacher judgement formation through online meeting centres'. *Journal of Learning Design*, 3(2). https://doi.org/10.5204/jld.v3i2.47

Adie, L. E. & Willis, J. (2016). 'Making meaning of assessment policy in Australia through teacher assessment conversations'. In Allal, L. & Laveault, D. (Eds.), *Assessment for Learning: Meeting the Challenge of Implementation. The Enabling*

Power of Assessment, Volume 4, 35–53. Switzerland: Springer. https://doi.org/10.1007/978-3-319-39211-0_3

Adie, L. E., Willis, J. & Van der Kleij, F. M. (2018). 'Diverse perspectives on student agency in classroom assessment', *The Australian Educational Researcher*, 45(1): 1–12. https://doi.org/10.1007/s13384-018-0262-2

Australian Institute for Teaching and School Leadership. *Australian Professional Standards for Teachers*. https://www.aitsl.edu.au/teach/standards

Biggs, J. (1998). 'Assessment and classroom learning: A role for summative assessment?'. *Assessment in Education: Principles, Policy & Practice*, 5(1): 103–10, https://doi.org/10.1080/0969595980050106

Black, P. J. (1998). *Testing: Friend or Foe? Theory and Practice of Assessment and Testing*, London: Falmer. https://doi.org/10.4324/9780203137840

Black, P. J. & Wiliam, D. (1998a). 'Assessment and classroom learning'. *Assessment in Education: Principles Policy and Practice*, 5(1): 7–73. https://doi.org/10.1080/0969595980050102

Black, P. J., & Wiliam, D. (1998b). *Inside the Black Box: Raising Standards through Classroom Assessment*, London: King's College London School of Education. https://doi.org/10.1177/003172171009200119

Black, P. J., Harrison, C., Lee, C., Marshall, B. & Wiliam, D. (2003). *Assessment for Learning: Putting It into Practice*. Buckingham: Open University Press.

Black, P. J. & Wiliam, D. (2009). 'Developing the theory of formative assessment', *Education Assessment Evaluation and Accountability*, 21: 5–31 https://doi.org/10.1007/s11092-008-9068-5

Black, P. J. (2015). 'Formative assessment – an optimistic but incomplete vision'. *Assessment in Education: Principles, Policy and Practice*, 22(1): 161–77, https://doi.org10.1080/0969594X.2014.999643

Brown, B. (2020). 'Steering at a distance', Australian school principals' understandings of digital technologies policies during the Digital Education Revolution'. *Journal of Educational Administration and History*, https://doi.org/10.1080/00220620.2020.1856796

Cope, B., & Kalantzis, M. (2016). 'Big data comes to school: Implications for learning, assessment, and research'. *Aera Open*, 2(2), https://doi.org/10.1177/2332858416641907

Gibson, A. & Willis, J. (2020). 'Ethical challenges and guiding principles in facilitating personal digital reflection'. In Burr, C. & Floridi, L. (Eds.), *Ethics of Digital Well-Being: A Multidisciplinary Perspective*. 151–73. Netherlands: Springer. https://doi.org/10.1007/978-3-030-50585-1_8

Gleeson, J., Klenowski, V. & Looney, A. (2020). 'Curriculum change in Australia and Ireland: A comparative study of recent reforms'. *Journal of Curriculum Studies*, 52(4): 478–97, https://doi.org/10.1080/00220272.2019.1704064

Graham, L., Tancredi, H., Willis, J. & McGraw, K. (2018). 'Designing out barriers to student access and participation in secondary school assessment'. *Australian Educational Researcher*, 45(1): 103–24. https://doi.org/10.1007/s13384-018-0266-y

Hopfenbeck, T. N. (2018). 'Classroom assessment, pedagogy and learning – twenty years after Black and Wiliam 1998'. *Assessment in Education: Principles, Policy and Practice*, 25(6): 545–50, https://doi.org/10.1080/0969594X.2018.1553695

Klenowski, V. (2002). *Developing Portfolios for Learning and Assessment: Processes and Principles*. United Kingdom, London: Routledge.

Klenowski, V. (2009). 'Australian Indigenous students: Addressing equity issues in assessment'. *Teaching Education*, 20(1): 77–93.

Klenowski, V. & Willis, J. (2011). 'Challenging teacher's assumptions in an era of curriculum and assessment change'. *The Primary and Middle Years Educator*, 9(1): 1–9.

Klenowski, V., Connolly, S. & Funnell, R. (2012). 'Examining the assessment opportunities for cultural connectedness for student learning: A sociocultural analysis'. In Boyle, C. (Ed.), *Student Learning: Improving Practice*, New York: Nova Science Publishers Inc.

Klenowski, V. (2012). 'Raising the stakes: The challenges for teacher assessment'. *Australian Educational Researcher*, 39(2): 173–92. https://doi.org/10.1007/s13384-012-0057-9

Klenowski, V. & Funnell, R. (2013). 'Exploring the conditions to support assessment for more equitable learning outcomes'. *Curriculum Perspectives*, 33(3): 33–45.

Klenowski, V. & Woods, A. (2013). 'Exploring the possibilities and methodological challenges of evaluation practice: A democratic question'. In Lai, M. & Kushner, S. (Eds.), *A Developmental and Negotiated Approach to School Self-Evaluation [Volume 14: Advances in Program Evaluation]*, 253–73. United Kingdom: Emerald Group Publishing.

Klenowski, V. (2013). 'Towards improving public understanding of judgement practice in standards-referenced assessment: An Australian perspective'. *Oxford Review of Education*, 39(1): 36–51. https://doi.org/10.1080/03054985.2013.764759

Klenowski, V. (2014). 'Towards fairer assessment'. *Australian Educational Researcher*, 41(4): 445–70. https://doi.org/10.1007/s13384-013-0132-x

Klenowski, V. & Ehrich, L. (2016). 'Transitioning towards ethical leadership: A collaborative investigation of achieving equity in times of high-stakes accountability'. *International Studies in Educational Administration*, 44(1): 41–54.

Matters, G. & Masters, G. (2014). *Redesigning the Secondary-Tertiary Interface: Queensland Review of Senior Assessment and Tertiary Entrance*. Melbourne: ACER.

Perrenoud, P. (1998). 'From formative evaluation to a controlled regulation of learning processes. Towards a wider conceptual field'. *Assessment in Education: Principles, Policy and Practice*, 5(1): 85–102. https://doi.org/10.1080/0969595980050105

Sadler, D.R. (1998). 'Formative assessment: Revisiting the territory'. *Assessment in Education: Principles, Policy and Practice*, 5(1): 77–84. https://doi.org/10.1080/0969595980050104

Starratt, R. J. (1996). *Transforming Educational Administration: Meaning, Community, and Excellence*. Maidenhead: McGraw-Hill Companies.

Starratt, R. J. (2004). *Ethical Leadership*. Volume 8. Hoboken, NJ: Jossey-Bass.

Starratt, R. J. (2014). 'Ethics and social justice: Strangers passing in the night?'. In I. Bogotch *International Handbook of Educational Leadership and Social (In)justice*, 67–80. Dordrecht: Springer. https://doi.org/10.1007/978-94-007-6555-9_5

Willis, J. (2011). 'Affiliation, autonomy and assessment for learning'. *Assessment in Education: Principles, Policy & Practice*, 18(4): 399–415. https://doi.org/10.1080/0969594X.2011.604305

Willis, J., & Adie, L. (2013). 'Negotiating the meaning of achievement standards in the Australian curriculum'. *Curriculum Perspectives*, 33(1): 52–62.

Willis, J., Adie, L. & Klenowski, V. (2013). 'Conceptualising teachers' assessment literacies in an era of curriculum and assessment reform'. *Australian Educational Researcher*. 241–56. https://doi.org/10.1007/s13384-013-0089-9

Willis, J. & Adie, L. (2014). 'Teachers using annotations to engage students in assessment conversations: Recontextualising knowledge'. *Curriculum Journal*, 25(4): 495–515. https://doi.org/10.1080/09585176.2014.968599

Willis, J., Crosswell, L., Morrison, C., Gibson, A., & Ryan, M. (2017). 'Looking for leadership: The potential of dialogic reflexivity with rural early-career teachers'. *Teachers and Teaching*, 23(7): 794–809. https://doi.org/10.1080/13540602.2017.1287695

Willis, J. & Klenowski, V. (2018). 'Classroom assessment practices and teacher learning: An Australian perspective'. *Teacher learning with classroom assessment: Perspectives from Asia Pacific*, 19–37, https://doi.org/10.1007/978-981-10-9053-0_2

Willis, J., McGraw, K., & Graham, L. (2019). 'Conditions that mediate teacher agency during assessment reform'. *English Teaching*, 18(2): 233–48. https://doi.org/10.1108/etpc-11-2018-0108

Willis, J. & Gibson, A. (2020). 'The emotional work of being an assessor: A reflective writing analytics inquiry into digital self-assessment'. In Fox, Jillian, Alexander, Colette & Aspland, Tania (Eds.), *Teacher Education in Globalised Times: Local Responses in Action*, 93–113. Singapore: Springer. https://doi.org/10.1007/978-981-15-4124-7_6

Willis, J., Gibson, A., Kelly, N., Spina, N., Azordegan, J. & Crosswell, L. (2020). 'Towards faster feedback in higher education through digitally mediated dialogic loops'. *Australasian Journal of Educational Technology*, 22–37. https://doi.org/10.14742/ajet.5977

10

Assessment for Equity: The Role of Formative Assessment

Dennis Alonzo, Chris Davison and Pasi Salhberg

Introduction

The work of Paul Black and Dylan Wiliam (1998) on formative assessment (FA) has been highly influential in shaping major assessment reforms in many educational systems, including in the UK, the United States, Australia, New Zealand, Hong Kong, Brunei, Singapore and many other countries. Building on their seminal research, many follow-up studies have been conducted into the role of FA in enhancing learning and teaching, with most findings reinforcing Paul and Dylan's original meta-analysis which highlighted the powerful impact of a range of FA practices and techniques on student learning (Hattie, 2008; Hattie & Timperley, 2007; Kippers, Wolterinck, Schildkamp, Poortman & Visscher, 2018; Rust, 2007).

In their meta-analysis Paul and Dylan (1998) highlighted the critical role of FA in enhancing the learning outcomes of low-achieving students, citing Bergan, Sladeczek, Schwarz, and Smith's (1991) study of 838 5-year-old students, primarily from disadvantaged backgrounds, drawn from six regions in the United States. In this study, students in the experimental group whose teachers were trained to implement FA had significantly higher scores in reading, mathematics and science than the control group. This potential use of FA to help support educationally disadvantaged students has been followed up in a few studies (e.g. Cumming, Dickson & Webster, 2013; Fenwick, 2011) but has never been explored systematically. While the use of FA to enhance student outcomes has a strong research base, there is little evidence about its use to ensure equitable support for educationally disadvantaged students.

The aim of this chapter is to investigate what specific research has been undertaken with students from low socio-economic backgrounds, using a scoping technique to review research evidence on how FA is used to address equity issues in the classroom internationally and some of the issues and challenges in doing so.

Formative assessment: The influence of Paul Black and Dylan Wiliam

Formative assessment has always been an implicit part of educational practice, but it was only in 1971 that Bloom, Hastings and Madaus formalized the term by adopting the concept from the field of evaluation along with summative assessment (SA). They describe the distinguishing features of SA versus FA, including the purpose and timing of assessments and the interpretability of data gathered by test items (Bloom, Hastings & Madaus, 1971). Since then, both terms have been used operationally to distinguish the types and functions of assessment. In general, those assessments being conducted by teachers regularly or daily to gather data aimed at improving learning were collectively referred to as FA while those assessments conducted to determine whether learning had occurred over a period of teaching were classified as SA.

The conception of and distinction between FA and SA in the United States spread to other countries, including Australia, which, during this period, was not very reliant on high-stakes tests, hence judgements about student learning involved a relatively large degree of teacher-based assessment, even for formal secondary graduation requirements. In Queensland, Sadler (1989) formalized the distinction between FA and SA, attributing it to the work of Ramaprasad (1983), who put feedback as the central feature of FA. Sadler argued that FA differs from SA in terms of purpose and effect (like Bloom et al., 1971) but excluded timing as a distinguishing feature. He further posited that 'many of the principles appropriate to summative assessments are not necessarily transferable to formative assessment, the latter requires a distinctive conceptualization and technology' (Sadler, 1989: 120).

The concept of FA has gained unprecedented attention because of the groundbreaking work of Paul and Dylan (1998). Their meta-analysis of over 250 studies on the effects of FA in learning and teaching explored the utilization of FA to improve student learning. Shortly after the publication of their seminal paper, which showed the powerful effect of FA in improving student learning and the benefits it had for low-achieving students, various educational systems adopted it as a centrepiece of their educational reforms. However, even before Paul and Dylan's work was commissioned, the value of

FA in the UK had been acknowledged. In fact, from 1970s until the release of their 1998 paper, despite the dominance of SA in UK educational systems, there had been numerous studies documenting the effects of assessment in supporting learning. In 1982, FA had started to gain considerable attention with the recommendation of the Inquiry into the Teaching of Mathematics in Schools in the UK that 'assessment should be diagnostic and supportive and teaching should be based on the scheme of work which is appraised and revised regularly' (Cockcroft, 1982: 243). However, Paul and Dylan's work marked the beginning of the formalization of FA. In their report, they offered a definition of FA as follows:

> We use the general term assessment to refer to all those activities undertaken by the teachers – and by their students in assessing themselves – that provide information to be used as feedback to modify teaching and learning activities. Such assessment becomes formative assessment when the evidence is actually used to adapt the teaching to meet the student needs.
> (Black & Wiliam, 1998: 140)

In 2003 Paul and his colleagues at King's College London extended this definition and emphasized the utilization of the results of assessment as feedback to improve student learning. There was a strong emphasis on using assessment to elicit evidence of student learning to be used to 'adapt the teaching work to meet learning needs' (Black, Harrison, Lee, Marshall & Wiliam, 2003: 2–3).

In 2009, Paul and Dylan made a slight revision of their definition, highlighting the active role of students in monitoring learning and using the results of assessment to make decisions about their learning. They also incorporated SA as part of FA, adjusting their earlier position that SA could not be used for formative purposes. They argued that the results of SA provide data of students' achievement and, therefore, can be used to elicit and give feedback. Also, they emphasized the value of SA to 'communicate to learners what is and is not valued in a particular discipline, thus communicating criteria for success' (Black & Wiliam, 2009: 8).

More recently, they have revisited the recommendation of Perrenoud (1998) and have retheorized the relationship between FA and SA with a wider theoretical lens, particularly in relationship to the theory of pedagogy (see Black, 2017 and Black and Wiliam, 2018), although Baird et al. (2017) argue that assessment and learning are still fields apart in their current forms. Paul and Dylan have clearly articulated how assessment needs to be linked into the broader pedagogical approaches of teachers, emphasizing that the distinction between FA and SA 'is not useful because all assessment would be about producing valid inferences about students' (Black and Wiliam, 2018:570). This then draws attention to the validity of different assessments used for diverse student populations and the question about the role FA in enhancing equity in education.

Equity in assessment

The study of equality and equity in education, concepts often wrongly assumed to be interchangeable, has a long tradition. Since James Coleman and colleagues' study in the United States in the 1960s about equality of educational opportunities (Coleman et al., 1966) there has been a consensus among researchers that differences in students' academic learning outcomes are intimately linked to their home backgrounds, especially parents' or caregivers' socio-economic status (Alexander & Morgan, 2016). Indeed, these factors outside the school gate influence significantly more what students learn at school than curricula, teachers, school leaders or other in-school features.

Research on school effectiveness since the 1970s has revealed much better understanding of how these various factors actually affect student achievement in school (Teddlie, 2010). Popham and colleagues (2014) remind us that because 'teachers account for only a little variance in students' test scores', they are not the most significant forces in accounting for the differences in students' standardized test scores at school (also Haertel, 2013; Coleman et al., 1966). Nevertheless, the interrelated nature of the quality of education outcomes and how evenly they are distributed across student populations has remained a controversial topic in education policy and practice until present.

The concept of equity in education has been widely discussed over the past half a century. In the context of schooling, several overlapping and interrelated aspects such as inclusion, fairness, non-discrimination and social justice appear in considerations of how school education should be distributed in societies (Levin, 2009; OECD, 2018; Sahlberg & Cobbold, 2021; UNESCO, 2018). Often these discussions have been specifically about the idea of 'equality of opportunity' in education. In short, equity in education is a term which has several different interpretations and has therefore been a subject of much philosophical debate (Anderson, 1999; Dworkin, 2000; Sen, 1992; Scanlon, 2018). While this chapter is not a place to review these debates in detail, for the purposes of this review we need to define equity in education in relation to the practical context of educational assessment policies and practices, especially regarding school education.

When the OECD launched its Programme for International Student Assessment (PISA) in 2000, it included student-level data about the association between their home backgrounds and academic performance in school. Since the publication of more systematic comparative findings of these associations, equity in education has become a central theme in national education policies and school-level practices (OECD, 2012, 2018; Schleicher, 2018). In a seminal review of equity and quality in education OECD (2012) defined equity in education by two dimensions: Equity as *inclusion* means ensuring that all students reach at least a basic minimum level of skills and equity as *fairness* implies that personal or socio-economic circumstances, such as gender, ethnic origin or family background, are not obstacles to educational success.

Another intergovernmental organization, UNESCO (2018), sees equity in education as the means to achieving equality. It intends, according to UNESCO, to provide the best opportunities for all students to achieve their full potential and act to address instances of disadvantage which restrict educational achievement. For the purposes of this chapter, we understand equity in schooling to mean 'ensuring that differences in educational outcomes are not the result of differences in wealth, income, power or possessions'. This definition of educational equity was used by the panel led by David Gonski in Australia that reviewed funding for schooling in 2011 (Australian Government, 2011). In other words, when equity in education system enhances, the strength of the relationship between student's family background (or economic, social and cultural status) and achievement in school gets weaker. This is also called equity of education outcomes. How these outcomes are measured then plays an important role in determining equity in education.

Research into equity in education has been steadily growing over the last two decades, with many studies exploring specific settings of education policy and practice, such as school funding, staffing and curriculum (OECD, 2021). However, much less attention has been given to exploring equity in assessment, and how different assessment methods might help or hinder its development. Equity in assessment is often confused with equality, where policymakers mandate the use of the same assessment instruments and protocols in the same way for all students, with only limited accommodations for students requiring special consideration due to illness, misadventure or special needs. This is the basic requirement in standardized assessment protocols, such as national tests or school leaving exams.

Equality in assessment can be defined as a situation where all students are assessed using the same assessment methods (e.g. standardized tests) steered by common policies. These include common required levels for minimum proficiency, standards for stage-level performance or final examination criteria that are same for all students. Students' success is primarily determined by comparing how they perform compared to other students. This supposedly guarantees fairness by providing all students with access to the same assessments. In contrast, *equity* in assessment refers to a situation in which students are assessed using methods and arrangements in accordance with the interests and needs of each student. These methods include a wider range of assessment tools that are suitable for different contexts and serve diverse learners, such as diagnostic assessments designed by teachers and various tools and techniques for FA. Student success is therefore primarily determined by comparing how they perform regarding their own potential. This strengthens teaching and learning by allowing students to demonstrate their progress in different contexts or in different ways.

Equity in assessment also requires education policies and school resources that enable teachers to use different assessment instruments and methods in accordance with the needs of each student at school. Another key concept related to equity in education is *inclusion* in assessment, which refers to a situation in which the diversity of students is embraced, and the educational system acknowledges and values the differences they bring to school so that all students can fully engage in meaningful life and learning. This requires giving all students more voice regarding assessing their learning and removing or avoiding elements in assessments that would be experienced as discrimination, cultural biases or structural barriers by students.

Montenegro and Jankowski (2017) argue that unless we examine issues of inclusion and equity, 'the students who may stand the most to gain from assessment efforts may have the least benefit since their learning is not accurately assessed, and feedback may not be relevant to impact learning' (p.5). They propose the deliberate adoption of a range of appropriate assessment tools or approaches that offer the greatest chance for various types of students to demonstrate their learning so that assessment results can be used to benefit students from all backgrounds. Formative assessment, for example, is promoted as being particularly helpful for students with special educational needs, additional/second language learners or lower-achieving students, in other words, being more equitable. It enables teachers to tailor the assessment tool to fit the type of task being assessed and to capture the individual students' existing knowledge and skills in relation to the performance of that task. Students can also be directly involved in assessments through self- and peer assessment, creating a more dialogic and highly contextualized relationship between teachers and students which enables students to have more meaningful feedback conversations which help them understand what they have learned, what they still need to learn and how to get there. This helps to realign the traditional top-down power relationships between teacher and student which have long been blamed for learner passivity and disengagement. With such an approach to FA, students learn to set goals, self-regulate their behaviour, participate in activities based on mutual support trust, respect and cooperation, and experience success.

The OECD (2008: 1) claims that by using the kind of FA approaches and techniques outlined above, teachers 'are better prepared to meet diverse students' needs – through differentiation and adaption of teaching to raise levels of student achievement and achieve a greater equity of student outcomes'. However, this in turn leads to questions as to the exact nature of the research basis upon which such optimistic views of the role of FA in enhancing equity are formed, the focus of this chapter.

Methods

In this review, we undertook a meta-analysis of journal articles which reported the results of an empirical investigation into the use of FA with students from low socio-economic status (SES) backgrounds. We limited the review to low SES as an indicator of disadvantage as that has been the primary focus of much research into equity in education and is a more widely accepted indicator of disadvantage than other student background characteristics, such as cultural background, ethnicity, race or disability. We sought answers to the following questions:

1. What has been reported in the literature about the use of FA to support students from low-SES backgrounds?
2. What are the issues and challenges in using FA to support students from low-SES backgrounds?

We used a scoping literature search to answer the research questions following the Preferred Reporting Items for Systematic Reviews and Meta-Analyses (PRISMA) guidelines (Moher et al., 2009).

Data sources and literature search

We used ProQuest, Scopus and Web of Science databases to initially search the literature. We limited our search from Black and Wiliam (1998) to the present. The combination of keywords, *assessment, FA, classroom assessment, teacher assessment, assessment for learning, assessment strategy, sharing learning* outcomes and success criteria, self- and peer assessment, feedback, questioning, and *low socio-economic status, disadvantaged students, equity*, was used to identify relevant papers in every database. Additional sources were taken from the reference sections of those articles.

Study selection

As shown in Figure 10.1, the initial search generated a total of 889 articles. After removing the duplicates, the titles and abstracts of the articles were reviewed if they met the criteria. Using the following exclusion criteria: published in English, empirical study, university and school setting, and availability of full text, twelve articles remain for full-text review.

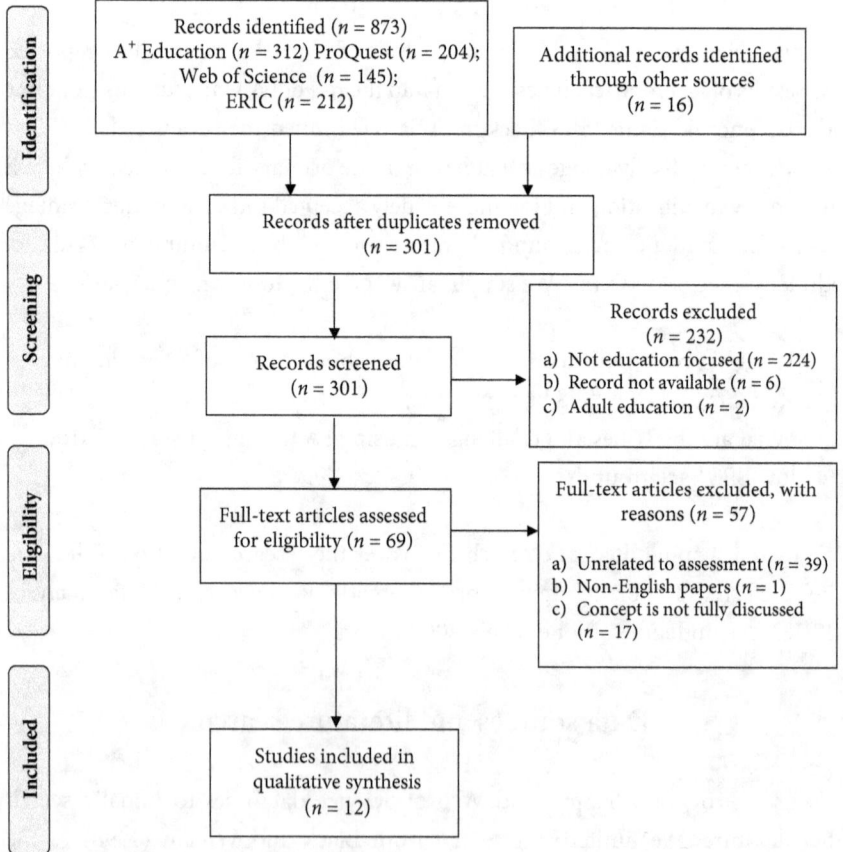

Figure 10.1 Selection process for articles.

Approach to analysis and synthesis

We read the sixty-nine articles that remained after the initial screening to assess if there was a clear articulation of the use of FA to support students with low socio-economic status. Papers that did not specifically highlight the relationship between assessment and student outcomes were excluded. Following the same shortlisting, twelve articles remained for final analysis.

Three stages of thematic synthesis in systematic reviews highlighted by Thomas and Harden (2008) were used. These three stages are (i) coding text, (ii) developing 'descriptive' themes and (iii) generating analytical themes. Descriptive and analytical themes were developed by two of the authors. Then, these data-driven themes and coding were reviewed again by all authors. The results of the thematic synthesis are presented in the following section.

Findings

As can be seen in Table 10.1, the meta-analysis found surprisingly few empirical studies about using assessment to enhance equity in education (and to support students from low SES backgrounds). Since Black and Wiliam (1998), only twelve articles have been published focusing on the intersection of assessment and students from low SES backgrounds. Most of the studies are from the United States (41.7 per cent) and South Africa (33.3 per cent). The very low number of published articles on this topic suggests a limited research interest in the issue of the use of FA to enhance equity in education, even to support the most educationally disadvantaged students.

Although the number of articles looking at FA and equity is relatively low, this meta-analysis demonstrates that using assessment to support disadvantaged students has a sound empirical evidence base for its effectiveness. For example, teachers' use of goal setting, self- and peer assessment, feedback, questioning and rubrics increased opportunities for disadvantaged students to learn resulting to higher achievement (Hilberg, 2012). This is consistent with the review of literature by Clark (2014) that establishing a formative learning environment enables this group of students to participate actively in their own learning progression by consciously monitoring and regulating product-oriented learning. There is also evidence that using assessment strategies increased students' academic readiness (Alexander, Badenhorst & Gibbs, 2005), engagement in learning (Norodien-Fataar & Daniels, 2016) and meta-

Table 10.1 Summary of research studies linking FA and equity.

Authors	Country	Research design	Assessment strategy reported	Outcomes reported	Recommendations if any
Clark (2014)	Japan	Review of literature from 1995 to 2021	Sharing learning outcomes, use of assessment criteria, self- and peer assessment	Formative learning environments enable economically and culturally disadvantaged students to participate actively in their own learning progression by consciously monitoring and regulating product-oriented learning	School staff should be organized to collaborate with parents/caregivers in two ways: (a) which foster understandings of a child's need for 'connectedness' in school; and (b) which establish and sustain legitimate partnerships between school and families which empower families and schools to oversee the academic progress of children collectively (p.123)
Hilberg (2012) PhD Thesis	The United States	Mixed method with classroom observation, interview and survey with seventeen teachers and eleven principals	Goal setting, self- and peer assessment, feedback, questioning, mastery learning, use of rubrics	Teachers' use of formative assessment strategies increased opportunities of disadvantaged students to learn and result in greater equity in achievement. 'Principals' formative use of assessment data with the goal of increasing learning, analysis of data disaggregated by ethnic, language, and socioeconomic groups ...	Consider the specific application of formative assessment strategies, such as questioning, feedback, and self- and peer assessment within various content areas including mathematics, science or language arts. Consider the affordances and constraints of formative assessment in different classroom organizations – working with

					specific group of disadvantaged students
Kirby and Downs (2007)	South Africa	Intervention using self-assessment; two cohorts, 219 and 222 university students for two different years	Self-assessment using criteria	Students' self-assessments varied and were significantly lower than marks awarded by staff	Implementing self-assessment requires clearly defined criteria and training students; integrate more feedback as part of the process of self-assessment
Alexander, Badenhorst, and Gibbs (2005)	South Africa	Intervention programme with thirty-two disadvantaged students	Test, feedback	Using tests and providing feedback increased students' academic readiness	Use intensive programme to support educationally disadvantaged students
Bloom, Unterman, Zhu, and Reardon (2020)	The United States	Randomized treatment of 12,003 students from 2006 to 2012	Data-driven instruction, i.e. instruction determined by assessment	Data-driven (assessment results are used to adjust learning and teaching activities) instruction increased graduation rate among disadvantaged students	More research is needed to account for individual school context

Authors	Country	Research design	Assessment strategy reported	Outcomes reported	Recommendations if any
Ng, Bartlett, Chester, and Kersland (2013)	Australia	Intervention study with seventy-six 5th year students	Strategy instruction	Provision of quality feedback from volunteer adults provided support for disadvantaged students	Consistently implement the intervention to sustain reading gains
Grayson (1997)	South Africa	Intervention programme with ninety-nine pre-university students	Self-assessment, peer assessment, frequent assessment and opportunity to resubmit their work	Assessment strategies developed students' ability to reflect on their learning (meta-cognitive skills)	Build students capacity for self-reflection for life-long learning
Stevens and Van Houtte (2011)	Belgium and UK	Comparative ethnographic school observations and interviews study with three tutor groups	Adapting assessment	Teacher perception/ understanding of their students' background enabled them to adapt their assessment	More research evidence is needed to support the results of this study
				Teachers whose assessment results are not used for accountability and state comparison better tailored their assessment (and teaching) to students' needs	De-standardization of student and school evaluation systems
Anderson and Pellicer (1998)	The United States	Secondary data analysis from twelve schools	Performance standards	Clear and high-performance goals facilitated teacher and student success	Use a conceptual framework where standards of programme, school culture, curriculum and teaching are supporting each other to support disadvantaged students
			Parental involvement, use of individual student records to monitor success, use of feedback	Bidirectional relationships between school and home are critical for student success	
				Teacher personal knowledge of students enabled them to adapt their teaching	

Baker and Logan (2006)	The United States	Intervention programme using action research with 112 students from 1996 to 2003	Use of action research to increase academic success of disadvantaged students	Teacher autonomy is needed for teachers to make decisions based on what is best for their students
				Data (attendance, level of participation, timely submission of assignments, ability to pass test) gathered from students were used to adapt teaching
				Students' active participation in the discussion of assignments facilitated peer-teaching. This increased students' self-esteem, making them to ask for more immediate feedback on their performance.
Norodien-Fataar and Daniels (2016)	South Africa	Interview with seven university students	Feedback discussion	Post-test feedback discussions increased student engagement
				Universities should support students to increase their engagement in learning
Tomlinson and Jarvis (2014)	The United States	Case study for four years using observation, interview and documentary analysis of three schools	Feedback, sharing learning intentions, testing, ongoing assessments linked to standards-based content	Using various assessment strategies provided access to a challenging curriculum for disadvantaged gifted students
				Implement schoolwide practice grounded in a shared vision for student success
				No recommendations related to use of assessment

cognitive skills (Grayson, 1997). In addition, students' active participation in the discussion of assignments facilitated peer teaching. This increased students' self-esteem, making them to ask for more immediate feedback on their performance (Baker & Logan, 2006). Similarly, an assessment data-driven instruction programme increased graduation rates among disadvantaged students (Bloom, Unterman, Zhu & Reardon, 2020).

There is also evidence that FA helped teachers adapt their teaching practices to address the learning needs of disadvantaged students (Anderson & Pellicer, 1998; Baker & Logan, 2006), although this was somewhat compromised by the accountability focus of assessment. Teachers whose assessment results were not used for accountability and state comparisons better tailored their assessment (and teaching) to students' needs (Stevens & Van Houtte, 2011). In other words, teachers need sufficient autonomy to make decisions on the basis of what is best for their students (Anderson & Pellicer, 1998).

One study demonstrated that principals' formative use of assessment data enabled them to develop intervention to enhance teachers' sense of responsibility for student learning (Hilberg, 2012). The principals used these data to monitor student progress and evaluate the effects of classroom, school and district efforts to achieve equity goals. Moreover, research shows that parental and community involvement in assessment supports disadvantaged students. Bidirectional relationships between school and home are critical for student success (Anderson & Pellicer, 1998). In addition, in an intervention programme implemented by Ng et al. (2013), community mentors were trained to provide feedback to disadvantaged students. Results showed that students valued such feedback from their mentors.

Finally, there is also evidence that using various student assessment strategies including eliciting and giving feedback, sharing learning intentions, testing, ongoing assessments linked to standards-based content, helped disadvantaged gifted students to access a challenging curriculum (Tomlinson & Jarvis, 2014). However, Kirby and Downs (2007) showed that students self-assessment results were not comparable to the results of their teachers' assessment, which implies students need to be well prepared to engage effectively in any FA activity.

In summary, our review provides some evidence that teachers' use of FA to support students from low SES backgrounds actually influences their learning, although much more research is needed in order to understand in more detail how different forms of FA could benefit disadvantaged students in particular and enhance equity in education in general. However, taken as a body of research on assessment and equity, this meta-analysis demonstrates that some issues need to be further explored.

Firstly, the studies reported have methodological limitations. Although interview data, observations and secondary data analysis provide a strong link between assessment and the achievement of students from low SES backgrounds, a more rigorous research design is needed to establish a causal relationship between using FA and improvements in students' achievement, ideally reporting the effect size of the assessment strategies used. Secondly, no study reported how assessment was affected by the context of these students' learning experiences. Modifications may be required for an FA strategy to be effective for a specific group of students or even for individuals, highlighting the need for teachers to be adaptive (Loughland & Alonzo, 2019) to continuously reflect on student characteristics and assessment data and adjust learning and teaching activities based on student learning needs and support. Broadly, more studies are needed to highlight the intersections of assessment and equity within a policy context as it shapes teachers' assessment practices (Alonzo et al., 2021a).

Another issue that remains relatively unexplored is the critical role of school leaders in building a strong assessment culture in schools that support teachers to implement FA with a strong focus on equity. Principals play a critical role in leading an assessment reform in their respective schools (Alonzo, Leverett & Obsioma, 2021). In particular, principals' use of data for formative purposes to develop equitable school programmes increases teachers' sense of responsibility for student learning (Hilberg, 2012) and presumably helps inform modifications to FA tool and techniques to make them more effective in improving equity.

Where to from here?

This meta-analysis has highlighted the potential of FA to support educationally disadvantaged students to enhance their learning and academic achievement. The reported impact of FA in enhancing student outcomes in these studies reinforces the earlier findings of Black and Wiliam (1998) and suggests far more attention should be paid to the role of FA in enhancing educational equity.

The time is now ripe for rethinking equity in assessment and the current role of FA in many education systems. The global pandemic has terminated or modified national testing and final examinations in many countries. For example, universities in the United States and some other countries are admitting students without traditional scholastic aptitude tests (SATs). In January 2021 the College

Board[1] released a statement that said, '[T]he expanded reach of (advanced placement) and its widespread availability for low-income students and students of colour means the Subject Tests are no longer necessary for students to show what they know.' This was widely considered as a call for more innovative and diverse assessment practices to support student learning in school and judge their overall readiness for further study and, indeed, for life. At the same time, demands to redesign entire national assessment systems, including in Australia, United States and Great Britain (Moss et al., 2021; Wilson, et al., 2021), have become even more pressing with proposals to replace often harmful high-stakes standardized testing with more intelligent assessments and professional accountability policies.

In all of these proposals the role of classroom-based, teacher-led FAs has been emphasized in order to make student assessments better serve the pursuit of both excellence and equity in education. What we need now is more high-quality studies which investigate this important area.

Note

1 A US nonprofit organization established in 1899 that runs fee-based SATs for college admission.

References

Alexander, K. & S. Morgan (2016). 'The Coleman Report at Fifty: Its legacy and implications for future research on equality of opportunity. RSF: The Russell Sage Foundation'. *Journal of the Social Sciences*. DOI: 10.7758/rsf.2016.2.5.01. https://socweb.soc.jhu.edu/faculty/morgan/papers/Alexander_and_Morgan_2016.pdf

Anderson, E. (1999). 'What is the point of equality?' *Ethics*, 109(2): 287–337.

Alexander, R., E. Badenhorst & T. Gibbs (2005). 'Intervention programme: A supported learning programme for educationally disadvantaged students'. *Medical Teacher*, 27(1): 66–70. DOI: 10.1080/01421590400016472

Alonzo, D. (2016). 'Development and application of a teacher Assessment for Learning (AfL) literacy tool'. (PhD). University of New South Wales, Sydney. http://unsworks.unsw.edu.au/fapi/datastream/unsworks:38345/SOURCE02?view=true

Alonzo, D., V. Labad, J. Bejano & F. Guerra (2021). 'The policy-driven dimensions of teacher beliefs about assessment'. *Australian Journal of Teacher Education*, 46(3).

Alonzo, D., J. Leverett & E. Obsioma (2021). 'Leading an assessment reform: Ensuring a whole-school approach for decision-making'. *Frontiers in Education*, 6(62). DOI: 10.3389/feduc.2021.63185

Anderson, L. W. & L. O. Pellicer (1998). 'Toward an understanding of unusually successful programs for economically disadvantaged students'. *Journal of Education for Students Placed at Risk (JESPAR)*, 3(3): 237–63. DOI: 10.1207/s15327671espr0303_3

Australian Government (2011). *Review of Funding for Schooling*. Final Report. Canberra: Department of Education, Employment and Workplace Relations.

Baird, J. A., D. Andrich, T. N. Hopfenbeck & G. Stobart (2017). 'Assessment and learning: Fields apart?' *Assessment in Education: Principles, Policy & Practice*, 24(3): 317–50. DOI: 10.1080/0969594X.2017.1319337

Baker, C. R. & L. B. Logan (2006). 'Using action research to promote increased academic success for educationally disadvantaged students'. *Global Perspectives in Education*, 3(1): 1–21.

Bergan, J. R., I. E. Sladeczek, R. D. Schwarz & A. N. Smith (1991). 'Effects of a measurement and planning system on kindergartners' cognitive development and educational programming'. *American Educational Research Journal*, 28(3): 683–714. DOI: 10.2307/1163154

Black, P. & Wiliam, D. (1998). 'Assessment and classroom learning'. *Assessment in Education: Principles, Policy & Practice*, 5(1): 7–74. https://doi.org/10.1080/0969595980050102

Black, P., C. Harrison, C. Lee, B. Marshall & D. Wiliam (2003). *Assessment for Learning: Putting it into Practice*. Oxford: Oxford University Press.

Black, P. (2017). 'Assessment in science education'. In K. S. Taber & B. Akpan (Eds.), *Science Education: An International Course Companion* (pp. 295–309). SensePublishers. https://doi.org/10.1007/978-94-6300-749-8_22

Black, P. & D. Wiliam (2009). 'Developing the theory of formative assessment'. *Educational Assessment, Evaluation and Accountability*, 21: 5–31.

Black, P., & D. Wiliam (2018). 'Classroom assessment and pedagogy'. *Assessment in Education: Principles, Policy & Practice*, 25(6): 551–75. https://doi.org/10.1080/0969594X.2018.1441807

Bloom, B. S., J. T. Hastings & G. Madaus (1971). *Handbook on Formative and Summative Evaluation of Student Learning*. New York: McGraw-Hill.

Bloom, H. S., R. Unterman, P. Zhu & S. F. Reardon (2020). 'Lessons from New York City's small schools of choice about high school features that promote graduation for disadvantaged students'. *Journal of Policy Analysis and Management*, 39(3): 740–71. DOI: https://doi.org/10.1002/pam.22192

Clark, I. (2014). 'Equitable learning outcomes: Supporting economically and culturally disadvantaged students in "formative learning environments"'. *Improving Schools*, 17(1): 116–26. DOI: 10.1177/1365480213519182

Cockcroft, W. H. (1982). *Mathematics Counts. Report of the Committee of Inquiry into the Teaching of Mathematics in Primary and Secondary School sin England and Wales*. London: HSMO.

Coleman, J. S., C. J. Hobson, J. McPartland, A. M. Moo, F. D. Weinfeld & R. L. York (1966). *Equality of educational opportunity*. National Center for Educational Statistics. Washington: U.S. Department of Health, Education, and Welfare.

College Board (2021). *An Update on Reducing and Simplifying Demands on Students*. College Board Communications, 19 January 2021. https://allaccess.collegeboard.org/update-reducing-and-simplifying-demands-students

Cumming, J., E. Dickson & A. Webster (2013). 'Reasonable adjustments in assessment: Putting law and policy into practice in Australia'. *International Journal of Disability, Development and Education*, 60(4): 295–311. DOI: 10.1080/1034912X.2013.846467

Davison, C. (2007). 'Views from the Chalkface: English language school-based assessment in Hong Kong'. *Language Assessment Quarterly*, 4(1): 37–68. DOI: https://doi.org/10.1080/15434300701348359

Dworkin, R. (2000). *Sovereign Virtue: The Theory and Practice of Equality*. Cambridge, MA: Harvard University Press.

Fenwick, L. (2011). 'Curriculum reform and reproducing inequality in upper-secondary education'. *Journal of Curriculum Studies*, 43(6): 697–716. DOI: 10.1080/00220272.2011.576773

Grayson, D. J. (1997). 'A holistic approach to preparing disadvantaged students to succeed in tertiary science studies. Part II. Outcomes of the science foundation programme'. *International Journal of Science Education*, 19(1): 107–23. DOI: 10.1080/0950069970190108

Haertel, E. (2013). 'Getting the help we need'. *Journal of Educational Measurement*, 50: 84–90. https://doi.org/10.1111/jedm.12002

Hattie, J. & H. Timperley (2007). 'The power of feedback'. *Review of Educational Research*, 77(1): 81–112.

Hattie, J. (2008). *Visible Learning: A Synthesis of over 800 Meta-analyses Relating to Achievement*. Hoboken: Routledge.

Hilberg, S. (2012). 'Formative assessment, equity, and opportunity to learn' (PhD). University of California, Sta. Cruz. https://escholarship.org/uc/item/3tr7r3qg

Kippers, W. B., C. H. D. Wolterinck, K. Schildkamp, C. L. Poortman & A. J. Visscher (2018). 'Teachers' views on the use of assessment for learning and data-based decision making in classroom practice'. *Teaching and Teacher Education*, 75: 199–213. DOI: https://doi.org/10.1016/j.tate.2018.06.015

Kirby, N. F. & C. T. Downs (2007). 'Self-assessment and the disadvantaged student: Potential for encouraging self-regulated learning?' *Assessment & Evaluation in Higher Education*, 32(4): 475–94. doi:10.1080/02602930600896464

Levin, H. M. (2009). 'The economic payoff to investing in educational justice'. *Educational Researcher*, 38: 5–20. https://doi.org/10.3102/0013189X08331192

Loughland, T. & D. Alonzo (2019). 'Teacher adaptive practices: A key factor in teachers' implementation of assessment for learning'. *Australian Journal of Teacher Education*, 44(7). DOI: http://dx.doi.org/10.14221/ajte.2019v44n7.2

Moher, D., A. Liberati, J. Tetzlaff, & D. G. Altman (2009). 'Preferred reporting items for systematic reviews and meta-analyses: the PRISMA statement'. *BMJ*, 339: b2535. https://doi.org/10.1136/bmj.b2535

Montenegro, E. & N. A. Jankowski (2017). *Equity and Assessment: Moving Towards Culturally Responsive Assessment (Occasional* Paper No. 29). Urbana, IL: University of Illinois and Indiana University, National Institute for Learning Outcomes Assessment (NILOA). https://www.learningoutcomesassessment.org/wp-content/uploads/2019/02/OccasionalPaper29.pdf

Moss, G., H. Goldstein, S. Hayes, B. M. Chereau, P. Sammons, G. Sinnott & G. Stobart (2021). *High Standards, not High Stakes: An Alternative to SATs That Will Transform England's Testing & School Accountability System in Primary Education & Beyond.* British Educational Research Association. https://www.bera.ac.uk/publication/high-standards-not-high-stakes-analternative-to-sats

Ng, C. H. C., B. Bartlett, I. Chester & S. Kersland (2013). 'Improving reading performance for economically disadvantaged students: Combining strategy instruction and motivational support'. *Reading Psychology,* 34(3): 257–300. DOI: 10.1080/02702711.2011.632071

Norodien-Fataar, N. & D. Daniels (2016). 'Exploring the educational engagement practices of disadvantaged students at a South African University'. *Alternation,* 23(1): 90–112.

OECD (2008). *Education at a Glance 2008: OECD Indicators.* Paris: OECD Publishing, https://doi.org/10.1787/eag-2008-en

OECD (2012). *Education at a Glance 2012: OECD Indicators.* Paris: OECD Publishing, https://doi.org/10.1787/eag-2012-en

OECD (2018). *Education at a Glance 2018: OECD Indicators.* Paris: OECD Publishing, https://doi.org/10.1787/eag-2018-en

OECD (2021). *Education at a Glance 2021: OECD Indicators.* Paris: OECD Publishing, https://doi.org/10.1787/b35a14e5-en

Perrenoud, P. (1998). 'From formative evaluation to a controlled regulation of learning processes. Towards a wider conceptual field'. *Assessment in Education: Principles, Policy & Practice,* 5(1): 85–102. DOI: 10.1080/0969595980050105

Popham, W. J. (2014). 'The right test for the wrong reason'. *Phi Delta Kappan,* 96(1): 46–52. https://doi.org/10.1177/0031721714547862

Ramaprasad, A. (1983). 'On the definition of feedback'. *Behavioral Science,* 28: 4–13.

Rust, C. (2007). 'Towards a scholarship of assessment'. *Assessment & Evaluation in Higher Education,* 32(2): 229–37.

Sadler, D. (1989). 'Formative assessment and the design of instructional systems'. *Instructional Science,* 18(2): 119–44. https://doi.org/10.1007/BF00117714

Sahlberg, P. (2018). *FinnishEd Leadership. Four Bold, Inexpensive Ideas to Transform Education.* Thousand Oaks: Corwin.

Sahlberg, P. & T. Cobbold (2021). 'Leadership for equity and adequacy in education'. *School Leadership & Management:* 1–23.

Scanlon, T. M. (2018). *Why Does Inequality Matter?* Oxford: Oxford University Press.

Schleicher, A. (2018). *World Class. How to Build a 21st-Century School System.* Paris: OECD Publishing.

Sen, A. (1992). *Inequality Re-examined*. Cambridge, MA: Harvard University Press.

Stevens, P. A. J. & M. Van Houtte (2011). 'Adapting to the system or the student? Exploring teacher adaptations to disadvantaged students in an English and a Belgian secondary school'. *Educational Evaluation and Policy Analysis,* 33(1): 59–75. DOI: 10.3102/0162373710377112

Teddlie, C. (2010). 'The legacy of the school effectiveness research tradition'. In A. Hargreaves, A. Lieberman, M. Fullan & D. Hopkins (Eds.), *The Second International Handbook of Educational Change*. Dordrecht: Springer.

Thomas, J. & A. Harden (2008). 'Methods for the thematic synthesis of qualitative research in systematic reviews'. *BMC Medical Research Methodology,* 8(1): 45. https://doi.org/10.1186/1471-2288-8-45

Tomlinson, C. A. & J. M. Jarvis (2014). 'Case studies of success: Supporting academic success for students with high potential from ethnic minority and economically disadvantaged backgrounds'. *Journal for the Education of the Gifted,* 37(3): 191–219. DOI: 10.1177/0162353214540826

UNESCO (2018). *Handbook on Measuring Equity in Education*. Quebec: UNESCO Institute for Statistics.

United Nations (2015). *Transforming Our World: The 2030 Agenda for Sustainable Development*. New York: United Nations.

Wilson, R., A. Piccoli, A. Hargreaves, P. T. Ng & P. Salhberg (2021). *Putting Students First: Moving on from NAPLAN to a New Educational Assessment System*. Sydney: Gonski Institute for Education, UNSW.

11

Changing the Culture of Classrooms, Changing the Responsibility of Students

Jo Boaler

Introduction

I think of student learning as a dance – a complex interplay between the knowledge students learn in classrooms and their beliefs about themselves as learners. This dance is fluid; it changes in each moment of learning for every student – one of the reasons that good teaching for all learners is so difficult, and studying learning is equally challenging. It used to be believed that student ideas and beliefs were separate from their knowledge and cognition, functioning in different parts of the brain, but we now know that they develop together and are complexly interrelated. In a study by Lang Chen and colleagues, for example, the neuroscientists found that positive attitudes were associated with increased engagement of the hippocampus (Chen, Bae, Battista, et al., 2018). This is an essential part of the brain when learning mathematics and other subjects. But what has this complex interrelationship of knowledge and beliefs got to do with Paul Black? To explain the critical role Paul has played in choreographing a beautiful dance for teachers and learners, worldwide, which facilitates the ideal interplay between knowledge and beliefs, I first need to explain the important role that teachers play in creating opportunities for students to develop positive beliefs – or, more specifically, growth mindsets.

Carol Dweck, the creator of mindset theories, is a colleague of mine at Stanford, and she once told me the story of the time she first considered students' 'mindsets' (Dweck, 2008). She told me that she had been interviewing some young children, giving them tasks to work on, and saw that many of the students withdrew when faced with a difficult task, but one young boy reacted completely differently. When he was given a challenging task he exclaimed, with glee, that he loved a challenge and he jumped in to work on the task. This young boy, unbeknownst to him, has played an important role in education worldwide, as he caused Carol to realize that students' different beliefs are important in learning, which led to the development of decades of research, by Carol and colleagues, on what came to be known as 'mindset'. When students have a growth mindset, they believe that they can learn anything and that belief strengthens them when learning is difficult, it protects them from damaging stereotypes, and it encourages persistence – all of which lead to higher achievement. The evidence for the impact of a change in students' mindsets, from fixed to growth, is overwhelming and has been noted in areas of education (Blackwell, Trzesniewski & Dweck, 2007), health (Zahrt & Crum, 2017), and social-emotional learning (Yeager, Trzesniewski & Dweck, 2013).

Despite the extent of important research, there is a dangerous misconception that many hold about mindsets in education – a damaging myth that a change in mindset is the responsibility of students, and it does not involve a change in teaching or the broader education system. Alfie Kohn has written about this phenomenon and the dangers of placing the responsibility for change on the shoulders of students (Kohn, 2015). When researchers deliver a mindset intervention to students, but their teachers do not change the way they teach and assess content, the intervention is minimized (e.g. see Sisk et al., 2018). This happens when students are told they can learn and grow but then are taught in narrow ways and tested with short questions in timed tests, leading students to think that learning is 'fixed'. Such teaching approaches and tests directly contravene growth mindset messages. Research confirms this, showing that the best way to help students develop a growth mindset and increase their achievement is to instil a mindset approach throughout the teaching of content, and through the assessment approaches that are used in classrooms. In an intervention enacted with fifth grade (students aged 10–11) teachers in California, the teachers changed their teaching and assessment, to a 'mathematical mindset' approach and their students significantly improved their achievement in response (Anderson et al., 2018).

As mindset ideas were developing and becoming known in education, in the early 2000s, teachers were eager to find ways to bring them into their classrooms and it quickly became clear that one of the areas most in need of a mindset influence was assessment. Traditional forms of assessment that dominated, then and now, were narrow, often emphasized speed and evaluated students by a number or grade. It is very hard to convince students they can learn anything, and that struggle is good for learning (a key mindset message) if they are marked down every time they make a mistake. Similarly, it is hard to teach a subject as a growth subject if students have no idea of the direction they are going, and the learning pathways they can take have not been set out for them. Fortunately for the world, the arrival of awareness of the importance of mindset came at the same time as Paul Black, with his co-scholar Dylan Wiliam, started to release evidence for the importance of Assessment for Learning (AfL), along with resources and teaching ideas. These two areas of research and practice – mindset and AfL – are a perfect partnership releasing students from fixed ideas and giving them responsibility to map out their own learning journeys.

The early release of ideas about mindset and AfL came at the time that I was working with Paul Black at King's College, London University. I was teaching maths in London comprehensive schools and undertaking a master's degree in the evenings. Paul was one of my mentors and when I started working on a PhD he became my lead PhD advisor (called a supervisor in England). At first, I was intimidated by the man who was a national leader, and something of a legend, but that soon changed when I experienced his mild demeanour, his kind smile and his encouragement of my ideas. Paul and I met many times over the three years of my PhD study, and now I am myself a professor, helping students with their studies at Stanford University; I share the messages and encouragement he once gave me as a PhD student.

When the ideas of AfL, and reflections from teachers, started to be shared, teachers noticed something important – the changed ideas about assessment fundamentally shifted students' roles in classrooms. Instead of receiving grades, scores and marks, as passive recipients of a teacher judgement, students started to realize that they had a role to play in their own learning and assessment. And while it may seem obvious that students can play a role in their own learning, traditional forms of assessment had given many students the opposite idea, that their achievement was decided by teachers, and they had little opportunity – or responsibility – to shape their own outcomes (Gardner, 2020). One of the most important changes brought about by an AfL approach is the laying out of knowledge students will be learning, so that students can see a pathway forward and reflect on where they are in that pathway. This is often achieved in classrooms by teachers designing rubrics for students, that communicate the work that they are doing, and that students can consider and reflect upon. This pathway is one that enables mindset messages to take root and flourish as students can hear that they can learn *and see* how that learning can happen.

There may be no subject more in need of this change than mathematics, a subject that is often taught as a set of methods to be memorized and followed. Students are often given questions with one answer and encouraged to use one method, and they are tested frequently through narrow, timed tests. This system, which I think of as closed mathematics, often leads learners to feel hopeless, unable to learn or to change their learning trajectory. It also results in many students – especially girls, students of colour and students from low-income backgrounds – to turn away from mathematics completely, further perpetuating gender, racial and class disparities in mathematics achievement (Boaler, 2022). Students change these ideas and their learning when teachers open mathematics questions and invite students to see them in different ways, discussing their different approaches with each other, and combine this teaching approach with assessment that values the creative ways students think. An open approach to mathematics (set out in Boaler, 2016, 2022) is inspiring for students and leads to higher achievement, but it is only fully successful when combined with an AfL approach to assessment (LaMar, Leshin & Boaler, 2020). Fortunately, for the world, there are many examples of innovative teachers who have moved to this open teaching and assessment approach and this chapter will share some of the impactful strategies they use. In the sections that follow I will give an example of an elementary teacher, a secondary mathematics department, a school and a collection of teachers, all of whom share their valuable approaches that support open teaching and assessment, putting into practice the ideas that Paul Black has shared.

Case 1. A teacher embraces change

Jean Maddox is a public school fifth grade teacher in the Central Valley of California. Elementary mathematics in the United States, and many other countries in the world, includes a substantial focus on arithmetic – dating back to decisions made about the content to be taught in 1895 (NEA, 1895). In many classrooms worldwide, arithmetic is taught in a closed way – with students working through repeated calculations with one valued method, one answer and a focus on speed. Jean has learned the neuroscience of mathematical thinking, in particular the importance of visual thinking, and she has learned to value the different ways problems may be approached and solved (Anderson, Boaler & Dieckmann, 2018). This has changed her teaching of mathematics completely and now she asks students to draw the way they see problems, as well as calculate and use standard methods, and to explain how the methods work. Jean has found her approach to be particularly beneficial for English learners – 'Students draw out what they understand first (because visualizing the math before calculation shows true understanding),' Jean recalls: 'I provide a process where students can share their thinking, whether it be by partner discussions, acting out the problem, explaining their drawings, and then finally doing the number work (calculations) is the last step' (Boaler et al., 2021). This process allows Jean to drop in on her students' thinking and determine the best steps for working with each student.

This is an ideal approach to the teaching of mathematics and one that Jean describes as creating 'amazing experiences' for students. Unfortunately for Jean – and her students – the idea that mathematics can be approached and solved in different ways, including visual approaches, is undermined by standardized testing, which requires students to solve problems in one way, at high speed. The mismatch between the mathematics assessed in standardized tests and the students' experiences in their classrooms – seeing and solving in different ways, absent from time pressure – was noticed by the fifth grade students in Jean's classroom who complained about their experience of standardized tests, which resulted in the district dialling back on their use (for more detail see Boaler, 2019). This was important as Jean knew the importance of partnering open mathematics with an AfL approach to assessment. When Jean gives her students summative tests, she names them: 'Show what you know' and always allows students to use manipulatives (such as Cuisenaire rods, multi-link cubes and other physical representations of numbers) as they work and to revise their work for a higher grade after they receive Jean's comments. She also shares with students that they can use any approach that makes sense for them. When Jean moved to this different approach to assessment, with opportunities to improve a grade, she shared that it was 'huge' for the students. Jean uses her classroom assessments formatively by following them with different classroom options – students who are 'totally comfortable with the material' are given their own assignments, while students who need more time experience targeted teaching opportunities with Jean. The next phase in Jean's journey involved eliminating grades and replacing them with feedback for students.

The transformation of Jean's teaching of mathematics – from a focus on calculations and one method, to an open approach of multiple methods and strategies and supporting visuals – took place over a number of years, with professional development provided by an online course (www.youcubed.org/resource/online-courses-for-teachers/) and in person professional development in her county (Anderson, Boaler & Dieckmann, 2018) and learning opportunities she found for herself. Importantly Jean was able to support this new approach to mathematics learning with an assessment approach that gave consistent messages – learning is a process of growth, and mathematics can be approached in a multitude of ways.

Case 2. A leader supports change

Jordan Benedict teaches students aged 11–18. He has worked as the head of mathematics at the *American School of Dubai and Shanghai American School* and at both schools has led teachers in developing opportunities for students to engage in self-assessment and reflection. He currently works as a learning and data coach. Jordan shared with me that in all schools he has worked with teachers to develop a key tool that allows students to own their learning pathways, which he described as a self-assessment/reflection/error analysis protocol. Importantly the tool, set out in Table 11.1, invites students to take an active role in their assessment, co-creating final marks and feedback with their teacher.

Jordan shared that this practice 'changes both teachers and students. By the second time the students participate in the protocol, they start seeing assessment as an opportunity to learn about themselves and about their current understandings (and misunderstandings). They see it as a growth opportunity and not a final judgment'.

The tool is not only used for major or summative assessments; Jordan shared that mini-versions of the tool are used when students work on tasks – at the end of lessons students are asked to self-reflect on the process with their peers and give themselves feedback before class ends. In both of the departments in which this approach to assessment has been used, giving students significant responsibility, standardized test results have improved, for students across the achievement range.

Case 3. A school-wide infusion of mindset and AfL

A few years ago I met a head teacher of a K-8 school in Canada who shared that he had worked to develop a mindset infused school and that it all started with a change in assessment. Mark Cassar, the head teacher, shared with me that he had totally embraced the research on the importance of mistakes and struggle (see Boaler, 2019), but the teachers found that 'it is hard to tell students that mistakes are really useful for learning, but then penalise them on tests for every mistake they make'. Mark and his teachers moved to a different approach to assessment, replacing tests with rubrics, setting out the important mathematics students were learning, with teachers providing diagnostic comments, as shown in figure 11.1.

Table 11.1 Jordan Benedict's self-assessment/reflection/error analysis protocol.

	Process	Additional notes
1.	The student receives their assessment back with few, if any, marks from the teacher.	They are given time to share their work and discuss their approaches (including areas of particular growth or challenge). No writing, just discussing.
2.	The students then receive a marking pen of their choosing and give themselves written feedback.	They write notes to themselves like 'remember that *share* means to divide'. During this time, they can also revise and add on to their work with their marking pen.
3.	The teacher then hands out 'model-cards'. These are exemplars with detailed explanations, not just correctly performed problems.	The students once again revise and may even have to revise some of their revisions! They continue with the same process from step 2, giving themselves feedback, adding on to their work, and consulting with peers.
4.	The students self-evaluate with a common rubric, answer reflection questions, and determine actionable next steps.	Teachers share either the common departmental rubric that breaks down the mathematics into practices and skills and the students highlight the areas that best represent their feelings on their work.
5.	The student conferences with the teacher, where they will determine final feedback and final marks.	Each student has a three-minute conference where they share their rubric and reflections. In most cases, the teacher has also filled in an identical rubric for comparison.
6.	Optionally the students may document their final marks on a data tracker, have a mini-conference with their parents or add their work to an online portfolio.	This step depends on individual teacher preferences and departmental agreements.
7.	Students have the option to show their growth through improving and resubmitting their work resubmission or reassessment.	In almost all cases, if a student completes their action plan, they can request a reassessment or resubmission. Each teacher has their own way they logistically organize this.

a. Grade 2 Rubric

Grade 2: Number Sense and Numeration Word Problem Rubric

Level 1	Level 2	Level 3	Level 4
		Used pictures, numbers, and words to demonstrate learning ✓	Next time please include more ways to represent the numbers. Try using a number line, tallies, hundreds chart
		Compose and decompose two-digit numbers in a variety of ways ✓	
		Represent, compare, and order whole numbers to 100 using contexts (e.g., real-life experiences, number stories)	

Well done Alex. You clearly showed you understand the UMCL model.
Next time Represent both 50 and 36 more than just pictures. Try using all the strategies learned in class. Great job in using a number sentence and telling me that Mrs Pileggi gave out more. :)

Parent Signature _____

b. Grade 4 Rubric

Toothpicks Problem (Patterning)
Assessment For/As Learning

Criteria	1	2	3	4	Feedback
Create, identify, extend patterns			✓		Can you build (or draw) a second pattern that looks different but follows the same pattern rule?
Make a table of values for a pattern			✓		how might you use the table of values to create the pattern rule?
Communicate math thinking in writing and pictures (communication and representation)		✓			how did you figure out it skip counts by 5? Your pictures in **bold** help make your answer clear.

1 = expectation not met; 2 = approaching expectation; 3 = meets expectation; 4 = exceeds expectations

c. Grade 8 Rubric

Math 8: Prime & Composite Numbers

Assessment

Criteria	Level 1	Level 2	Level 3	Level 4
Understanding	demonstrates a limited understanding of prime and composite numbers in a problem solving environment	demonstrates some understanding of prime and composite numbers in a problem solving environment	demonstrates clear understanding of prime and composite numbers in a problem solving environment	demonstrates thorough and exceptional understanding of prime and composite numbers in a problem solving environment
Problem Solving/Thinking	uses 1 strategy, has many errors	uses 2 strategies with failed errors	correctly uses 1 strategy to solve the problem/find answers	correctly uses 2 or more strategies
Communication	provides limited or inaccurate explanation; justification that lacks clarity or has many errors	provides partial or incomplete explanation/justification that exhibit some clarity and logical thought	provides appropriate, complete and clear explanation/justification of thinking	provides clear, thorough, complete, insightful, and logical explanation/justification that may be beyond grade level expectations
	uses minimal words, pictures, symbols, and/or numbers/technology	uses simple words, pictures, symbols, and/or numbers/technology	uses appropriate words, pictures, symbols, and/or numbers/technology	uses an extensive range of words, pictures, symbols and/or numbers/technology
	uses few or no mathematical vocabulary and/or lacks clarity and precision	uses some mathematical vocabulary with some clarity and precision	uses mathematical vocabulary with clarity and precision	uses a broad range of mathematical vocabulary to communicate clearly and precisely

- explain why or how showing the factor rainbows helped you.

- you picked a challenging #

- explanations are limited → explain further what it shows you (strategies).

Figure 11.1a–c Rubrics used at St Alphonso School, Toronto.

Mark shared that at first the students looked for a number, to evaluate themselves, but gradually they realized that the rubric gave them more important insights into their learning journeys, and the teacher comments helped them improve. In a powerful video (see www.youcubed.org/resources/an-example-of-a-growth-mindset-k-8-school/) some of the students share the changes they perceived, from the closed mathematics they had known in their previous school, to an open mathematics approach with AfL assessment. One of the students reflects on the difference in this way:

> We would get worksheets, hand it in to our teachers, they would say you got it wrong, next time try to … next time … they didn't give us tips for next time. But here they will give us tips for what we'll improve on.

The young boy being interviewed realized, as he was talking, that his previous school did not help him improve; they would merely evaluate his current achievement, but that his new school 'gave him tips' to help him improve. I think of individually crafted diagnostic comments from teachers as one of the greatest gifts they can give to students. They take more time than giving a score or a grade, but they are a powerful tool for learning and for communicating the growth that is possible for students. Ellen Crews, a middle school teacher who moved to an approach of rubrics and comments (see Boaler, 2016, 2022), reflected that they take more time but can be given less often. More detail of Mark's school and the impressive work of his teachers can be seen at: www.youcubed.org/resources/an-example-of-a-growth-mindset-k-8-school/

Case 4. The widespread influence of Paul Black's work

When I was preparing for this chapter, I asked, on Twitter, if teachers would share with me any changes they had made as a result of Paul Black's work. The response was incredible, with teachers from across the world immediately sharing a range of initiatives they now employ, six of them are summarized in Table 11.2, from work in Canada, England, the United States and Australia.

These six teachers, from four different countries, describe important ideas that have come from a framing of AfL and, in many cases, mindset. Their reflections on the change it has created for students are powerful, with Dave Martin describing the change as the 'most profound' of his whole career. Laura talks about the permeation of AfL ideas 'irrevocably, wonderfully', permeating all of her teaching and lesson planning, allowing her to 'center my students exactly as they are'. Dan says the A4L changes 'transformed' his teaching, Matt describes

Table 11.2 Teachers sharing their approaches to AfL.

Teacher	Form of A4L	Description
Dave Martin, President of the Math Council of Alberta, Canada. High school vice principal.	Moving from grades to diagnostic feedback	In 2014–2015 I moved to an entire written response assessment strategy grouped by outcomes. Instead of one part multiple choice, one part numerical response, and one part written, I only assessed with questions that forced students to make their understanding visible. It was in this year, I truly started to sit next to my students and provide them written and verbal feedback that pushed their learning forward instead of simply saying 'here are the X questions you answered incorrectly and here are the correct answers'. My feedback was focused on learning, not on which questions they answered wrong.

Simply put, I stopped writing grades, learning levels or any other ranking system on student work. Instead I only provided feedback and asked questions that pushed learning forward. Even if a student demonstrated 'mastery' of an outcome, I would still provide feedback or leave them with a question that pushed them beyond the scope of the outcome.

This was the most profound transformation I have ever experienced in my entire career. |
| Laura Duffy, Algebra 1 and Algebra 2 in an all-girls school in Brooklyn, New York, USA | Using photos of problem-solving to stimulate conversation and class discussions, celebrating mistakes. | I ask students to submit photos of their problem-solving and then hold diagnostic conversations: e.g., 'There's an error in #7 do you see it?' I then coach the student individually and celebrate students' mistakes by building class discussions around them.

I also use Google forms to ask students to self-report what they understand and what they don't. For example, I ask students:

What do you find interesting?

What is boring?

What's a way we could make something more interesting?

I check in on students' social-emotional learning, using a 'Google Ask' to ask the students questions such as: 'If your mood was a colour what would it be and why?'

In closing, Laura reflected: |

Dan Wilson: Secondary maths teacher and developer of amPIL Tracker Cheshire, England	Bringing A4L to summative assessment	I don't have anything super fancy that I do regarding my use of A4L. Rather A4L as a mindset has irrevocably, wonderfully, permeated every thought regarding task design and lesson planning, allowing me to centre my students exactly as they are, not where I expect them to be, nor where my curriculum map or department chair tells me they 'should' be. This is the greatest gift A4L has given me: the practice of seeing students exactly as they are and exactly where they are at. Throughout my teaching career I have always bought into the notion that assessment should be used first and foremost to provide learning opportunities. I spent a lot of time helping transform our department's formative assessment strategies in the classroom. Craig Barton's outstanding of diagnostic questions platform is an incredibly powerful tool, which fundamentally allows you to immediately assess and address misconceptions with AfL strategies at its heart. We felt we were getting a lot right, all thanks to the strategies introduced to us by Paul Black and Dylan William. My attention then turned to the summative assessments which I felt we were simply not using as a full learning opportunity. When the Key Stage 2 exams (in the UK) changed a few years ago, schools were provided with a question-level analysis for every student from the Key Stage 2 exam. When I found out about this, I immediately set to work creating an Excel tracker file which linked this to our scheme of works so we could predict how the students are likely to find upcoming topics using the prerequisites. This approach transformed my teaching. When I knew all/most students had secure foundations, I pitched my series of lessons at a higher level. I also made sure I checked in with those students who were less secure. It helped me really get to know my students and pre-empt any stumbling blocks we might have along the way.
Lindsay LaPorte: Instructional coordinator, Colorado, USA (former secondary mathematics teacher)	Highlighting mistakes on tests, students present evidence of learning.	My goal as a mathematics teacher has always been to focus on learning over scores and grades. When I was teaching in California, about 5 years ago, I saw a video from Edutopia, 'Highlighting mistakes – a grading strategy' and I immediately implemented the strategy into my classroom for all assessments (formative and summative). I found that students initially struggled, as they were conditioned to look for the grade on any assignment before looking for feedback or where they had space to grow. It didn't take long for students to switch their focus. They wanted to know why things were highlighted, what errors they made and (most importantly) how to fix those mistakes. The goal was always mastery regardless of initial performance.

Teacher	Form of A4L	Description
Matt Rector Math teacher and Department Chair at Grant Union High School, California, USA	Offering a 'three-read approach'	In the summer of 2018 I worked with some colleagues to develop evidence outcomes for each course that I was teaching. Students would use this spreadsheet to track their progress and give themselves a score of understanding. They could use quizzes, tests, homework, videos they created to demonstrate their understanding, or any other piece of evidence they had to prove their level of mastery. HERE is the evidence of understanding I used for my math 8 class. At the end of the topics, students would meet with me one on one to present their evidence and explain why they scored themself the way they did. We would talk about their understanding of the topic and agree on a 50–100 point score that would go into the gradebook. I was consistently impressed with how well students were able to identify their understanding and grade themselves on a topic. About 85 per cent of the time I would be thinking of a score for a student and they would say the same number within 1 to 2 points. For homework and quick checks, students would work to attempt problems, check their answers and reflect on their learning. I wanted students to be self-assessing and believed they needed the tools to know if they were on the right track or not. I found that by not grading homework or quizzes students became less focused on points and grades and more focused on how to improve their understanding. In addition to student conferences and self-assessment, students completed bi-weekly reflections for my class. HERE is the document I used with reflection questions. I would give students feedback on their responses and they were always given time to refine their responses until they were complete. After a deep dive into our data I found that 96 per cent my students were judged to be below standard on their 8th grade SBAC math assessment. When looking at their transcripts I found that most had failed or received a 'D' in all of their previous math classes. This had been going on for as far back as I could find. So after I gave another twenty-problem test that I spent 20 hours grading only to confirm that they weren't passing without a significant curve I decided that things needed to change. The old fashion test model was not moving learning forward. All I was accomplishing was re-enforcing what they already knew: 'They couldn't do math.'

Last year I was involved in a research project with CPM for Math Literacy and developed a graphic organizer for a three-read system – for example: https://teacher.desmos.com/activitybuilder/custom/5fd6402a1654230d50f7344f?collections=5f7dd5a332c9050cbcfa9e6b

'The Three Read Protocol is one way to do a close read of a complex math word problem or task. This strategy includes reading a math scenario three times with a different goal each time. The first read is to understand the context. The second read is to understand the mathematics. The third read is to elicit inquiry questions based on the scenario' (San Francisco Unified Mathematics three-read math).

At the same time I was reading A4L which led me to a new assessment model based around the three-read graphic organizer. As the school year went on I refined the model and it produced amazing results in multiple ways. The most significant of which is that I helped students believe that they could do math and solve problems.

AfL is an everyday practice for me. My career has taken place in an environment that is slowly evolving over time to focus more and more on individual growth of the student rather than one of everyone being on the same page at the same time.

Instead of the teachers necessarily being the owners of what the students know, we are putting it back in the hands of the students. Students are given time to determine at what point of their learning they are currently at and analyse what they know and can do and set goals accordingly. These goals are shared among their teachers (secondary setting), so they have multiple teachers) and thus give students an opportunity to have influence over their learning.

We also use Microsoft Teams and OneNote and are training students up on how to record their own progress. What is the standard you are at currently, what is the next standard you are aiming for, what do you need to do to be able to get there and what evidence can you use to demonstrate you have got there. We have found in our initial work that students are empowered by this, and by being able to explicitly state what their next step in learning is, they are far more likely to get there.

Gaining a deeper understanding of using AfL has been a foundation of my growth as a teacher and something that I try and pass on to those I work with. I find it hard to imagine working in a classroom where I am not using assessment to inform next steps in learning because it seems so foundational that unless I know where my students are at, how am I going to know what they need next?

Ashley Foote Senior leader Transdisciplinary Learning Victor Harbor High School, South Australia	Students see standards and record their own progress

'amazing results' and Ashley reflects that she could not imagine 'working in a classroom where I am not using assessment to inform next steps in learning'. Lindsey shares that one of the biggest impacts of AfL has been students taking ownership of their learning and becoming 'masters at identifying their strengths and areas of growth'. These teachers are exemplary in the creative work they have done to allow students to own their learning and the opportunities they provide for students to work with teachers in advancing their learning. The teachers have all changed their assessment from a measurement approach to one that is focused on student thinking, and students are provided with information that helps them develop their thinking. This is not a mere assessment change; it is a change in the learning environment, the culture of classrooms and the responsibility of students. When teachers communicate to students that they are interested in the growth in their thinking, and they provide them with opportunities to grow and extend their thinking, students feel supported and the classroom environment is a nurturing and caring place. For many decades mathematics has been taught as a performance subject, and students have not felt supported in their learning of mathematics, making these changes especially significant in the context of mathematics learning. Put simply, they change mathematics for students from a performance subject to a learning subject, and there are few more necessary or important changes in education.

Conclusion

In all of the chosen teaching examples, teachers change the culture of classrooms and encourage students to play a central part in their own learning. Teachers who achieve such changes do not do so by following rules or prescriptions for practice; they all share the ways they have created their own classroom methods, which embody the principles of AfL. Teachers are creating ways for students to take responsibility as they themselves take responsibility for the creation of teaching and assessment methods that encourage their students' growth and learning. Students in their classrooms do not passively try to learn the content a teacher shares and hope for a good assessment result; they reflect on their learning pathways, assessing their own progress and using teacher ideas to improve. This is how all learning should happen, and Paul Black's work, highlighting the importance and methods of A4L, has allowed this culture change – for millions of students. Such changes need to be made carefully, with support for teacher learning and access to high-quality professional development (Anderson, Boaler & Dieckmann, 2018) but they need to be made in many more schools across the world. The fact that assessment can be so transformative points to the key role it plays in students' learning. In a film entitled *The Gatekeeper*, which examines the damaging role traditional mathematics teaching and assessments play, a middle school student called Delia shares her reaction to receiving an F in her math class. She says:

> When I saw the F on my paper I felt like a nothing. I was failing in that class so I thought I may as well fail in all my other classes too. I didn't even try.
>
> (Delia, middle school student, *The Gatekeeper*, Reel Link Films)

This statement is so important – as Delia shares that one 'F' in her class caused her to give up on all of her learning and to feel like 'a nothing'. This is the harsh impact that grades can play. Imagine if, instead, Delia had received a note from her teacher, giving careful attention to her individual thinking and setting out what she needed to learn next. Experiences like Delia's are especially tragic when we consider the number of students across the world who receive failing grades in mathematics classes. In the United States, some districts report that 40 per cent of students receive 'D's and 'F's in algebra classes (Waxman, 2019) which limits their access to STEM courses and often to college admission (Sawchuck, 2018). This barrier to learning has significantly contributed to the inequities in mathematics and in STEM more broadly (Boaler, 2016, 2022). Paul Black and his colleagues have shared a form of assessment with the world, which leads to completely different experiences for students – whereby they are encouraged and enabled to understand their own learning and take responsibility for their own progress. This is the form of learning and assessment that leads to the development of growth mindsets and that has the potential to encourage so many more girls and students of colour, into high-level futures. An often-quoted statistic is the impact of a country moving to an AfL approach, which, it is estimated, would raise the achievement of the country in international comparisons from the middle of the group to a place in top three (Black & Wiliam, 2010). I contend that this increase in achievement would be accompanied by a diversification of high achievement, with doors opening for many more girls and students of colour, who had previously been held back. The teachers I interacted with quite rightly described the change to AfL as 'transformative'. This transformation has impacted millions of students worldwide, and could impact many more, and it is due, in no small part, to the incredible legacy of Paul Black.

Helpful Links

Dave Martin:
http://realteachingmeansreallearning.blogspot.com/2018/05/differentiating-assessment.html?m=1
&
https://teacher.desmos.com/activitybuilder/custom/5fd6402a1654230d50f7344f?collections=5f7dd5a332c9050cbcfa9e6b

Dan Wilson
https://www.ampil.co.uk/

Lindsay LaPorte:
Highlighting mistakes:
www.youtube.com/watch?v=BO2gndc4d9I
https://docs.google.com/spreadsheets/d/1BuXJd9fdNn8bvAybs6JyptDAA0mDq46GFxn7aKBJutI/edit#gid=189950396
Reflection questions:
https://docs.google.com/document/d/14BF5BqMoOpCCCdjjW9QD4-UmzCa6RXcYMDAK8uBlUWk/edit

Matt Rector
http://realteachingmeansreallearning.blogspot.com/2018/05/differentiating-assessment.html?m=1
Three-read mathematics: https://teacher.desmos.com/activitybuilder/custom/5fd6402a1654230d50f7344f?collections=5f7dd5a332c9050cbcfa9e6b

References

Anderson, R. K., J. Boaler & J. A. Dieckmann (2018). 'Achieving elusive teacher change through challenging myths about learning: A blended approach'. *Education Sciences*, 8(3): 98.

Boaler, J. (2016). *Mathematical Mindsets: Unleashing Students' Potential through Creative Math, Inspiring Messages and Innovative Teaching*. Chappaqua, NY: Jossey-Bass/Wiley.

Boaler, J. (2019). *Limitless Mind. Learn, Lead and Live without Barriers*. London: Harper Collins.

Boaler, J. (2022). *Mathematical Mindsets: Unleashing Students' Potential through Creative Math, Inspiring Messages and Innovative Teaching – New Edition*. Chappaqua, NY: Jossey-Bass/Wiley.

Boaler, J., N. Brynelson, D. Fisher, N. Frey, K. Kennedy, L. Martinez, C. Williams & H. Yopp Slowik (2021). *California Digital Learning Integration and Standards Guidance*. Adopted by the State Board of Education, 12 May 2021. https://www.cde.ca.gov/ci/cr/dl/documents/dlintegrationstdsguide.pdf

Black, P. & D. Wiliam (2010). 'Inside the black box: Raising standards through classroom assessment'. *Phi Delta Kappan*, 92(1): 81–90.

Blackwell, L. S., K. H. Trzesniewski & C. S. Dweck (2007). 'Implicit theories of intelligence predict achievement across an adolescent transition: A longitudinal study and an intervention'. *Child Development*, 78(1): 246–63.

Chen L., S. R Bae, C. Battista, et al. (2018). 'Positive attitude toward math supports early academic success: Behavioral evidence and neurocognitive mechanisms'. *Psychol Sci*, 29(3): 390–402. [PMC free article] [PubMed] [Google Scholar]

Dweck, C. S. (2008). *Mindset: The New Psychology of Success*. Random House Digital, Inc.

Gardner, T., Ed. (2020). *Leading in the Belly of the Beast*. Washington, DC: Rowman & Littlefield.

The Gatekeeper. https://beyondtheracetonowhere.org/the-gatekeeper/

Kohn, A. (2015). 'The perils of "Growth Mindset" education: Why we're trying to fix our kids when we should be fixing the system'. https://www.salon.com/2015/08/16/the_education_fad_thats_hurting_our_kids_what_you_need_to_know_about_growth_mindset_theory_and_the_harmful_lessons_it_imparts/

LaMar, T., M. Leshin & J. Boaler (2020). 'The derailing impact of content standards – an equity focused district held back by narrow mathematics'. *International Journal of Educational Research*, 1. https://www.sciencedirect.com/science/article/pii/S2666374020300157?via%3Dihub

National Education Association of the United States Committee of Fifteen on Elementary Education. (1895). 'Report of the committee of fifteen on elementary education, with the reports of the sub-committees'. [New York, Cincinnati etc. Pub. for the National education association by the American book company] [Web.] Retrieved from the Library of Congress. https://lccn.loc.gov/04003882

Sawchuck, S. (2018). 'Students of color face persistent disparities in access to advanced STEM courses'. Education Week, April, 2018. https://www.edweek.org/leadership/students-of-color-face-persistent-disparities-in-access-to-advanced-stem-courses/2018/04

Sisk, V. F., A. P. Burgoyne, J. Sun, J. L. Butler & B. N. Macnamara (2018). 'To what extent and under which circumstances are growth mind-sets important to academic achievement? Two meta-analyses'. *Psychological Science*, 29(4): 549–71.

Waxmann, L. (2019). 'Changes in math curriculum paying off in increased participation, but access to calculus remains an issue'. San Francisco Examiner. https://www.sfexaminer.com/news/changes-in-math-currin,%20Lculum-paying-off-in-increased-participation-but-access-to-calculus-r San Francisco Examiner, 11 January 2019.

Yeager, D. S., K. H. Trzesniewski & C. S. Dweck (2013). 'An implicit theories of personality intervention reduces adolescent aggression in response to victimization and exclusion'. *Child Development*, 84(3): 970–88.

Zahrt, O. H. & A. J. Crum. 'Perceived physical activity and mortality: Evidence from three nationally representative US samples'. *Health Psychology*, 36(11): 1017.

12

Using Research to Inform Practice and Teaching to Shape Research

Paul Spenceley and Chris Harrison

Moving from research to practice – Introduction from Chris Harrison

Teaching is a highly personal activity where teachers bring together and make sense of notions of curriculum, pedagogy and assessment. While there has been an increasing focus on research-informed practice in recent years (Gittner & Harrison, 2019), attitudes and beliefs about teaching are largely derived from classroom experiences (Guskey, 2002). The majority of teachers are pragmatic in their approach to professional development, in that they seek concrete ideas and examples that they can use in their classrooms immediately. Professional development can introduce teachers to new ways of working but often it is difficult for teachers to visualize what new practice might look like and this includes how they might make space within their current practice for new routines and activities (Harrison, 2015/16).

In 1998, Paul Black and Dylan Wiliam published a review of formative assessment practices that took in a wide range of classroom studies from the previous ten years that had been shown to be productive in raising attainment. From their distillation of these research studies a number of areas of classroom practice were highlighted as areas that might be useful for teachers to focus on in terms of classroom assessment practices (Black & Wiliam, 1998a). The difficulty that faced the researchers was how to turn these ideas into professional learning opportunities when these practices were quite wide ranging and only briefly described and exemplified within the research literature.

Paul was clear, from the start, that any action to bring about change in classrooms required close collaboration with teachers and extended programmes of professional learning and he wrote in *Inside the Black Box* (Black & Wiliam, 1998b:17–18) – a small booklet where he and Dylan had captured the main ideas from their formative assessment review:

> [E]ach teacher finds his or her own ways of incorporating the lessons and ideas ... into her or his own patterns of classroom work. This can only happen relatively slowly, and through sustained programmes of professional development and support. ... What they need is a variety of living examples of implementation, by teachers with whom they can identify and from whom they can both derive conviction and confidence that they can do better, and see concrete examples of what doing better means in practice.

It was from these early thoughts by Paul that the King's-Medway-Oxfordshire Formative Assessment Project (KMOFAP) was designed. We worked with science and mathematics teachers in six schools in Medway in Oxfordshire, beginning with a six-month exploratory phase and a school year experimental phase. Our interest was in how these teachers, two science and two mathematics teachers, from each school made sense of and implemented more formative approaches in their classrooms.

At the time, Paul Spenceley, already an experienced teacher, was Paul's PhD student and had just completed the data collection exploring classroom assessment practices in lower secondary school science. In KMOFAP we were aware that the participant teachers were likely to have to make fundamental changes to the ways they worked in their classrooms. Formative assessment focuses on collecting evidence to inform future teaching and learning rather than measuring attainment. We were therefore asking the participant teachers to revolutionize how assessment worked in their classroom and this would require them to rethink how they interacted with learners and how they adapted or replaced assessment activities and routines. Understandably it was difficult for the teachers to conceptualize formative assessment fully before they began to develop it and so were unable to perceive the types of changes they needed to make in their day-to-day practice. Our solution was to try to model formative practices so that the participant teachers came to understand both how to work in a more formative way in their assessment and teaching.

Our research question was: How do teachers take ideas generated in professional development meetings and establish them in practice? Project meetings happened every 6–8 weeks with school visits every 3–4 weeks, so that we were able to capture teachers' initial ideas and intentions and were able to observe and discuss what happened in each classroom over the weeks that followed. We saw this as an example of participatory action research where practitioners are involved in the research process from the initial design through to final conclusions and actions arising out of the research. The idea was for both teachers and researchers to benefit from this collaboration through the interplay of professional learning and research. Teachers were introduced to new ideas and helped in making sense of these in their own context. At the same time, researchers were helped in understanding how research ideas translated into practice and how the principles worked within authentic and complex environments. This was in essence classroom-informed research or what calls close-to-practice research. Through the KMOFAP project, we were able to explore translation of research ideas into practice by the teachers in the first six-month period and how this practice was adapted and refined over a school year with one class. Each of the teachers found their own way of evolving formative practices within their teaching. The next section exemplifies how involvement in this close-to-practice research was embodied by Paul Spenceley.

Working with researchers – Paul Spenceley's story

I always knew I wanted to be a biology teacher, which is why, in 1977, fresh from school, I started out on the first year of a four-year degree in biology and education at Chelsea College – Centre for Science Education in London. As a new undergraduate, I was assigned a personal tutor, whom I could always check in with if I had any personal problems. My personal tutor was Paul. Because he was physicist, and I am biologist, our paths did not cross that often. I can only recall meeting him once or twice, to 'check how I was getting on', and this generally met with the obligatory teenage response of 'Okay'. It would be fair to say that at this stage in my educational journey, Paul had not really made much of an impact on me or my career.

Fast forward over twenty years, and I was an experienced science teacher, at a comprehensive 11–18 school in the southeast of England. Probably because of my training at Chelsea, which had always encouraged an 'inquiring' attitude towards teaching science, I had always been interested in guiding individual students to reach their potential. One way I had approached this was by always writing detailed feedback on students' work. So, when my school was asked by King's College London to supply two science teachers for a new project on assessment, my head teacher decided that I was the 'natural choice'. So off I went for a day's meeting with other teachers to King's, where I was surprised by two things. First, what I thought was going to be a one-day training course turned out to be a four-year research project, and second, that the person leading the project was none other than Professor Paul Black! What happened over the next four years, during the KMOFAP made a profound, and literally life-changing, impact on everything I was to do as a teacher. It enabled me to work closely with Paul, Dylan, Christine Harrison and the King's College London team and revolutionized how I interacted with my students and influenced every aspect of my teaching.

It did not take long in the early days of the project for me to realize how little I really understood about formative assessment. For the first time since I started teaching, I was introduced to studies and ideas that might help my students to improve, but I was also given the time to reflect on and consider how such ideas might work in my classes. Each time our group of mathematics and science teachers attended one of the project meeting days at King's, we were encouraged to take back one or two of the ideas discussed and attempt to implement these in our own classrooms. Being given the time to discuss what worked, how and why, and to listen to other teachers' reports on their trials of the ideas was both exciting and invaluable. Without a doubt, this unique opportunity for trial and reflection, which Paul and his team gave us, as teachers, was undoubtedly what led to the success of the project. Gradually, each teacher found ways of making formative assessment work for them and their classes. This approach was later consolidated as Assessment for Learning.

Initially the project encouraged me, and my science colleague, David Tuffin, to concentrate on ways to improve our use of questioning during lessons, by using more open-ended questions, longer wait times, and using a variety of techniques to get more students involved in the discussions. Many – although not all – of the techniques we tried, and reflected on, made clear and obvious impacts in our lessons, and most importantly, on the learning achieved by our students. Meeting at King's on several occasions each year was backed up by classroom observations by the research team and Sue Swaffield, the local authority science advisor, providing the sort of precise and dedicated professional feedback, which I had not received previously.

After the first six months, because KMOFAP was exploring what constituted formative practice, the researchers asked the teachers to focus their new practice on one or two classes. This was at the start of a new school year and we were asked to teach our target classes in a formative way throughout the year and all other classes as we had done prior to the project. Quickly, however, it became clear that to do so simply felt wrong. I felt that my 'control groups' were missing out on the best I had to offer. During the whole of the project, this was the only aspect, which I struggled with. As far as I was concerned, I was learning techniques, which were not just improving me as a teacher but starting to change my whole outlook on teaching. At the time I summed this up in an article I wrote, which appeared in the Science Teacher Education publication in April 2000. In this article, I described myself as feeling like a hamster in a wheel, <u>prior</u> to the King's project – completing units of work with a group of students, moving on to the next, etc. with the only real focus being to 'get everything done' before the next exam. I went on to say how the project had changed this, and had made me feel more like a 'free-thinking rat', free to concentrate my teaching on what was actually beneficial at that time to my students and their progress. It sounds odd now to think of it in this way, but without a doubt, being involved in the King's project made me realize that it made no difference if I was the best 'teacher' in the world, unless my students were 'learning'. This shift in focus from my lessons being about how well I could teach to becoming about how well my students were learning was to change the remainder of my career.

As the King's project developed, Paul and the team encouraged us to develop, and reflect on, ever more formative assessment techniques: comment-only marking, self- and peer assessment techniques, and the formative use of summative tests. Each technique was trialled, analysed, adapted, honed, re-trialled, allowing each of the project teachers to build their own Assessment for Learning repertoire.

I was lucky that David (the other science teacher volunteered by my school) and I were both passionate about all that the KMOFAP project could offer us as teachers. Together we would work on ideas and share our thoughts, successes and failures. David was the school's Head of Science at the time, and we were lucky to have a young department, with teachers who were interested to know what the two of us were doing and keen to also become involved. Well before the KMOFAP project ended, we had a whole science department who were changing the way they approached their teaching, with superb results for our students. Very soon, the science department were being held up as 'beacon of excellence' within the school and across the local authority. Along with David, I was asked by the King's team to talk at various national and international events as they disseminated the project ideas more broadly.

By the time that KMOFAP finished, leading to the publication of the seminal *Working Inside the Black Box* booklet, I had not only changed my whole approach to teaching but become a passionate advocate of the newly named 'Assessment for Learning'. For the remainder of my career, I would continue to strive to develop the four cornerstones, which the project had focused on: questioning, self- and peer assessment, feedback and the formative use of summative tests.

I think it is fair to say that my second encounter with Paul had rather more influence on me as a science teacher than my first had! Indeed I always felt that my career split perfectly into two sections, 'BK' (Before King's) and 'AK' (After King's).

Continuing to work inside the black box

By the completion of the KMOFAP, I was already a changed teacher. The project did much more than simply change the way in which I taught; it changed the way I thought about students' learning. As a result of this, instead of simply picking up a number of formative assessment techniques, to improve my teaching, I became somebody who continually looked for new and better ways to improve my students' chances of learning. Until my retirement in 2017, I would strive to develop methods to improve the learning of my students. I have chosen to summarize some of the key ways in which the work I had done with Paul, and his team, continued to guide me.

Questioning – What makes a good-quality science discussion?

As I have already mentioned, this was the first formative assessment technique that I tried to develop during the original KMOFAP project. As time went on, however, I began to realize that there was more to good-quality questioning than just making sure more open-ended questions were used, and students were given longer wait times. One of the first things, which I changed about my teaching, regarding questioning, was the fact that I started to keep a record of good-quality questions, which resulted in high-quality class discussions, which in turn gave really useful information about student learning. Even all these years later, it is still interesting to see the reaction of teachers when you ask them to identify which questions or answers to questions really helped learning. I still remember observing a young science teacher, who was doing work on magnets with a low attaining group of 12-year-old. At the end of the lesson, rather than just asking them to recall what happened when the poles of magnets were put near to each other, she asked the group, 'What might happen if a magnet was cut in half?' This question created an intense discussion where ideas about magnetism were explored and challenged that allowed the students to consolidate their learning and provide the teacher with useful evidence about where to go next. How sad to think that this question may have been lost forever in the moment if it had not been department policy to keep records of and share such superb examples.

During the King's project, I had already experimented with meta-cognition and self-regulation, asking students, for example, 'What was tricky/easy about that idea?' 'Who is confident to make a start on this explanation?' This was another area of interaction I would develop over the years. My final teaching groups were all too aware that they might be asked to evaluate their confidence in their knowledge or understanding. For example, 'Who feels so confident of their answer, that they will "bet" that everybody else on their bench could be given an extra question for homework, if they get it wrong?' Students would see these as a 'fun challenge', and they would certainly add to the enjoyment of the lesson, but more seriously, they would provide me with information about the level of understanding of individual students, on particular topics.

One area, which I continued to develop throughout my teaching, was getting more students involved in discussions. After initially realizing during the King's project that longer wait times after questions got more students involved, I became interested in other techniques to get more students to participate. The first method I developed to get more students involved in discussions was simply to tell the students that the discussion was important. I discovered that explaining to students that communication and discussion were central to learning science changed the whole atmosphere during class, with far greater direct student involvement and improved active listening.

This led in turn to a second technique designed to get even more students involved, which was telling students what they needed to do and get out of the discussion. For example, 'This discussion is important, because at the end of it, you will be expected to use what you hear to answer three short questions about ….' The difference this made to participation was amazing.

Self- and peer assessment

In the early days of the King's project, this aspect of formative practice tended to centre on variations of using 'traffic lights' to get students to consider how well they, or somebody else, had achieved a particular task. As time went on, this developed into using 'traffic lights' in a more metacognitive manner, for example, asking students to judge their confidence with various skills or learning.

Over the years, however, I have realized that the best self- and peer assessment involves students summarizing their ideas not with 'traffic lights' or smiley faces, but in writing (further elaboration later). Here, as with questioning, I found that many science teachers naturally assumed that students would be able to self- or peer-assess. With this in mind, I have worked on a whole range of techniques to develop students' capability to self- or peer-assess. What has become clear over time is that no matter the age, or capabilities of the students, self- and peer assessment is something which they need regular training, support and guidance with. This allowed students to model and practise giving feedback as well as provide the context for them to recognize what a quality piece of work should look like across a range of topics and activity types. Not only were these techniques important in helping students become active learners; they were integrated into the science curriculum, so that they became an important part of the learning experience of the students and therefore requiring considerable curriculum time.

Feedback

Although I had always provided my students with a lot of written feedback, even before my involvement on the King's project, what I learned then, and continued to develop, was the importance of linking feedback to *learning*. Nor could I ever forget Paul Black's words of wisdom when he said, 'Written feedback should make students think.' As with all the best ideas, it seems obvious when you consider it, but these two points became my focus for providing ever better written feedback to my students.

One key aspect that the King's project made me realize was that none of these techniques or ideas about formative assessment could be taken separately. So, in order to ensure that my written feedback was focused on students learning, I realized that this would involve making sure that the students were comfortable with using a 'language of learning'. To do this involved making sure that learning objectives, at the start of the lesson, were precisely worded, becoming more like success criteria, rather than vague lesson aims. This in turn meant that the way in which I planned my lessons also subtly altered to make lessons more about learning and less about teaching. Regularly using the language of learning meant that when students came across the same type of language in their written feedback, they saw this as a natural part of the lesson, rather than a separate 'add on'. This highlights the ways in which what had started out as a few 'formative assessment techniques' in the early KMOFAP days had become a total approach to my teaching.

One aspect of written feedback, which altered during my career, was what students were expected to actually do about the feedback they received. This settled down to become known as the 'student response' and basically meant that students were expected to actually response to the teacher's advice. One simple technique, which I developed, was to encourage teachers to use the word 'by', in their feedback, so that students had some hint or instruction about what they should do. For example: 'I want you to improve your description of the rock cycle *by* including examples of all three types of rock.' This obviously fits with Paul's 'making the students think' point, and the impact on student responses, by using this simple idea, was enormous. It moved marking from correction of work to guiding students to improve.

Although it quickly became apparent to me, following the King's project, that the formative techniques we had been trialling were far from 'bolt ons' to my lessons that required me to approach every aspect of my teaching in a different way, it is fair to say that the area, which I developed most during the rest of my career, was the link between summative and formative assessments. In science, especially, these are often totally isolated from each other. This soon became my ultimate AfL passion – developing ideas to merge the two in practicable ways.

As with many science teachers, when faced with marking a Year 11 mock school leaving exam, I became frustrated not just with the students' lack of knowledge but also with the number of 'silly' marks which seemed to be lost, by not reading questions properly, by making errors in maths or with graphs, by lack of clarity, and by incorrect use of scientific terminology. This led to my development of a system of marking exam papers using a system I invented called MARCKS, which recognized where marks were lost and so where improvement could be gained. These letters stand for the following:

M – Maths or graph error
A – Application of science error
R – Not reading the question properly
C – Lack of clarity/use of scientific terminology
K – Lack of revision of the required knowledge
S – Statements per mark (three-mark question needs three facts, etc.)

When summative assessments were marked, the students would get a tick for a correct answer, and one (or more) letter(s) for an incorrect answer, or for marks lost, rather than a cross.

Over time, this idea was used across the age range, from years 7 to 13, and proved to be highly successful, so that students moved away from being concerned simply about their grade to begin to focus on which of the six areas had lost them marks. Although this tended to be Knowledge mostly, many students were surprised how often other aspects of their work had cost them marks.

This idea developed further, with a school I worked with, which had many low-attaining, unmotivated, girls doing science. When receiving their mock exams back, with a grade, and their MARCKS information, they were also told how many more actual marks they needed to make the 'small step' to the next grade. They were then given the free choice of which questions, or part questions, they improved in order to get this improved grade. The effect on the girls was amazing. Many realized that by reading a couple of questions more carefully, or using a calculator to check some basic maths, they could easily have achieved the next grade up. Once again the focus was on improvement indicating to students where their efforts would pay dividends.

Sharing good practice

One final aspect of my teaching, which I recognized as key in KMOFAP, was the importance of sharing good practice with colleagues. Not just good questions to use during classroom discussions, but anything which helped students to learn science better. Teaching and professional learning became a much more collaborative endeavour for me.

It quickly became obvious to me that although sharing good practice over a coffee, etc., was very useful, it was often a bit haphazard. Looking around for a better forum for sharing of ideas and professional learning, I decided to scrap some of the administrative tasks from our monthly departmental meetings. Instead I instigated a session where members of staff could 'share good practice' with the rest of the department; this would always be the first item on our departmental agenda. There was no obligation on teachers to lead on this, but often most would want to do so. Whether it was mentioning a 'good question', which had sparked a really good discussion, or suggesting how a 'fish-tail diagram' had been used as an excellent revision tool in a specific topic, these sessions quickly began to be valued as the most important part of our departmental time. The sessions were almost like mini versions of the original KMOFAP meetings!

I feel that my involvement in the KMOFAP project helped me become a better teacher of science. I have also used my experiences over the years, to support many other schools, none of which would have been possible, had it not been for the impact of Paul and his team. But at the end of the day, it has to be said that whether I thought of myself as a 'better teacher' or not was somewhat irrelevant. What really mattered was that my involvement in the project had actually benefitted my students. In 2010, I had moved to a new school, a very high-achieving selective grammar school. Following disappointing science 'A' level results in 2011, the head teacher asked me to push every aspect of Assessment for Learning across the department. Over the next few years, all the main four pillars from *Working inside the Black Box* were developed, using the range of techniques, which I have briefly mentioned above. Figure 12.1 shows the results

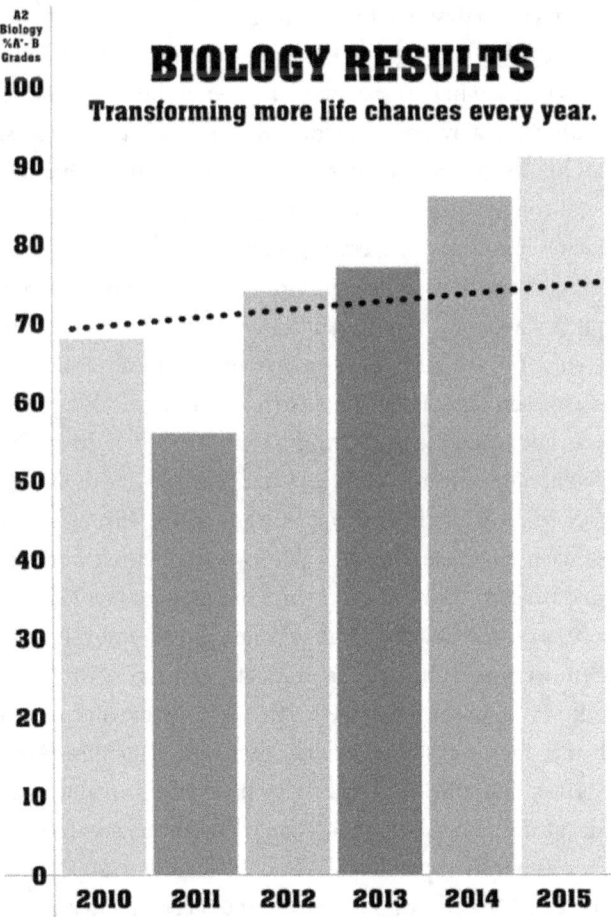

Figure 12.1 School biology 'A' level result improvement from 2010 to 2015.

of the impact of the techniques, and approaches to teaching, on the percentage of students gaining a grade A or A* in biology 'A' level, their final high-stakes examination, over the following few years.

Professional learning through the KMOFAP project – Chris Harrison's reflections

Teaching draws on a 'well-thought-through' and coherent conceptual framework that combines elements of technical 'know-how' with knowledge of research and theory (Orchard & Winch, 2015). Because teaching is grounded in classroom practice, both past and present, teachers cannot learn teaching simply by studying it, analysing it or planning for it; a different kind of knowing emerges during classroom engagement with students (Lampert & Graziani, 2009). Decisions reached in the classroom are filtered through a teacher's current thinking, building on a range of evidence from past experiences. Practical wisdom of this kind supports teachers in acting in practically appropriate ways across a range of contexts. This gradually prepares teachers for the challenges of attending to many minds at work, establishing relationships and trust over time and encouraging interactions as key components of the learning process.

This is explicitly apparent throughout the Paul Spenceley's description of the teacher involvement in the KMOFAP project and his recognition of the impact of this research and professional ways of working on his teaching and classroom practices. It was not as simple as providing training in how to teach differently but rather reflection on research ideas and consideration, with others, what and how some of these ideas might play out in classrooms. Through trialling small changes to his teaching, the teacher was able to evaluate what worked, providing opportunity and time for the lived experience of these changes to be adapted and embedded in his practice. Teacher change is not about removal of old practices and replacement with new but rather a gradual evolution – which could lead to lasting revolutionary changes – that blends in new ways of working into previous routines such that there can be an explicit focus on principles. Any change in classroom routines can affect all aspects of how teaching and learning work together, while, at the same time, such changes might be subtle as the changes build on already established practices. White & Gunstone (2000) report similar findings (2000, p. 302): 'The way research influences practice in education is not through discovery of a detailed and specific mode of teaching but through substantiation of principles that pervade thinking about teaching and learning.'

It is clear that as a project teacher, Paul Spenceley was able to exemplify how the research ideas he was introduced to played out in practice, and he, along with other teaching colleagues, developed the language to describe how the decision-making and actions they have taken fostered and supported learners. The project teacher came to realize that his job was to learn about his students and use the evidence he collected to prepare for teaching and learning, each and every time that teaching took place. The various moves he made, beginning with improving questioning in class, were analysed and evaluated by him as he worked out how to strengthen formative assessment in his classroom over time. This transformed the way he taught as he recognized what helped his learners and how he might support progress.

Conclusion

Paul Black's influence on how assessment is used to inform teaching and learning has transformed how many teachers now think about and use evidence of learning in their classroom. The importance of this is captured in the first author's reflections below.

I think it is clear to see the impact of all that I had learned and developed from Paul Black, and his King's College London team, more than ten years after my initial involvement with the KMOFAP project.

Personally, I could never thank Paul Black, Dylan Wiliam, Chris Harrison and the other researchers enough for the impact that they made on my life as a teacher. However. what is ultimately more important is that ALL has improved the life chances of hundreds of students. On behalf of every one of them, I can only say THANK YOU!

References

Black, P. J. & Wiliam, D. (1998a). 'Assessment and classroom learning'. *Assessment in Education: Principles Policy and Practice,* 5(1): 7–73.

Black, P. J. & Wiliam, D. (1998b). *Inside the Black Box: Raising Standards through Classroom Assessment.* London: GL Assessment.

Gittner, A. & Harrison, C. (2019). 'How do you develop research-informed practice?'. *School Science Review,* 100(373): 61.

Guskey, T. (2002). 'Professional Development and Teacher Change'. *Teachers and Teaching Theory and Practice,* 8(3): 381–91.

Harrison, C. A. (2015). Assessment for Learning in Science Classrooms. *Journal of Research in STEM Education*, 1(2).

Lampert, M. & Grazziani F. (2007). 'Instructional Activities as a Tool for teacher and teacher Educators Learning'. *The Elementary School Journal*, 109(5): 491–509. Chicago: Chicago Press.

Orchard, J. & Winch, c. (2015). 'What training do teachers need?: Why theory is necessary to good teaching'. *Impact*, 15(22).

White, R. Gunstone, R. (2000). *Probing Understanding*. London: Falmer Press.

13

Mapping the Roads of Learning: Linking Learning Progressions with Assessments

Mark Wilson

Introduction

The contents of this chapter represent a sampling of the work of a collaboration between Paul Black, a group of California-based researchers and me.[1] The interactions started in 1997 when Paul and I were both selected to be members of a U.S. National Research Council (NRC) committee that gathered to formulate the ways that educational assessments should be changing with the new insights from cognitive psychology and the learning sciences, and also under the (then nascent) influences of innovations in information technology. The resulting committee report, *Knowing What Students Know* (NRC, 2001), has been very influential within the assessment literature (e.g. 3,997 citations to date, according to GoogleScholar). One of the major themes of that report is that curriculum, pedagogy and assessment must work together to improve education and that a strengthened focus on (a) assessment and (b) its crucial connections to the other two aspects is needed, as this had been missing over the last decades.

We worked off and on for several years on a follow-on project that we intended to serve as a demonstration of these central ideas in that report. Of course, Paul's contributions to assessment, particularly to formative assessment, are well known (witness many other chapters in this volume), but the focus of our project was the development of an infrastructure that spanned all three parts: curriculum, pedagogy and assessment (CPA). Initially, we worked intensively, though intermittently, mainly in the dining room of Paul's house in Wimbledon, in an attempt to align the two trajectories of work that we brought to the (dining room) table, interspersed by cups of tea and delightful conversation sparked by Paul's wife Mary. What I brought was a body of work mainly focused within the technical world of psychometrics and its applications to both summative and formative (e.g. teaching unit quizzes) assessments. What Paul brought was his deep engagement in what happens in classrooms, especially in the ways that in-classroom assessment activities can provide feedback to both the teacher and the students about how the learning is progressing. After some period of circling around this area, we came to agree that one crucial element that has been missing from both literatures has been a concrete way to align the relevant parts of the curriculum (C) with instructional activities (i.e. the pedagogy – P) and assessments (A). We labelled this infrastructure the *roadmap*,[2] and we gathered our work and thoughts together on this topic and summarized them in a focus paper (Black, et al., 2011) to establish the *Roadmaps Project*, and which was published alongside twelve commentaries by a group of distinguished and insightful colleagues from the fields of educational assessment, psychometrics and cognitive science.

The next section of this chapter is composed of a brief summary of that paper along with some illustrations of the examples we worked on during that time. The next two sections of the chapter represent (a sampling of) follow-on segments of the roadmap work, one from an early episode and one from a recent episode:

(a) an example of how complex the relationship between curriculum plans and assessment findings can be and
(b) a description of the issues we are facing in current ongoing roadmaps work linking the outcomes of the assessments to teacher instruction in the classroom.

The chapter finishes with a conclusion discussing next steps along the road.

Highlights of the 'roadmap' idea

In reflecting on the widely lauded success of the work on formative assessments by Paul and his colleagues (Black, et al., 2003; Black & Wiliam, 1998), Paul was concerned about a strand of criticism that was summed up by Perrenoud (1998):

> This [feedback] no longer seems to me, however, to be the central issue. It would seem more important to concentrate on the theoretical models of learning and its regulation and their implementation. These constitute the real systems of thought and action, in which feedback is only one element.
>
> (p. 86)

In addition, he was also concerned about the difficulties that teachers faced when they had to tangle with the twin needs for formative and summative assessments within their classrooms. Many commentators have bemoaned the dominant effects of summative assessments (especially those from forces external to the classroom; e.g. Herman, 2008; Koretz, 2017; Wilson, 2004, 2018). To represent his perspective on this Paul developed a new diagram to express this force. To see this, look at Figure 13.1 (left panel): here we see the 'standard' conception of the cyclical and supportive relationship among curriculum, pedagogy and assessment. However, in the 'vicious triangle' (see Figure 13.1, right panel), the beneficial relationships among these are altered and the pedagogy gets 'squeezed' between the usual pressure from curriculum and very demanding and direct pressure from (summative) assessment! In fact, one of the motivations for the *Assessment for Learning* (AfL) movement (e.g. Assessment Reform Group, 2006) has been to counter these effects and to focus on the practices and bounties of in-classroom formative assessment. Yet Paul's concern was that this effort was doomed to eventual failure if it was constituted principally as a counter to summative assessment – the better solution was to create an infrastructure for schooling that included support for both summative and formative assessments, and capitalized on the virtues of each, while disparaging neither, a view later revisited in Black and Wiliam (2018). It is this insight that was the driving force behind the 'Roadmaps' paper (Black et al, 2011) – it contains (besides a strong account of the forms and importance of classroom assessment) an account of (a) a theoretical infrastructure for education (i.e. for linking CPA) and (b) an example of the way that this might work in the topic area of Structure of Matter in science education.

Our task, then, was to discern a way to relate elements of a curriculum (C) to the design of assessments (A), so as to facilitate the instruction by the teachers (P). The theoretical structure that we chose as the basic underpinning (effectively, the 'grain-size') of the relationship between assessment and

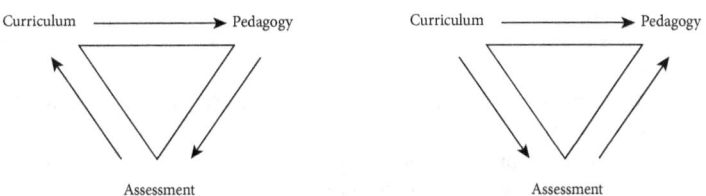

Figure 13.1 The traditional CPA triangle (left panel) and the 'vicious' triangle.

curriculum is the *construct map* (Wilson, 2004). A construct map (see example shown in Table 13.1 and discussed in the next paragraph) is a way to structure a topic in a curriculum to emphasize its nature as set of developmental levels that progresses from less sophisticated to more sophisticated. To be useful to teachers in designing and implementing their instructional plans, it must (a) embody an important curriculum topic, (b) be expressed in a way that facilitates understanding of the sequence of development involved in that topic and (c) guide the creation of observational events (ranging from formative in-classroom discussions to summative tests) that can lead to evidence about a student's likely location on the map, and hence (d) provide an evidentiary basis for what the next pedagogic step should be. There is an assumption that the topic is relatively unitary, in the sense that there is a peak level of sophistication[3] that is to be attained by students, and, in the main, levels of sophistication below that are discernible, though there may be complex ways in which those levels exist and are manifested. Thus, these construct map levels must be chosen to be useful to teachers in the classroom and must relate to teachers' goals in designing their instruction. Of course, there is more than one such unitary topic in any curriculum, so these will be represented by multiple construct maps, and these may have complex interrelationships.

A visual representation of an example construct map in the science topic of Structure of Matter (at the middle school level) is shown in Table 13.1. This is a generic version of the specific construct called Changes of State, and it is based on a review of the relevant science education literature (summarized in Black et al, 2011). It is important to note that although the relevant literature contains many examples of empirical studies that investigate smaller-scale relationships among concepts and skills in this area, the construct map is itself a new educational product depending on a very deliberate synthesis of the literature, aimed to provide a representation of typical instructionally-relevant development within

Table 13.1 The generic construct map for Changes of State.

Level	Description
3	Both material and mass are conserved.
2	Partial evidence of conservation: either material or mass is conserved, but not both.
1	Can use appropriate terminology, but no evidence of conservation in terms of either material or mass.
0	Neither material nor mass is addressed.

that topic. And, once the literature review and the construct map design are concluded, it must then be seen as a *hypothesis*, yet to be confirmed (or altered/denied) by direct empirical testing. Moreover, in this case the levels shown in Table 13.1 represent a coarse-grained hypothesis – that is, one may well expect some variation across different manifestations of state change, such as melting, evaporation or condensation, although this will likely depend on the grain size of the levels. Table 13.1 shows just one of the construct maps that were hypothesized (based on the literature) in that paper. An illustration of the other constructs and their relationships in the Structure of Matter roadmap is given in Figure 13.2. Each of the boxes in the figure represents one construct map. For a description of these constructs and their relationships see Black et al. (2011).

It is a significant aspect of the roadmap idea that an assessment task associated with a construct map will be designed to prompt student responses that relate to two or more of the levels (as for Changes of State in Table 13.1).[4] An example task is shown in Figure 13.3: This is an assessment task with two questions, the first is a multiple-choice item and the second is a short-response open-ended item. The responses to both can be mapped to the levels in Table 13.2. When a construct map (especially a generic one, as in Table 13.2) is realized in terms of specific items, the description of the levels can often take on a more complicated look, though the principles are the same. For example, for the open-ended question (Question 2), the responses can be categorized into all four levels of the

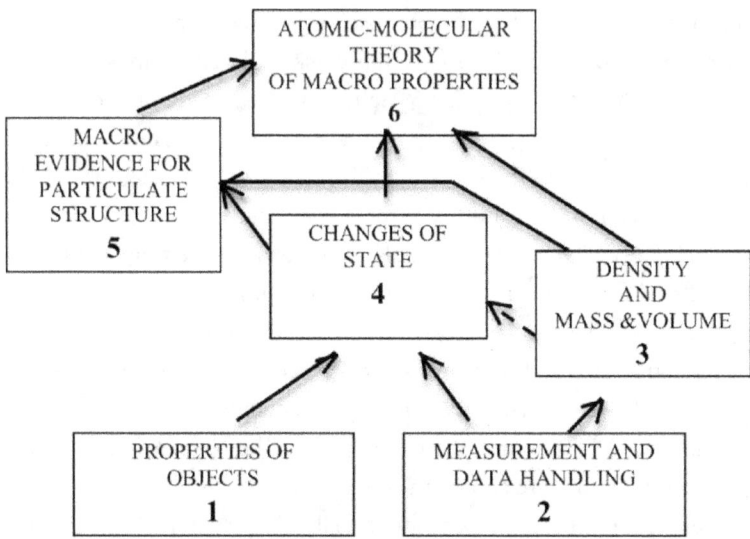

Figure 13.2 The initial Structure of Matter roadmap.

> Carmen wants to know what happens to the mass of something when matter changes from one form to another. She puts three ice cubes in a sealed bag and records the mass of ice in the bag to investigate this. Once the ice cubes have melted, she records the mass of the water in the bag.
>
> 1. Which of the following best describes the result?
>
> (a) The mass of the water in the bag will be less than the mass of the ice in the bag.
> (b) The mass of the water in the bag will be more than the mass of the ice cubes in the bag.
> (c) The mass of the water in the bag will be the same as the mass of the ice cubes in the bag.
>
> 2. Describe your thinking. Provide an explanation for your answer.

Figure 13.3 An example of a Changes of State task with two questions.

construct, as shown in Figure 13.4 (where the numbers in the right-hand column indicate the construct map levels and some are followed by letters indicating that there are different sub-categories in that level for that item). The responses to the multiple-choice question (Question 1) can also be mapped onto the construct map levels; in this case response (c) is mapped to level 2C, responses (a) and (b) to 1A, and any other response to 0. As can be seen, formative interpretations in terms of construct levels for responses to individual items are immediately available to teachers, once the responses are scored. These can be used as feedback regarding individual students or accumulated across a classroom as feedback for how the whole group is performing.

Empirical results for the test composed of the assessment tasks related to Changes of State for the study reported in Black et al. (2011) are summarized in Figure 13.5. In this figure, resulting Wright maps are shown for two sub-parts of the construct – for Melting items (left-hand side) and Evaporation items (right-hand side), respectively.[5] The two (vertical) sets of X's are histograms of student locations and each of the columns to the right of each of the histograms shows the results for a single item. For example, looking at the Melting Dimension first (i.e. the left-hand side of Figure 13.5), the column immediately to the right of the histogram shows that for the item labelled '219MC' (i.e. the ordered multiple-choice version[6] of item 219), the threshold between the lowest level and level 1 is at approximately -3.6 logits. And, going up that column, the threshold between level 1 and level 2 is at approximately 0.5 logits. The patterns for the next four items in this construct are shown in the next four columns, and the pattern is quite different in each case. Skipping then to the Evaporation Dimension (on the right-hand side), we see a pattern that is equally varied.

Description	Typical student responses	Level
Both same mass (or weight) and same material explicitly	'(Students chose c) Mass will be the same because they are the same substance but in a different form.' (students chose c) The mass of the matter will be the same as the ice cubes' mass because only its state of matter changed and not the molecules themselves.'	3
Both different (larger or smaller) mass (or weight) and same material explicitly	'(Students chose b) The water will have more mass because the water will have more mass if turned into liquid.''(Students chose a) I think the mass of the water in the bag will be less because the pressure changes. It's still the same amount of water, but the molecules move.'	2B
Same mass (or weight) but not explicit about same material	'(Students chose c) I think that the mass will stay the same because matter cannot be destroyed or created and if nothing can escape the bag it will stay the same in mass at least.' '(Students chose c) Even if matter changes to another, the mass will still be the same because there are the same number of molecules in there.'	2C
Same mass but not same material	'(Students chose c) It stays the same because you put an amount in there and just because the molecules change doesn't mean the amount has.'	2A
Different (larger or smaller) mass (or weight) but not explicit about same material	'(Students chose b) Mass is space taken up. So I think it's b, since water fills up the bag but the ice cubes take less mass since it's bundled up into.' '(Students chose a) Ice is solid and weighs more than liquid.'	1
Any response that indicates the term 'melting' incorrectly used/I don't know/Off-topic response	'I don't know why.' 'I guessed.'	0
Blank		0

Figure 13.4 The scoring guide for the open-ended Changes of State question in Figure 13.3.

In order to link the individual item outcomes (as in the previous paragraph) to a broader interpretation of the results by a teacher, looking across all the items, and (in this case) looking across both Melting and Evaporation, a higher-level summary of the pattern of results is needed. This is what is provided by a standard-setting exercise called 'banding', and the results are indicated in Figure 13.5 by the three grey horizontal lines. These lines are judged to divide the Changes of State outcome scale into four segments where the students are learning the four levels of the Changes of State construct (and the four segments are demarcated by the grey thresholds). Starting first at the bottom,

(i) the students in the histograms located below the lowest grey line are at level 0 on the construct map (i.e. they are not yet even learning the relevant terms), and
(ii) those above this line are in the process[7] of achieving level 1 in the construct (i.e. they are learning the relevant terms, but have no conservation), while
(iii) those above the middle line are in the process of achieving level 2 (i.e. learning partial conservation, either mass or material, but not both), and
(iv) those few students above the highest grey line are in the process of achieving level 3, and would be seen as learning conservation (i.e. both material and matter are conserved).

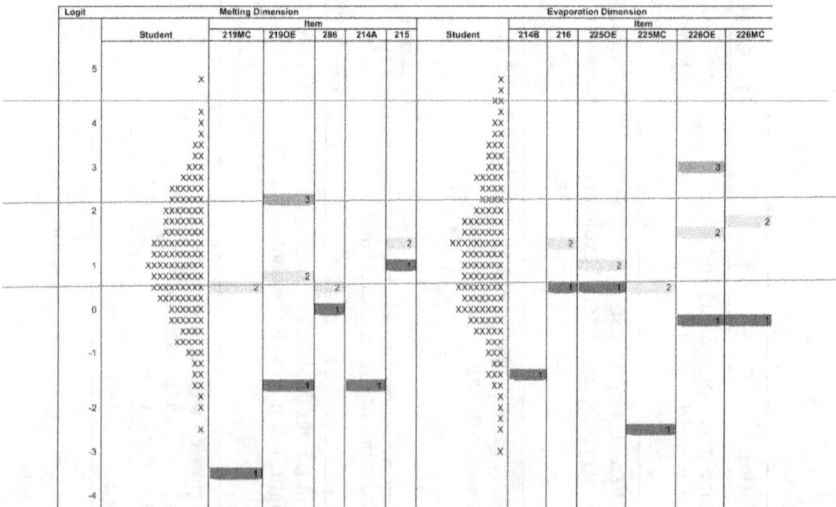

Figure 13.5 Twin Wright maps for the melting and evaporation tasks in Changes of State.

The account given above, starting with a construct map, developing items, and mapping them into 'bands' on a Wright map, is a brief example of the steps to build a roadmap, as described in Black et al. (2011). However, this was deliberately chosen to make the steps clear – it is not always so clear, as is shown in the example in the next section.

Revising the Roadmap

Unfortunately, this clarity of results is often not found to be the case, especially in the first instances where one is examining the empirical information about how items serve as indicators of a construct. In this section, I recount a less simple story, where our expectations, based on the literature (and the judgements of the assessment task developers), were not upheld, and we were forced to go back to the drawing board about the construct in question. This section is based on a research working paper (Black, 2013) and associated other publications and presentations (as noted below).

The construct in question is called Particulate Explanations of Chemical Changes (ECC), and it is a part of a revised roadmap based on subsequent empirical data and analyses after the initial one shown in Figure 13.2 was devised. The new roadmap is shown in Figure 13.6 – as can be seen, ECC is the new peak construct in the roadmap. The hypothesized construct map for the ECC construct is shown in Table 13.2.

If all went perfectly well, then we might 'expect'[8] to see a resulting Wright map for ECC that looks like the one in the top panel of Figure 13.7 (Wilson et al., 2013). After collecting a new data set including new assessment tasks developed to be indicators of the constructs in Figure 13.6, we analysed the data and found the results shown in the bottom panel of Figure 13.7!

Table 13.2 The initial construct map for Particulate Explanations of Chemical Changes.

Level	Description
5	Chemical changes produce different molecules
4	Chemical and physical change – Particulate explanations of differences
3	Atoms and molecules.
2	Chemical and physical change – Observable differences
1	Conservation of matter.
0	Matter not conserved.

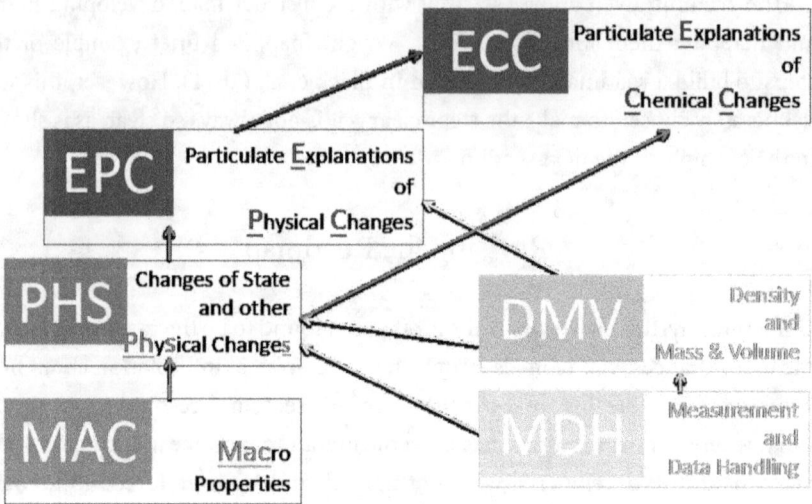

Figure 13.6 Subsequent roadmap for the Structure of Matter.

Needless to say, this was quite a disappointment for the project members, and this presented the project with a knotty problem – how to 'untangle' the many levels in the bottom panel of Figure 13.7?

Paul's reaction to this shock was typical – he bounced back with four suggestions about what had happened (Black, 2014):

> bad map
> bad items
> different students
> bad idea!

In his typical fashion, Paul then leapt into the problem (he quoted the old adage – 'Keep calm and carry on'), told the project members to lower our immediate expectations, and led us back to a deep engagement with the empirical results (described in Black (2013)) to refine items that seemed oddly located in the Wright Map in Figure 13.7 and start the constructs design over again, this time basing it on the empirical findings. These investigations resulted in a split in the construct into three new 'smaller' constructs ('strands') as shown in Figure 13.8). The resulting Wright map is shown in Figure 13.9. Here we can see that indeed Paul and the project had developed a set of constructs where

(i) the ordering of levels *within* each of the three constructs is consistent with empirical observation; and

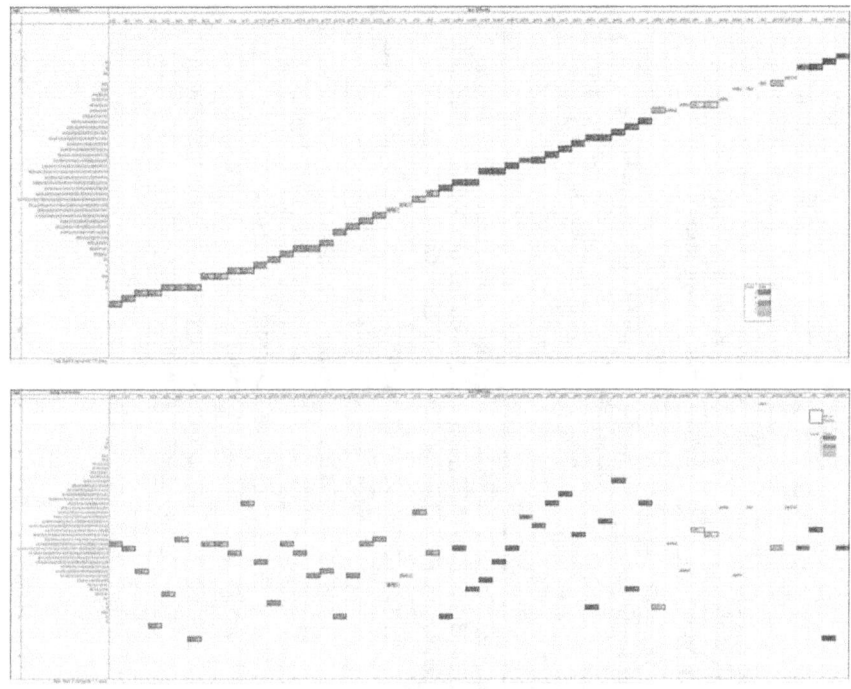

Figure 13.7 What we 'expected' to get (upper panel) and what we got (lower panel).

(ii) the top levels of the three constructs are in the order expected; but
(iii) the lower thresholds overlap a great deal in terms of difficulty (i.e. students are learning all three at once).

After a further interlude of investigation and discussion, the resulting new roadmap is shown in Figure 13.10. An important conceptual advance in conceiving of the roadmap was to recognize that, although the ideas and skills in the Density and Mass & Volume (DMV) and the Measurement and Data-Handling (MDH) constructs are *requirements* for the Structure of Matter roadmap, they were themselves not a part of the structure. Instead, they play facilitative roles, enabling students to carry out calculations and solve problems that are needed to assess students' Structure of Matter knowledge. This is indicated in Figure 13.10 by linking them to the *arrows between* boxes rather than to the boxes containing the other constructs.[9] Of course, the material in these constructs must still be addressed as part of the instruction required by students learning Structure of Matter.

The resolution of this knotty problem in the mapping of a construct has left us with an interesting conclusion. The neat and tidy plan for Particulate

ECC-A Chemical or physical changes: knowing that atoms and molecules do or do not change in these two types of change	ECC-B chemical or physical changes: changes in macroscopic properties	ECC-C molecular representations of elements and compounds
Knowing that in a chemical change the atoms stay the same but in different molecules, while in physical change the atoms stay in the same molecules, but that in both changes the numbers of atoms involved stay the same.	Can recognize that properties all differ after a chemical change Can distinguish chemical from physical change in unfamiliar cases.	Can recognize and distinguish between representations of one or two elements or compounds, or of mixtures between these.
Understands that in a chemical change the atoms or molecules change the way they combine and so form new materials	Can distinguish chemical from physical change: where it is not clear whether or not a new material has been produced. Knowing that mass is conserved in all cases.	Knows that atoms and molecules have weight, that in solids and in liquids there are empty spaces between atoms and molecules. Knows that different molecules can be made of the same atoms or of different atoms. Can recognize a representation of an element with diatomic molecules.
Understands that two different materials will be made of the different molecules, but that these can be made of the same atoms or of different atoms.	Can distinguish chemical from physical change: where it is clear whether or not a new material has been produced.	Knows that atoms and molecules are not usually visible and may have different sizes. Recognizes a representation of an element with monatomic molecules.

Figure 13.8 The revised set of constructs for Particulate Explanations of Chemical Changes.

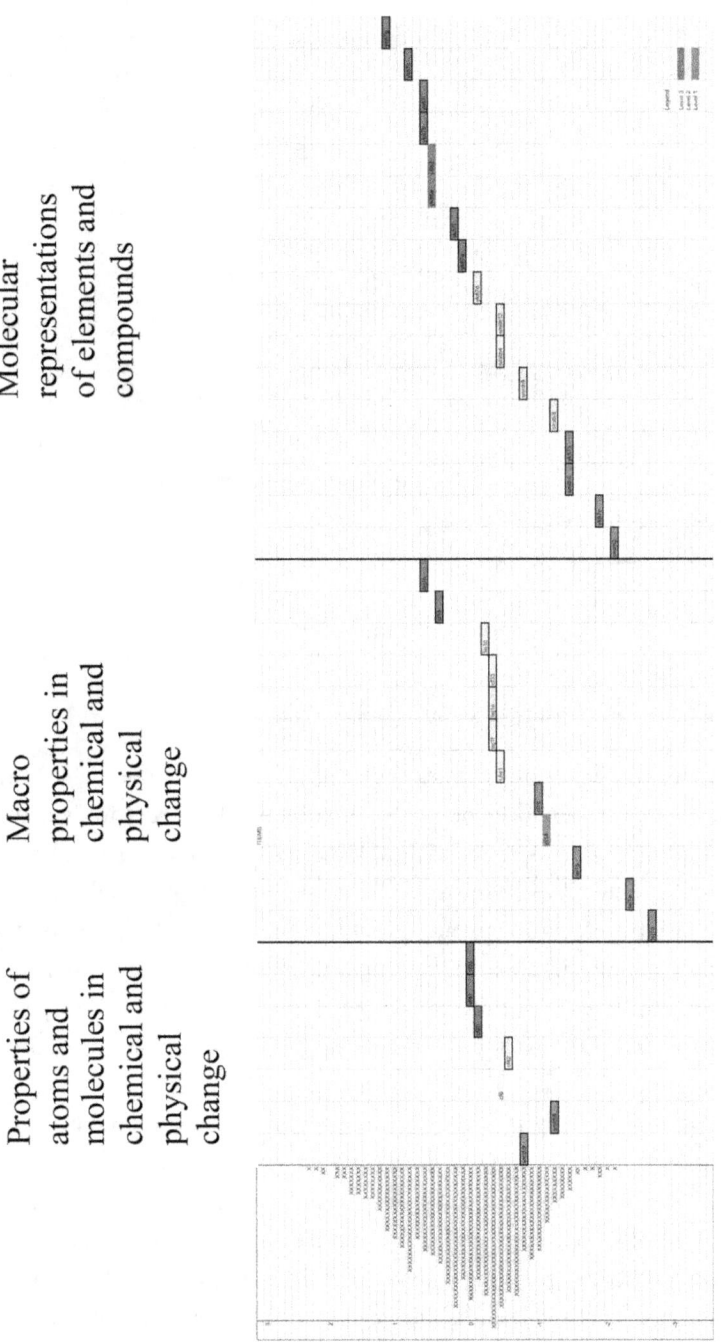

Figure 13.9 The Wright map for the three new constructs in Particulate Explanations of Chemical Changes.

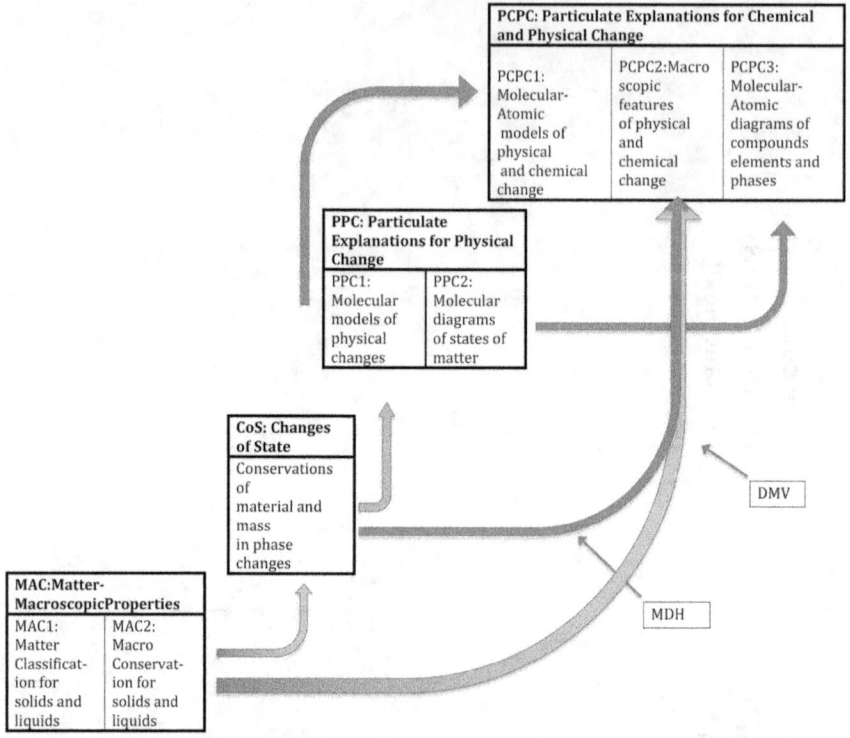

Figure 13.10 Latest roadmap for Structure of Matter.

Explanations of Chemical Changes shown in Table 13.2 is not viable, and we have had to revise our ideas of what is the highest construct in Structure of Matter to now encompass three highest levels! (Although there is still one that seems most difficult to reach the top of.[10]) These strands represent three 'parallel' constructs that students are learning simultaneously, so teachers will need to be aware of the complexity that students are learning three different strands at the same time. This is an important consideration for teachers when they planning their instruction for this topic, and when they are interpreting individual student responses.

Looking more deeply into the constructs and item sets representing them, some challenges yet remain, as next steps beyond what has been discussed above: (a) the discernment of a dividing line (both in terms of definition and empirical results) between molecular models representing differences and molecular models representing changes and (b) the discernment of a dividing line (in terms of empirical results) between items with pictures of models versus written descriptions. These are not illustrated or discussed here but are included to signify the continuing nature of the research on this topic.

Linking the outcomes of the assessments to teacher instruction in the classroom[11]

In this section, I lay out the basis for the way the project is conceptualizing its work in capitalizing on the strengths of the construct maps and other associated assessment materials (such as the items and Wright Maps, as exemplified above) to build up teacher resources for use in their classrooms. The aim of the work discussed here is presented as only an attempt (as this is part of the continuing work of the project) to answer the following question:

> How are the results for Structure of Matter and Ecology[12] to be used in teachers' classroom work on these subjects?

The ways in which the results are used by teachers in their classroom work will depend on the model(s) of pedagogy within which they may be found useful. If a teacher uses a 'delivery' model, results of the kind reported above in Sections 2 and 3 (i.e. the 'Highlights of the "roadmap" idea' section and the 'Relationships between curriculum plans and assessment findings' section) can be seen as advice on the optimum instructional order for organizing what students they must learn, and the assessment items developed in the project will be useful tools to check, by summative assessments, that the learning has happened. Even at this superficial delivery-like approach to learning, problems of measurement can arise – for example, given a multiple-choice question, a number of students may choose the correct option, but when asked to explain their choice, the number who can provide a valid explanation may be smaller – although how much smaller may depend on the nature of the topic and of the multiple-choice formulation; thus the validity of those multiple-choice questions is problematic

If, however, the teacher is interested in helping students to develop their capacity to learn, the topic may then be chosen either to engage students in activity which will help their development as learners or to develop a deep understanding of the topic involved, or to serve both purposes. What follows is an elaboration of some of the characteristics of a pedagogy which aims to serve both purposes. These characteristics are presented under four main headings: this structure, however, does not imply either that the earlier headings are the more important of the four, or that these four represent a time sequence in which the four are to be applied. On the contrary, there are deep and multiple inter-connections between these four so that they constitute a four-dimensional space within which any given pedagogic episode may be located.

A. Group work and collaborative learning

In classroom discussions between students working in small groups, students are learning from one another. A teacher may pose a question to a class, and after (say) an answer is offered, react neutrally to whether it is a correct, a partially correct or a completely wrong response, and proceed rather by asking 'Can anyone else suggest a different answer?'. If the question builds upon, but demands more than, ideas that have already been grasped by most of the class, then two or more responses may be offered. The teacher may then invite students to work in small groups (e.g. about five per group) to compare and contrast the different answers and to produce an agreed group ranking of, or commentary on, them. In so doing, the teacher is helping students to be resources for one another through 'collaborative learning'. There is good evidence that lecturing to students is largely ineffective, and that there is much value in classroom interactivity and in the value of group work (Blatchford, et al., 2006; Chi, 2009; Johnson & Johnson, 2009; Mercer, et al., 2004).

The construct maps and assessment tasks provide a rich set of materials on which to base such group work and collaborations. For example, Figure 13.3 is based on a scenario that can be readily adapted for a classroom exercise for small groups of students, and the Changes of State construct map then becomes a mental resource for teachers listening in and participating in students' interactions during the group work.

B. Dialogue

International comparisons of classroom dialogue have shown that it differs greatly between different countries (Alexander, 2000). However, Alexander also argued, in common with many others, that dialogue is itself a mode of learning and not simply superficial talk – with learning happening only when one was writing down one's thinking. He emphasized this as follows:

> Children, we now know, need to talk, and to experience a rich diet of spoken language, in order to think and to learn. Reading, writing and numeracy may be acknowledged curriculum 'basics', but talk is arguably the true foundation of learning.
>
> (Alexander, 2006, p. 9)

He later developed the argument in a more fundamental explanation:

> Talk vitally mediates the cognitive and cultural spaces between adult and child, among children themselves, between teacher and learner, between society and

the individual, between what the child knows and understands and what he or she has yet to know and understand.

(Alexander, 2008, p. 92)

This level of explanation is explored more fully in the literature on the psychology of learning (e.g. Greene & Azvedo, 2007; Vygotsky, 1962; Wood, 1998). In these dialogues, construct maps can serve as boundary objects (Star & Griesemer, 1989) – crucial supports for students and teachers trying to understand one another's perspective, and the items that the students are familiar with can provide useful concrete reference points for them to refer to in their discussions.

C. The formative-summative spectrum

The development of the concept of formative assessment has been a notable feature of assessment discussions over the last 20 years. The prominence that some discussions give to it as a distinct form of assessment can be misleading. Assessment in education is the elicitation of evidence about students' learning: any such evidence can be interpreted and then used for the formative purpose of guiding the next activity to develop that learning, or for the summative purpose of evaluating the achievement of the learning of the material assessed. Any particular evidence may be used for both purposes, although the design of the assessment may be guided by the priority given to one purpose over the other. So, for example, an informal assessment designed to summarize the learning achieved at the end of the teaching of a particular topic may reveal that one of the ideas involved has been misunderstood by many of the students in a class, so that the teacher may spend time on further discussion of that idea before proceeding to the next topic.

Some authors seem to regard formative and summative as fundamentally different (e.g. Scriven,1967). The argument that Paul and I were promoting was that assessment is just the gathering of information about students' learning – the formative use and the summative use may be seen as the two ends of a spectrum of the uses of assessment information, with any one use lying somewhere within that spectrum (see e.g. Black, 2018b). This view does not apply solely to classroom discussions: students' written work, whether within the classroom in (say) an informal test or outside the classroom with the products collected and assessed by the teacher, may be used to give feedback, either to individual students or to a class as a whole, and, either formatively or summatively. Item banks that are developed within this approach can be used, in concert with the construct maps to facilitate the coordination of results between summative and formative, and, where efforts have been made to calibrate both open-ended and selected responses together, teachers can relate rich formative results (i.e. from the open-ended items) to more distal results of selected response items used in summative assessments (Wilson, Morell, Osborne, Dozier & Suksiri, 2019).

D. Validity

An outstanding criterion for judging the quality of feedback, whether written or oral, and/or at individual or classroom level, is its validity (AERA/APA/NCME, 2014; Crooks, et al., 1996; Messick, 1989). The development of an assessment system with the features used in the roadmaps projects ensures that access to and testing of critical validity evidence are 'baked in' by the sequence of standard steps carried out within the BAS – the five aspects of validity evidence (plus fairness) that are present in the 'Testing Standards' are generated by a BAS-guided assessment development. This, then, also would apply to a context where a new curriculum was accompanied by the development of such assessments, leading to a double-bonus payoff – the curriculum has a valid assessment that can be used to evaluate the effectiveness of the curriculum, and also, and perhaps even more important, the curriculum can be deployed with a valid formative and summative assessment system to accompany it. Although the former is extremely important and would represent a critical step forward compared to the typical use of 'standardized assessments' in curriculum evaluations (Sussman & Wilson, 2019), the latter is the asset that is more interesting and useful to the teachers who will actually use the curriculum to enhance student learning.

The project's findings and outcomes have provided valuable tools for enhancing teachers' classroom work. However, there are several problems to be considered if their dissemination and wider use are to be encouraged.

Potential users have to understand that these tools aim to provide (a) the optimum sequence of components (or sub-topics) in which any main topic should be presented and (b) questions which have been tried and tested to assess the several stages in understanding which students may or may not have reached. Once teachers have been able to select those questions that seem neither too easy or far too demanding for the classroom they are teaching, then these questions can be used to raise issues for discussions whereby students will explore and thereby develop their existing understanding. It follows that, in implementing a plan for progression in classrooms, it is often essential to adjust the plans using formative feedback.

As Paul and I stated in our earlier publication (Black et al., 2011), the studies on progression in student learning have revealed that not much was known about how to choose good sequences for the development of students' understandings of a topic (Black et al., 2011). The studies that Paul and I carried out during our collaboration often revealed many inconsistencies between what seemed a clear sequence and what was empirically the case, so that the assumed sequence must be revised over several cycles of modification and empirical verification. The resulting roadmap of the complex succession of the multiple component concepts can then be used as a guide by teachers for their planning. Such maps have also been produced by work in England (Johnson & Tymms, 2011), Germany (Hadenfeldt et al., 2016) and the United States (Lehrer et al., 2014; Morell et al., 2017). In most cases, the relevant state curricula provide no more than a general and hypothetical foundation on which teachers can choose a progression sequence in promoting students' learning.

However, the activities presented in the above paragraph entail assumptions about the pedagogic approach that a potential user chooses to employ. The traditions of different schools, and between different school subjects within a school, will influence and/or constrain the choice, as will the degrees of support, and/or constraint, which any state or school district may provide. We might worry that our project's findings are limited because they were mainly developed within a single large and diversified school district: We doubt that this is a serious constraint in the light of widespread experience of the curricula and assessments in science education, and the centrality of the Structure of Matter to all curricula. However, any wider dissemination would have to acknowledge where, and with which communities of teachers, the findings were established, while arguing also for their wider relevance.

Conclusion

The three sections above are a (very) small sampling of the thoughts, interactions and plans that were laid out within the collaboration between Paul and I over a twenty-year period. Each represents a different step along the way, as well as different aspects of the work of the project. The first represents a coming together of the core ideas comprising (a) a theoretical infrastructure for education and (b) the development of materials for science education. The chapter then addressed some of the challenges inherent in developing this infrastructure, focusing on the critical need for empirical evidence to support the construct maps. Finally, it focused on next steps needed – the development of teacher-ready materials and professional development. The project has moved forward on this challenge, and it has initiated studies of teacher use of outputs from the roadmap infrastructure.

Of course, this 20+-year project has involved complexities beyond those mentioned above. In order to convey some of the scope of the full project, a listing of project publications and presentations is given in Appendix A.[13] The final judgement of the success of this project will depend on (a) whether the idea of an infrastructure for curriculum, pedagogy and assessment becomes a standard basis for conceptualizing education, (b) whether roadmaps designed on the basis of construct maps become a part of the intellectual technology that forms that infrastructure, and (c) whether the roadmaps that have been developed in this project find popular use, even just as ideals. At the present time, these ideas are still percolating into the science education research and development world.

Notes

1. I must acknowledge the work and insights of the following as we have gone along this path: (at UC Berkeley) Linda Morell, Shih-Ying Yao, Tina Collier (Chiu) and Weeraphat Suksiri, and (at Stanford University) Jonathan Osborne, Brian Henderson, Anna McPherson and Sara Dozier. Of course, Jonathan Osborne was at King's College London, before we were working together, and has since retired from Stanford.
2. This term was seen by Paul and I as being closely related to the two terms 'learning progression' from science education, and 'learning trajectory' from mathematics education, but we coined this term to emphasize how it can be of use to teachers in classrooms as they navigate the challenges of teaching students complex topics.
3. Sometimes called an 'upper anchor'.
4. This is one of the tenets of the BEAR Assessment System (BAS; Wilson, 2005) which has been used by the project as the guiding measurement approach.
5. For more detail about interpreting these Wright maps, see Black et al. (2011) and Wilson (2005).
6. An ordered multiple-choice item is one where the different options have been classified as being of different degrees of 'correctness' and hence can be scored into more than just the traditional two scores, correct and incorrect (Briggs et al., 2006). In this case, the scores are the construct map levels for melting.

7   I.e. these students are succeeding on the relevant (Level 1) questions at approximately 50 per cent, which we take as an indication point for active learning (Wilson, 2005).
8   I.e. expect with some minor variations of course, hence 'expect'.
9   This had been hinted at in Figure 13.6 by the 'greying' of those constructs.
10 See discussion of this possibility in the text regarding Figure 13.7 in Wilson (2008).
11 The following section of this chapter is lightly adapted from the text of a working paper by Paul Black, devoted to discussing the future work of the project (Black, 2018a), with minor edits to improve continuity with the current chapter.
12 I.e. Ecology was a second content topic explored by the project.
13 Although our collaboration was initially sparked by shared interests, Paul and I had the benefit of initial funding via the Strategic Education Research Partnership Foundation, followed by two rounds of funding from the U.S. Federal Institute of Education Studies, and now it is continuing with funding from U.S. National Science Foundation.

References

Alexander, R. (2000). *Culture and Pedagogy: International Comparisons in Primary Education*. Oxford: Blackwell.

Alexander, R. (2006). *Towards Dialogic Thinking: Rethinking Classroom Talk*. York: Dialogos.

Alexander, R. (2008). *Essays in Pedagogy*. Oxford: Routledge.

American Educational Research Association, American Psychological Association, & National Council on Measurement in Education. (2014). *Standards for Educational and Psychological Testing*. Washington, DC.

Assessment Reform Group. (2006). *The Role of Teachers in the Assessment of Learning*. London, UK: Institute of Education.

Black, P. & Wiliam, D. (1998). 'Assessment and classroom learning'. *Assessment in Education*, 5: 7–71.

Black, P. (2013, March). *ECC Road Map Lessons*. Learning Progressions in Science Working Paper, Berkeley: University of California.

Black, P. (2014, July). *Levels for Assessment*. Paper presented to the Association for Science Assessment, Hatfield, UK.

Black, P. (2018a, September). *What Next?* Learning Progressions in Science Working Paper, Berkeley: University of California.

Black, P. (2018b). 'Helping students to become capable learners'. *European Journal of Education*, 53: 144–59.

Black, P., Harrison, C., Lee, C., Marshall, B. & Wiliam, D. (2003). *Assessment for Learning*. London: Open University Press.

Black, P. & Wiliam, D. (2018). 'Classroom assessment and pedagogy', *Assessment in Education: Principles, Policy & Practice*, 25(6): 551–75, DOI: 10.1080/0969594X.2018.1441807

Black, P., Wilson, M. & Yao, S. Y. (2011). 'Road maps for learning: A guide to the navigation of learning progressions'. *Measurement: Interdisciplinary Research and Perspectives*, 9: 71–123.

Blatchford, P., Baines, E., Rubie-Davies, C., Bassett, P. & Chowne, A. (2006). 'The effect of a new approach to group-work on pupil-pupil and teacher-pupil interaction'. *Journal of Educational Psychology*, 98: 750–65.

Briggs, D., Alonzo, A., Schwab, C. & Wilson, M. (2006). 'Diagnostic assessment with ordered multiple-choice items'. *Educational Assessment*, 11(1): 33–63.

Chi, M. (2009). 'Active-constructive-interactive: A conceptual framework for differentiating learning activities'. *Topics in Cognitive Science*, 1: 73–105.

Crooks, T. J., Kane, M. T. & Cohen, A. S. (1996). 'Threats to the valid use of assessments'. *Assessment in Education: Principles Policy and Practice*, 3: 265–85.

Greene, J. A. & Azvedo, R. (2007). 'A theoretical review of Winne and Hadwin's model of self-regulate learning: New perspectives and directions'. *Review of Educational Research*, 77(3): 354–72.

Herman, J. L. (2008). 'Accountability and assessment in the service of learning: Is the public interest being served?'. In K. Ryan & L. Shepard (Eds.), *The Future of Test-Based Accountability*, 211–31. New York: Routledge/Lawrence Erlbaum.

Hadenfeldt, J. C., Neumann, K., Bernholt, S. & Liu, X. (2016). 'Students' progression in understanding the matter concept'. *Journal of Research in Science Teaching*, 53: 683–708.

Johnson, D. W. & Johnson, R. T. (2009). 'An educational psychology success story: Social interdependence theory and cooperative learning'. *Educational Researcher*, 38(5): 365–79.

Johnson, P. & Tymms, P. (2011). 'The emergence of a learning progression in middle school chemistry'. *Journal of Research in Science Teaching*, 48: 849–77.

Koretz, D. (2017). *The Testing Charade: Pretending to Make Schools Better*. Chicago, IL: University of Chicago Press.

Lehrer, R., Kim, M-J., Ayers, E. & Wilson, M. (2014). 'Toward establishing a learning progression to support the development of statistical reasoning'. In A. Maloney, J. Confrey & K. Nguyen (Eds.), *Learning Over Time: Learning Trajectories in Mathematics Education*, 31–60. Charlotte, NC: Information Age Publishers.

Mercer, N., Dawes, L., Wegerif, R. & Sams, C. (2004). 'Reasoning as a scientist: Ways of helping children to use language to learn science'. *British Educational Research Journal*, 30: 359–77.

Messick, S. (1989). 'Validity'. In R. L. Linn (Ed.), *Educational Measurement* (3rd ed., 13–103. Washington, DC: American Council on Education/Macmillan.

Morell, L., Collier, T., Black, P. & Wilson, M. (2017). 'A construct-modeling approach to develop a learning progression of how students understand the structure of matter'. *Journal of Research in Science Teaching*, 54: 1024–48.

National Research Council (NRC). (2001). *Knowing What Students Know: The Science and Design of Educational Assessment*. In J. Pellegrino, N. Chudowsky & R. Glaser, (Eds.), Washington, DC: National Academy Press.

Newton, P. (2012). 'Clarifying the consensus definition of validity'. *Measurement: Interdisciplinary Research and Perspectives*, 10: 1–29.

Perrenoud, P. (1998). 'From formative evaluation to a controlled regulation of learning processes. Towards a wider conceptual field'. *Assessment in Education: Principles, Policy and Practice*, 5(1): 85–102.

Scriven, M. (1967). 'The methodology of evaluation'. In R. W. Tyler, R. M. Gagné & M. Scriven (Eds.), *Perspectives of Curriculum Evaluation*. Vol. 1, 39–83. Chicago, IL: Rand McNally.

Shea, N. A. & Duncan, G. A. (2013). 'From theory to data: The process of refining learning progressions'. *Journal of the Learning Sciences*, 22: 7–23.

Star, S. L. & Griesemer, J. (1989). 'Institutional ecology, "Translations," and boundary objects: Amateurs and professionals on Berkeley's museum of vertebrate zoology, 1907–39'. *Social Studies of Science*, 19: 387–420.

Sussman, J. & Wilson, M. (2019). 'The use and validity of standardized achievement tests for evaluating new curricular interventions in mathematics and science'. *American Journal of Evaluation*, 40(2): 190–213. doi:10.1177/1098214018767313

Vygotsky, L. (1962). *Thought and Language*. Cambridge, MA: MIT Press.

Wilson, M. (Ed.). (2004). *Towards Coherence between Classroom Assessment and Accountability. 103rd Yearbook of the National Society for the Study of Education, Part II*. Chicago, IL: University of Chicago Press.

Wilson, M. (2005). *Constructing Measures: An Item Response Modeling Approach*. Mahwah, NJ: Erlbaum. (now published by Taylor and Francis, New York).

Wilson, M. (2009). 'Measuring progressions: Assessment structures underlying a learning progression'. *Journal for Research in Science Teaching*, 46(6): 716–30.

Wilson, M. (2018). 'Making measurement important for education: The crucial role of classroom assessment'. *Educational Measurement: Issues and Practice*, 37(1): 5–20.

Wilson, M., Black, P. & Morell, L. (2013, April). *A learning progression approach to understanding students' conceptions of the structure of matter*. Paper presented at the American Educational Research Association's Annual meeting (San Francisco, CA).

Wilson, M., Morell, L., Osborne, J., Dozier, S. & Suksiri, W. (2019, April). *Assessing higher order reasoning using technology-enhanced selected response item types in the context of science*. Paper presented at the 2019 Annual Meeting of the National Council on Measurement in Education in Toronto, Ontario, Canada.

Wood, D. (1998). *How Children Think and Learn*. Oxford: Blackwell.

Appendix A
Papers and presentations based on work of the roadmap projects

Publications in Refereed Journals

Black, P., Wilson, M. & Yao, S. (2011a). 'Comments and thoughts'. *Measurement: Interdisciplinary Research and Perspectives*, 9: 169–172.

Black, P., Wilson, M. & Yao, S. (2011b). 'Road maps for learning: A guide to the navigation of learning progressions'. *Measurement: Interdisciplinary Research and Perspectives*, 9: 71–123.

Wilson, M. (2012). 'Responding to a challenge that learning progressions pose to measurement practice: hypothesized links between dimensions of the outcome progression'. In A. C. Alonzo & A. W. Gotwals, (Eds.), *Learning Progressions in Science*, 317–43. Rotterdam, The Netherlands: Sense Publishers.

Wilson, M. (2013). 'Seeking a balance between the statistical and scientific elements in psychometrics'. *Psychometrika*, 78(2): 211–36.

Yao, S-Y., Wilson, M., Henderson, J. B. & Osborne, J. (2015). 'Investigating the function of content and argumentation items in a science test: A multidimensional approach'. *Journal of Applied Measurement*, 16(2): 171–92.

Morell, L. & Wilson, M. (2016). 'Assessment as a tool to understand students' conceptions of the structure of matter'. *Journal of Physics: Conference Series* 772: 012049. doi:10.1088/1742-6596/772/1/012049

Morell, L., Collier, T., Black, P. & Wilson, M. (2017). 'A construct-modeling approach to develop a learning progression of how students understand the structure of matter'. *Journal of Research in Science Teaching*, 54(8): 1024–48. doi:10.1002/tea.21397

Shin, H.-J., Wilson, M. & Choi, I. H. (2017). 'Structured constructs models based on change-point analysis'. *Journal of Educational Measurement*, 54(3): 306–32.

Collier, T., Morell, L. & Wilson, M. (2018). 'Exploring the item features of a science assessment with complex tasks'. *Measurement*, 114: 16–24.

Wilson, M. (2018). 'Making measurement important for education: The crucial role of classroom assessment'. *Educational Measurement: Issues and Practice*, 37(1): 5–20.

Invited Presentations

Wilson, M. (2009, June). *Structured Constructs Models (SCM): A Family of Statistical Models Related to Learning Progressions*. Invited Plenary Address at the Learning Progressions in Science (LeaPS) Conference, Iowa City, Iowa.

Wilson, M. & Osborne, J. (2013, April). *Learning Trajectories and Formative Assessments for Physical Science and Argumentation*. Paper presented at the SERP Sandpit, San Francisco, California.

Wilson, M. & Osborne, J. (2013, September). *Some Examples of the Development of Assessments for Learning Progressions in Science*. Presentation in the 'Assessing Learning Progressions in Mathematics and Science' session at the Institute of Education Sciences Principal Investigator Conference, Washington DC.

Wilson, M. (2015, December). *Reconciling Formative and Summative Assessments*. Anaheim, California: Keynote address at the annual meeting of the California Educational Research Association.

Wilson, M. (2016, October). *Roadmaps to Help Develop Assessments for Learning Progressions in Science*. Paper presented in the 'Assessing experimental science in 11–18 education: New research directions' Conference, Wellcome Trust, London.

Wilson, M. (2017, April). *Making Measurement Important for Education*. Presidential address given at the NCME annual meeting, San Antonio, TX.

Refereed Conference Presentations

Black, P. & Wilson, M. (2009, April). *Learning Progressions to Guide Systems of Formative and Summative Assessment*. Paper presented at the annual meeting of the American Educational Research Association, San Diego, California.

Chiu, T., Morell, L. & Wilson, M. (2013, April). *Coding Student Responses: An Iterative and Construct-Driven Approach That Uses Multiple Sources of Data*. Paper presented at the Annual meeting of the American Educational Research Association, San Francisco, California.

Dozier, S., Morell, L., Suksiri, W., Osborne, J. & Wilson, M. (2020, March). *Automated Assessment of Argumentation in School Science: Developments and Challenges*. 2020 Paper accepted for presentation at the NARST Conference, Portland, Oregon.

Morell, L. & Wilson, M. (2016, August). Assessment as a tool to understand students' conceptions of the structure of matter. Paper presented at the IMEKO TC1-TC7-TC13 Joint Symposium, Berkeley, CA.

Morell, L., Suksiri, W., Dozier, S., Osborne, J. & Wilson, M. (2019, January). *Addressing the NGSS Practice of Arguing from Evidence Using Forced-Choice Item Formats: Challenges and Successes*. Paper presented at the IES Annual Principal Investigators Meeting, Washington, DC.

Wilson, M. & Black, P. (2007, March). *The Idea of a Learning Progression as a Core for Both Instruction and Assessment*. Paper presented at the annual meeting of the American Educational Research Association, Chicago, Illinois.

Wilson, M. (2008, March). *Measuring Progressions*. In A. C. Alonzo & A. W. Gotwals (Chairs), Diverse perspectives on the development, assessment, and validation of learning progressions in science. Symposium conducted at the annual meeting of the American Educational Research Association, New York. Retrieved March 30, 2008, from http://myweb.uiowa.edu/alonzo/aera2008.html

Wilson, M. (2013, April). *Challenges and Opportunities of Learning Progressions for the Psychometric Community*. Paper presented at the annual meeting of the American Educational Research Association, San Francisco, California.

Wilson, M., Black, P. & Morell, L. (2013, April). *A Learning Progression Approach to Understanding Students' Conceptions of the Structure of Matter*. Paper presented at the annual meeting of the American Educational Research Association, San Francisco, California.

Yao, S-Y. & Wilson, M. (2013a, April). *Developing and Validating a Learning-Progression-Based Assessment of the Structure of Matter*. Paper presented at the annual meeting of the American Educational Research Association, San Francisco, California.

Yao, S-Y. & Wilson, M. (2013b, April). *Validation of a Learning Progression in Science: A Latent Class Analysis Approach*. Paper presented at the annual meeting of the American Educational Research Association, San Francisco, California.

14

Certificating Learning on the Basis of Teacher Assessment

Paul E. Newton

Introduction

For decades, Paul Black has insisted that we should make far greater use of teacher assessment (TA) for high-stakes certification purposes (e.g. Black, 1998a; 1998b). During the 1980s and 1990s, policymakers in England were receptive to this view, and we did begin to make far greater use of TA. Since then, however, it appears to have fallen out of favour, and the belief that exams are the 'best and fairest way for young people to show what they know and can do' seems to be widespread (see DfE, 2020, quoting then Education Secretary, Gavin Williamson).

Paul has always recognized the importance of being able to 'sell' TA to the public and has encouraged 'forays to explore what might command confidence' (Black, 1993a:425). The present chapter responds to this challenge by considering case studies of TA policies that have failed to command confidence and by asking why.[1]

The chapter is presented in three main sections. The first explains why the 1980s and 1990s were a heyday (or sorts) for TA. The second presents three short case studies – based on coursework, controlled assessment and vocational assessment – which illustrate how confidence in TA has waned since then. This section proposes that the fate of each of these three TA practices was sealed by a 'toxic narrative' that captured escalating indignation over assessment error. The third extends the literature on qualification purposes to consider why arguments that may appear incontrovertible to certain stakeholders – concerning the benefits of TA – might simultaneously appear less than convincing to others. It explores the idea of assessment-related indignation in more detail, proposing that TA is highly susceptible to toxic narratives concerning a certain kind of assessment error, which is likely to ignite high levels of indignation among parents, students and members of the public more generally.

A heyday (of sorts) for TA

The 1980s was a period of substantial change in England – as far as educational assessment was concerned – and TA was embraced more warmly and widely than ever before. Indeed, the 1980s and 1990s were a heyday, of sorts, for TA, which was prominent in plans: for assessing the new national curriculum (TGAT, 1988), for the reform of vocational qualifications (Jessup, 1991), and for the new General Certificate of Secondary Education (GCSE) end of lower secondary education qualification at the age of 16 (Kingdon & Stobart, 1988). TA became integral to the end of upper secondary education 'A'-level qualification at age 18 too (Opposs, 2016).

Admittedly, TA was not universally welcomed even during its heyday, and some of the bolder experiments were reigned in quite soon. For instance, Prime Minister John Major insisted, in 1991, that GCSEs included far too much coursework, and coursework weightings were subsequently reduced somewhat. At key stages 1 to 3, TA received less attention from policymakers than many felt it needed (Daugherty, 1995). Problems mounted as overly specified curriculum frameworks spawned bureaucratic and time-consuming assessment approaches (Shorrocks-Taylor, 1999). The 1993 review of the national curriculum and its assessment reasserted the central importance of TA (Dearing, 1994). Yet, with limited commitment to enhancing its quality (Daugherty, 1997), and the introduction of a more traditional approach to testing for the core subjects, TA fell further into the background. Even the new vocational qualifications were not spared. For instance, the terms of reference of the 1995 review of National Vocational Qualifications (NVQs) required it to examine how external assessment might be integrated within these qualifications (Beaumont, 1995). This was a period of evolution rather than revolution. Where TA was warmly welcomed, this was largely as a complement to traditional testing, not as a replacement for it. In other words, the primary justification for TA during this period was that it should assess the parts other assessments cannot.

Despite bolder ambitions being reigned in, policy support for the idea of TA continued during the 1990s. For instance, although all sorts of problems beset GCSE coursework right from the very outset (Kingdon & Stobart, 1988; Scott, 1991;

Crisp, 2008), it was not until the mid-2000s that major interventions occurred. This presumably reflected a widespread belief that teething problems 'would be resolved with the passing of time and the growth in familiarity and professional confidence' (QCA, 2006:9). Even in 2005, when coursework was officially judged to be in need of strengthening, the Qualifications and Curriculum Authority (QCA) still assumed that its benefits 'generally outweigh any drawbacks' (QCA, 2005:5).

However, as the following section explains in more detail, policy support for the idea of TA has waned since the mid-2000s. GCSE coursework was replaced by controlled assessment in 2009. Controlled assessment was abandoned just a few years later. Nowadays, that which is pointedly referred to as 'non-exam assessment' is permitted within GCSEs and 'A' levels only by exception. Even certain vocational qualifications – including BTECs[2] with an established tradition of TA – have recently been required to incorporate external examining. In short, over the past couple of decades, TA has increasingly been designed out of national qualifications in England.

Reforms initiated by Michael Gove, during his tenure as Education Secretary (2010 to 2014) within a Conservative-Liberal Democrat coalition government, have played a significant role in the reduction of TA. However, it would be wrong to claim that this trend is straightforwardly party political. Note that the Conservatives presided over the embrace of TA during its heyday (see Daugherty, 1997). Furthermore, the very idea of assessing the work of a course, which characterized early ambitions for GCSE coursework, was formally abandoned under a Labour administration and replaced by the far more restricted notion of completing a controlled assessment. It is fair to say that debates concerning school-based assessment during the 1980s – which was the period just before a national curriculum was established in England – sometimes confounded teacher control of assessment and teacher control of the curriculum and these debates did feel deeply ideological at times (e.g. Bowe & Whitty, 1984). However, the idea that the embrace of TA was a straightforward party political preference – Labour aye, Conservative no – does not really hold water. We need to seek a more sophisticated explanation than this.

Toxic narratives

The body that was responsible for overseeing England's qualification system during the mid-2000s was the Qualifications and Curriculum Authority (QCA). When the QCA was dissolved, responsibility for securing qualification standards and for promoting public confidence transferred to Ofqual, the new qualifications regulator. We turn now to concerns that led QCA, and then Ofqual, to exclude TA from, or to reduce its role within, many of England's national qualifications.

The proposal that I will develop is that issues of public confidence weighed heavily on these decisions, and I introduce the idea of a 'toxic narrative' to explain this. More specifically, I propose that, when evidence of assessment error in high-stakes qualifications comes to light, this is liable to ignite a certain amount of indignation among members of the public (and rightly so). Sometimes, however, levels of indignation continue to escalate, enveloping the focal qualification within a toxic narrative. When this happens, major qualification redesign presents itself as an obvious route to restoring public confidence.

Toxic narratives provide no more than a partial explanation for why certain qualifications have ended up being redesigned over the years. However, these narratives are powerful because they help to construct a tipping point, whereby public opinion shifts from tolerance to intolerance. In exactly this sense, I suggest that

1. the 'cheating students' narrative sealed the fate of coursework,
2. the 'cheating schools' narrative sealed the fate of controlled assessment, and
3. the 'grade inflation' narrative sealed the fate of 100 per cent TA within certain vocational qualifications.

Cheating students

On the basis of a 2-year investigation into the roll-out of coursework at GCSE, Scott (1991) identified a litany of implementation challenges. Although many of these issues related to standardization – with practices diverging across subjects, schools and teachers – an important issue related to concerns expressed by teachers was that parents were unduly influencing coursework assignments. This included anecdotes of parents writing and rewriting English projects, revisiting fieldwork sites with their children, and providing detailed answers to history tasks. Having said that, Scott also concluded that these practices were not widespread.

When GCSEs were introduced for first teaching, in 1986, the World Wide Web did not exist. By the mid-2000s, however, more than half of UK households accessed the internet.[3] In this new context, many sympathized with the high master of St Paul's school in London, who described the internet as 'a gift to plagiarism', adding his name to a growing list of people who wanted coursework to be abolished (BBC News, 2004). The 'cheating students' narrative had begun to take root.

QCA set up a review to explore stakeholder views of coursework, which reported in 2005. Although the review spanned a variety of potential concerns, its report focused heavily on authentication – ensuring that any work submitted is genuinely the work of the candidate – and noted, for example, that 5 per cent of parents of GCSE students admitted drafting some of their children's coursework (QCA, 2005). According to *The Mail*, the Education Secretary Ruth Kelly responded by demanding 'a crackdown on cheating' (MailOnline, 2005).

A subsequent review recommended that – within the suite of reformed GCSEs that were to be taught from September 2009 – TA would only be used where it was the 'most valid' form of assessment (QCA, 2006:22). This clearly represented a tightening of the principle that TA should assess the parts other assessments cannot. Where TA remained, additional controls would be considered across four processes – task setting, task taking, task marking and assessor training (Colwill, 2007). GCSE 'coursework' was dead – long live 'controlled assessment'.[4] As a headline in *The Telegraph* put it: 'GCSE coursework scrapped to stop cheating' (Paton, 2007).

By the late-noughties, the idea that that coursework had become 'plagued by plagiarism' had become deeply engrained in the national psyche (as per the title of a report from the Association of Teachers & Lecturers, 2008). Having said that, student cheating was not the only reason why coursework was abandoned. Indeed, a reform of GCSE coursework had been on the cards since early 2005; yet, at that point in time, burden had been the primary concern (DfES, 2005). Yet the cheating student narrative is what came to animate public debate, both reflecting and fuelling an escalation of indignation, and ultimately sealing the fate of coursework (and shaping its successor, controlled assessment).

Cheating schools

Increasing levels of control over TA limited opportunities for plagiarism. For instance, where students were only permitted to work on assessment tasks in school, this obviously prevented parents from directly drafting work for them. Yet the cheating narrative continued. After all, under certain circumstances, students could still engage in plagiarism prior to the assessment. This might involve 'memorising vast chunks' in advance of the write-up and regurgitating this information under controlled conditions in school (IpsosMORI, 2011: 21).

An important reason why the cheating narrative proved hard to shift concerned genuine ambiguity over where the borderline lay between good practice and bad, when providing support to students in completing their assignments, including support from teachers. Ambiguity of this sort has bedevilled the use of TA within GCSEs, 'A' levels, and vocational qualifications (Mansell, 2007; Torrance et al., 2005; Torrance, 2018). As Scott (1991) had previously observed, what one teacher might think of as formative assessment another might judge to be cheating. Indeed, research on 'playing the system' by Ingram et al. (2018) concluded that practices that were described within a school as being for the good of students might well be described as 'gaming' when referring to their use by other schools.

The 'cheating schools' narrative began to crystalize and turn seriously toxic for controlled assessment in 2012. Reformed GCSE English qualifications had been introduced for first teaching in 2010, and qualification results were first awarded in June 2012 (Bramley, et al., 2014). Problems arose when unit grade boundaries were set far higher in June 2012 than corresponding ones had been in January 2012 – in an attempt to ensure the credibility of results from this new qualification – and this included controlled assessment units (which made up 60 per cent of the qualification in total) where it was widely assumed that boundaries should stay the same.

Details of the crisis and its resolution were complex (Ofqual, 2012; Isaacs, 2014). Ofqual's report noted how the exam boards' rules on controlled assessment were ambiguous and could be interpreted differently by schools. In fact, it claimed that some schools sought to 'stretch' their interpretation of the rules to create an advantage for their students. This claim was backed up with evidence from interviews with teachers, and commentators on the TES Forum, who said things like:

> When I've dared to suggest that the CAs [controlled assessments] should be done in exam conditions and that lots of schools are doing that, I'm told that that is rubbish, that CAs are really coursework, and that we have to cheat because other schools will be doing so, and we cannot afford to let our results slip at all.
>
> (Ofqual, 2012:61)

Ofqual's report was encapsulated in national newspaper headlines such as 'How teachers felt forced to "cheat" on GCSE English marking' (Hardman, 2012), and 'Fiddling of GCSE grades "is common" and extends beyond English, watchdog reveals' (Clark, 2012), and 'Pressure on teachers blamed for rash of cheating' (Garner, 2012). Subsequently, during 2013, headlines such as 'Rise in number of teachers claiming they are under pressure to inflate grades' (Syal, 2013) and 'Radical action is needed now to stop schools cheating at GCSEs' (Millar, 2013) helped to keep toxicity levels high.

In this context of heightened concern, Ofqual commissioned research to investigate teachers' experiences of and attitudes towards strategies that could be used to help maximize qualification results, which included 'gaming' and blatant malpractice (Meadows, 2015). Survey results suggested that teachers had plenty of first-hand experience of strategies that they tended to consider unacceptable, which included students receiving extensive parental support, teachers giving students hints during controlled assessment and teachers providing wording for students to include in their assignments (Meadows & Black, 2018). Furthermore, 40 per cent of respondents described at least one more unacceptable activity relating to controlled assessment, most of which were teacher-led (rather than student- or school-led).

In fact, the fate of controlled assessment had largely been determined by June 2013. Ofqual's *Review of Controlled Assessment in GCSEs* specified that non-exam assessment would only be used where it was the 'only valid' form of assessing 'essential elements' of the subject (Ofqual, 2013a:4). This applied the principle that TA should assess the parts other assessments cannot even more tightly than recommendations from 2006. The policy position was confirmed in November, and it was announced that assessment in most of the new GCSEs would 'be by exam only' which 'will make it easier to ensure exams are conducted fairly' (Ofqual, 2013b:4).

As with the cheating students narrative, the cheating schools narrative was certainly not the only reason why controlled assessment was abandoned. Yet it was the cheating schools narrative that animated public debate, both reflecting and fuelling an escalation of indignation, and ultimately sealing the fate of controlled assessment.

Grade inflation

Grade inflation has proved to be an especially toxic narrative for qualifications in England over the past couple of decades. By 2012, it had undermined the credibility of procedures for maintaining standards over time within GCSE and 'A'-level qualifications (Newton, 2021). In 2015, it struck BTECs:

> Students taking BTEC vocational qualifications are more than twice as likely to score top marks as they were seven years earlier, says a new study. [...] While debate about grade inflation has largely centred around GCSEs and A levels, the Hefce [Higher Education and Funding Council] report suggests that the phenomenon may be far more prevalent in vocational qualifications.
>
> (Grove, 2015)

Ofqual responded by investigating the possibility of grade inflation via a series of complex statistical analyses (Cuff, Zanini, & Black, 2018). The report on this research concluded fairly definitively that there had been an element of grade inflation within these 'older style' BTEC qualifications and suggested that the underpinning TA model might be at least partly responsible.

As far back as 2011, the Department for Education had concluded that many vocational qualifications needed strengthening. It decided that 'only those qualifications that provide evidence of substantial amount of external assessment […] will be counted' in school and college performance tables (DfE, 2011:4). Thus, by 2018, external assessment had already been leveraged into many vocational qualifications, including 'new style' BTECs.

In 2020, the inclusion of external assessment also became a formal regulatory requirement, established by Ofqual, for any Technical Award that was approved for inclusion in Department for Education performance tables at Key Stage 4, including BTECs and Level 1/2 qualifications from other awarding organizations. Ofqual required

> an assessment by examination through which at least 40% of the total marks for the qualification are available in the final assessment series and that the result achieved in the assessment by examination in that series is used towards the student's overall qualification grade.
>
> (Ofqual, 2020:27)

The justification for this decision was specifically to enable awarding organizations

> to manage perverse incentives for schools when delivering and marking non-exam assessments and, in doing so, provide awarding organisations with greater control over qualification standards.
>
> (Ofqual, 2020:27)

Ofqual's decision to specify external assessment as a regulatory requirement was taken in the immediate wake of concerns over grade inflation in 'older style' BTEC qualifications. By then, grade inflation was already well established as a toxic narrative, and the need to respond to it was self-evident. By requiring external assessment within related qualifications – in this instance, Level 1/2 Technical Awards, but subsequently other types of qualification too – the intention was to prevent them from becoming undermined by the grade inflation toxic narrative. In other words, this was a pre-emptive strike to prevent the kind of escalation of public concern that had characterized the demise of coursework and controlled assessment.

Indignation

As a distinguished scholar and teacher educator, it is perhaps not surprising that Paul Black has repeatedly diagnosed distrust of TA in terms of ignorance (assessment illiteracy) as though education might be the key to solving this problem. According to this logic, an educational campaign would be needed to improve understanding of the limitations of external examining, as well as of the strengths of TA (Black, 1993b; Black, Gardner & Wiliam, 2008; Black & Wiliam, 2018). It is true that assessment literacy is low, generally, and that we should take steps to improve it (Newton, 2005; 2015). Yet the challenge for TA runs deeper than merely improving knowledge and understanding of the facts.

The following sections suggest a quite different kind of explanation for the fragility of public confidence in TA, when used as a basis for certificating learning. It relates to the different perspectives that stakeholders adopt on the principal purposes that qualifications serve, and the different values that they bring to bear when judging various kinds of assessment error. This is where the idea of indignation comes into play, as the foundation upon which toxic narratives are built. Indignation is a natural reaction to evidence of assessment error in high-stakes qualifications. Yet, depending on the importance attached to the particular variety of error that has been implicated, people are liable to experience differing levels of indignation. Members of the public, I will argue, become especially indignant when they hear of assessment errors of a particular variety, to which TA happens to be especially prone.

Multiple perspectives

The idea that a qualification might be used to serve a variety of different purposes – job selection, course placement, teacher evaluation, school evaluation and so on – has been well understood for a very long time (Latham, 1886). Less well understood is the principle that qualifications need to be designed differently to render them fit for different purposes (Newton, 2007). Even less well understood is the paramount importance of understanding qualification purposes – and therefore policymaking – from a variety of quite different, potentially conflicting, perspectives (Newton, 2017a).

The perspectives that I have written most about are the information perspective, the expertise perspective and the engagement perspective (Newton, 2017b). Towards the end of this section I will introduce a new one, the contractual perspective, which is rarely discussed yet absolutely fundamental. Each of these perspectives has a different focus, as well as different champions. The information perspective focuses on the type of decision that a particular qualification is intended to be used to make, e.g. selection, placement or evaluation. To be fit for a purpose of this sort, qualifications need to be designed so that their results provide high-quality information – in effect, measurement information – about learners. For assessment in education, this information typically concerns how well a student has mastered a domain of learning. The champion of the information perspective is typically an expert on measurement, who is concerned with the design of the assessment procedure and who wishes to ensure that results provide qualification users with high-quality measurement information.

The expertise perspective focuses on the body of expertise (domain of learning) that the qualification is intended to provide information about, e.g., astrophysics, violin playing or site carpentry. To be fit for a purpose of this sort, qualifications need to be designed so that their syllabus targets the most appropriate body of knowledge and skills, as determined by a suitable community of practice, e.g. the Institute of Physics, Royal Academy of Music or the Construction Industry Training Board. The champion of the expertise perspective is typically a subject expert, who is concerned with the design of each syllabus, and who wishes to ensure that learners acquire exactly the right constellation of valued learning outcomes.

The engagement perspective focuses on the features and processes built into a qualification in order to influence its uptake and to motivate and direct its teachers and learners. To be fit for a purpose of this sort, qualifications need to be designed so that their assessment procedure and learning outcomes result in positive impacts on uptake, teaching and learning. The champion of the engagement perspective might well be an expert on instruction, who is concerned with both assessment and syllabus design decisions and who wishes to ensure that both teachers and learners remain as engaged as possible when teaching and studying the course.

Effective qualification design requires contributions from all three of these perspectives. Yet the stakeholders who champion each perspective have different ultimate objectives in mind: valid measurement, authentic curriculum, and optimal teaching and learning, respectively. Consequently, when forced to accommodate real-world constraints on qualification design – teaching costs and burdens, assessment costs and burdens, health and safety legislation, and so on – they are likely to favour different kinds of compromise and trade-off.

Qualification design is necessarily a collaborative exercise, involving measurement experts, subject experts and experts in instruction. However, there are other perspectives on qualification purposes, which – despite their importance – often remain far more implicit, especially where they are not actively championed by an expert stakeholder group. The contractual perspective is perhaps the most fundamental of qualification purpose perspectives yet perhaps also the most implicit. It focuses on the role that qualifications play in organizing society.

The core idea is that education involves an implicit social contract between each individual learner and the society that their education equips them to become an active member of. In an important sense, students demonstrate their agreement to become an active member of this society by learning what they are asked to learn at school. To incentivize the acquisition of societally valued competencies, the implicit social contract rules that students will be celebrated and rewarded for the breadth and depth of the competence that they are able to acquire by the end of key educational phases. In particular, it specifies that higher levels of competence will be rewarded with correspondingly more, or better, opportunities following the completion of critical educational phases when students transition into subsequent educational phases or into employment. In this approach to organizing society, qualifications play a critical role as arbiters of the acquisition of competence. Education selectors comply with this implicit contract when they specify minimum grades for course entry and when they preferentially select students with higher grades over students with lower ones. Employment selectors do similarly.[5]

To be fit for a purpose of this sort, qualifications need to be designed so that their assessment procedure and learning outcomes are as transparent as possible, and so that teaching, learning and assessment arrangements follow the established 'rules of the game' without partiality, prejudice or blatant malpractice. This ensures that all stakeholders understand the nature of the contract that learners implicitly enter into, and that the deliverables specified in the contract can be allocated accordingly, on the basis of qualification outcomes that are seen to be fair. The champions of the contractual perspective are not experts, per se, but the parents who consent to their children entering into the implicit social contract of education, as well as the students themselves. By focusing on parents and students, we are effectively focusing on 'the public' more generally.

Conflicting values

Assessment in education is not, and never could be, error free. Perfect assessment is not the ultimate objective of qualification design. Instead, we design assessment procedures to produce results that are as accurate as possible: in relation to a set of intended purposes (e.g. selection, motivation) and given a variety of real-world constraints (e.g. financial costs, resource availability, the law). Qualification design is therefore inherently a matter of trade-off and compromise. As noted above, it is not simply that different kinds of concerns are traded off against each other; it is that different stakeholders contribute to debates on qualification design from quite different perspectives, championing quite different values.[6]

I have come to suspect that the stronger a person champions a particular perspective, the harder it becomes for them to recognize the legitimacy of an alternative one, as they are driven by a quite different hierarchy of values. For instance, subject experts and measurement experts often clash over highly valued learning outcomes that are extremely hard to measure with sufficient accuracy. The subject expert bottom line – and the primary vector of their indignation – is that not assessing those learning outcomes constitutes an unacceptable risk from the expertise perspective, as well as from the engagement perspective via negative backwash on teaching and learning. Conversely, the measurement expert bottom line – and the primary vector of their indignation – is that attempting to assess those learning outcomes constitutes an unacceptable risk from the information perspective if it means that results will be insufficiently accurate to be credible.

Intolerance of bias

What has this got to do with Paul Black's insistence that we should make far greater use of TA for high-stakes certification purposes and his question concerning how best to 'sell' this policy to the public? Well, champions of the contractual perspective – including parents, students and members of the public more generally – are likely to have a quite different bottom line. If so, then the primacy vector of their indignation – the kind of assessment error that they are least likely to tolerate – is likely to be different again. This has a bearing on the persuasiveness of the arguments that Paul has mounted in favour of TA, and on why education, per se, is only part of the story.

For example, a critical component of Paul's case for TA concerns its potential to assess the valuable parts that external exams simply cannot. Yet parents, students and members of the public more generally are unlikely to value 'highly valued' learning outcomes as much as a subject expert like Paul does. For them, the goal of the 'education game' is first and foremost to acquire competence –

as it is the acquisition of competence that unlocks opportunities – so the exact nature of the competence that is acquired is of secondary importance. That is not to say that champions of the contractual perspective fail to see any value in the outcomes that champions of the expertise perspective value so highly. It is simply that this is not their bottom line. So the principle that TA should assess the parts other assessments cannot is unlikely to tip the balance for them, as it might for a subject expert. Indeed, predictable construct underrepresentation – where certain valued learning outcomes are rarely if ever assessed by the exam – is not too problematic from the contractual perspective. As long as all students are in the same boat of not being taught those elements, qualification results should still differentiate accurately between those who have acquired higher and lower levels of competence (even if it happens to be a narrower competence) as required by the implicit social contract.

Another core component of Paul's case for TA is the promise of its superior reliability – specifically, when it is embedded within everyday teaching and learning, and the dream of integrating formative and summative assessment has been realized. This should, in theory, be attractive from the contractual perspective to the extent that it promises to improve the accuracy with which students of differing levels of competence are differentiated via qualification results. Having said that, the promise of superior reliability only follows from a particular kind of continuous assessment, and even here, the underpinning argument remains to be comprehensively developed and evidenced (Newton, 2003). If, instead, the argument is simply that TA is no more or less reliable than external examining, then it becomes substantially less powerful, particularly given the following point.

Although Paul certainly acknowledges the possibility of bias in results from TA, he tends not to pay it the same attention as he pays to the possibility of unreliability in results from external examining. Conversely, with support from the earlier discussion of toxic narratives, I propose that parents, students and members of the public more generally tend to be less tolerant of systematic, non-random error (bias) and therefore more tolerant of unsystematic, random error (unreliability), particularly where this bias is viewed as an instance of partiality, or prejudice or, worse still, blatant malpractice. Indeed, I propose that this disposition follows naturally from the contractual perspective on qualification purposes.

The contractual perspective concerns the role that qualifications play in organizing society. Societies all around the world have turned to qualifications as a primary mechanism for allocating future educational and occupational opportunities, particularly following the completion of critical educational phases when students transition into subsequent educational phases or into employment. This represents an explicit rejection of alternative mechanisms for distributing opportunities, such as nepotism, bribery and other less-equitable routes to gaining social advantage. It therefore follows that certain kinds of assessment error – especially those that appear to arise from partiality, or prejudice, or blatant malpractice – are likely to be viewed extremely negatively by members of the public. Bias of this sort undermines the most fundamental purpose of a qualification system when viewed from the contractual perspective. Unreliability also undermines the system, of course, but not in a manner that threatens its very raison d'être. Indeed, it is only slightly ironic to say that unreliability (unsystematic, random error) is almost fair by definition in the sense of demonstrating neither prejudice nor partiality.

The contractual perspective – which underpins a qualification system like the foundations of a house – helps to explain why certain critical narratives on TA appear to have been sufficiently toxic to undermine public confidence. Indeed, even a nagging feeling that 'the school down the road' might be inflating TA grades can be sufficient to undermine credibility – if this feeling is widespread enough – even when concrete evidence of malpractice is minimal.[7]

Toxic narratives are not limited to TA contexts. However, TA is highly susceptible to toxic narratives concerning a certain kind of assessment error – systematic inflation or deflation of results (bias) arising from partiality, prejudice or blatant malpractice – and this kind of assessment error tends to ignite high levels of indignation among parents, students and members of the public more generally. TA is susceptible to accusations of bias for a variety of reasons. Teachers are only human, and what they know about their students, or what they feel about them, does have the potential to skew their assessment judgements. In addition, because teachers are often judged on the basis of their students' grades, there is an inevitable perverse incentive to be generous when making assessment judgements. Furthermore, because TA is inherently less standardized, or controlled, than an external exam (see QCA, 2007), more opportunities arise for subverting the assessment process, either consciously or unconsciously. In short, the more potential there is for partiality, prejudice or blatant malpractice, the more susceptible an assessment procedure will be to suspicions of this sort, and the greater the likelihood of a toxic narrative taking hold. All three of the narratives discussed above – cheating students, cheating schools and grade inflation – arose from suspicions of this sort.

Conclusion

From an expertise perspective on qualification purposes, and an engagement one too, there are very strong arguments for using TA as a basis for certificating learning. Indeed, even from a measurement perspective, there is a persuasive case in favour of TA, which goes beyond the principle of needing to assess parts that other assessments cannot. If there are reasonable grounds for believing that results can be made sufficiently reliable, and if the empirical evidence of bias is not overwhelming, then why not make far greater use of TA, especially if the effective integration of summative and formative has the potential to revolutionize teaching and learning, as argued by Paul Black?

The present chapter has argued that there is another perspective on qualification purposes, which is rarely discussed yet absolutely fundamental, and which helps to explain the nature of the challenge associated with using TA as a basis for certificating learning. This is the contractual perspective. It is championed by parents and students themselves, for whom qualifications function as a reward for competence acquired and as a key that unlocks future opportunities, as specified in the implicit social contract that is education. Given the role that qualifications play in organizing society – particularly as an alternative to nepotism, bribery and other less-equitable routes to gaining social advantage – any suggestion that they are being operated with prejudice or partiality would inevitably weigh heavily on the public mind. From this perspective, bias represents more of a threat to public confidence than unreliability. Indeed, even the mere suspicion of bias may be sufficient to undermine confidence in a qualification. Incidentally, it is worth noting that most of the examples discussed in the present chapter have focused on partiality or malpractice (cheating schools, grade inflation, cheating students). Had space permitted, a separate section could have been written on prejudice and an emerging 'discrimination' toxic narrative (e.g. Daley, 2018, Lee & Newton, 2021).

One final observation concerns the use of qualifications for holding schools and colleges to account. This has become increasingly prevalent since the 1980s, raising particular challenges for TA. Ofqual now has bespoke rules for certain types of qualifications that are counted in school performance tables to ensure that they can withstand the pressure that accountability exerts. Yet, as important as this context is, it would be wrong to assume that TA would flourish, once again, if only these accountability mechanisms were removed. Indeed, although the 'cheating schools' and 'grade inflation' narratives certainly were fuelled by accountability concerns, the same could not be said of the 'cheating students' narrative.

Policymakers are very sensitive to credibility threats arising from partiality, prejudice or blatant malpractice – as the three toxic narratives at the heart of this chapter illustrate – and rightly so. Having said that, while the contractual perspective is clearly important to policymaking, so too are all the other purpose perspectives. Qualification design decisions can only be made effectively with input from a full complement of perspectives. The challenge is how to weight each one satisfactorily, to ensure that the compromises and trade-offs that characterize policymaking are judged to be acceptable by as wide a range of stakeholder groups as possible. Consistent with Paul's work, we can improve the quality of policy decisions by improving assessment literacy, curriculum literacy, instructional literacy and so on. More important than this, however, is the need to promote mutual understanding, and empathy, as a foundation for rational policy debate, and fair-minded resolution.

Notes

1 This is a personal account, informed by my experiences of working on a range of teacher assessment policies from the turn of the millennium onwards. I joined the Qualifications and Curriculum Authority (QCA) as a researcher in 2002. Later, in 2008, my division metamorphosized into the fledgling regulator, Ofqual. I stayed until Ofqual finally closed its doors in London and migrated to Coventry in 2009. Subsequently, I rejoined Ofqual in 2014 and have worked there ever since. Although I have drawn upon my experiences of working in assessment agencies and regulatory bodies since the mid-1990s, the arguments that I develop here are my own and should not be attributed to any of my employers, past or present.
2 BTECs were originally developed by the Business and Technician (subsequently Technology) Education Council in England.
3 See https://www.statista.com/statistics/275999/household-internet-penetration-in-great-britain/
4 In fact, because there were fewer concerns over coursework at 'A' level (and because 'A' level was on a different reform timetable) controlled assessment was only actually rolled out at GCSE. The coursework label was retained at 'A' level until its next major reform. When new GCSEs and 'A' levels were first taught, from 2015, the 'non-exam assessment' label came into general use across both qualification types.
5 The 'selection' purpose can therefore be understood in terms of both the information perspective (effective decision-making) and the contractual perspective (just deserts).

6 These debates are constructed in different ways and via different media, including books, journals, magazines, newspapers, broadcasts, podcasts, social media and so on. When developing policy positions, organizations like Ofqual engage directly with experts from various perspectives, speak with multiple stakeholder groups and invite contributions from members of the public, including parents and students. Subsequently, when making policy decisions, organizations like Ofqual take a full complement of perspectives into account before deciding upon a suitable compromise position.
7 There is also the risk that it sets up a vicious circle, whereby the nagging suspicion that 'most schools' are inflating grades somehow legitimizes the behaviour, increasing its likelihood in the future.

References

Association of Teachers and Lecturers. (2008). School work plagued by plagiarism – ATL survey. 18 January.

BBC News (2004). 'Top head attacks exam coursework'. 3 September. (Available from: http://news.bbc.co.uk/1/hi/education/3624116.stm)

Beaumont, G. (1995). *Review of 100 NVQs and SVQs: Report Submitted to the Department for Education and Employment by Gordon Beaumont.* Chesterfield: Gordon Beaumont.

Black, P. J. (1993a). 'Assessment policy and public confidence: Comments on the BERA Policy Task Group's article "Assessment and the improvement of education"'. *The Curriculum Journal*, 4(3): 421–7.

Black, P. J. (1993b). 'Formative and summative assessment by teachers'. *Studies in Science Education*, 21(1): 49–97.

Black, P. J. (1998a). *Testing: Friend or Foe? The Theory and Practice of Assessment and Testing.* London: Falmer Press.

Black, P. J. (1998b). 'Learning, league tables and national assessment: Opportunity lost or hope deferred?'. *Oxford Review of Education*, 24(1): 57–68.

Black, P., Gardner, J. & Wiliam, D. (2008). Written Evidence to the House of Commons Children, Schools and Families Committee Inquiry into Testing and Assessment (Session 2007–08). (Available from: https://publications.parliament.uk/pa/cm200708/cmselect/cmchilsch/169/169we03.htm)

Black, P.J. (2013). 'Formative and summative aspects of assessment: Theoretical and research foundations in the context of pedagogy'. In J. H. McMillan (Ed.). *SAGE Handbook of Research on Classroom Assessment*, 167–79. Thousand Oaks, CA: SAGE Publications, Inc.

Black, P. J. & Wiliam, D. (2018). 'Classroom assessment and pedagogy. Assessment in education: Principles'. *Policy & Practice*, 25(6): 551–75.

Bowe, R. & Whitty, G. (1984). 'Teachers, boards and standards: The attack on school-based assessment in English public examinations at 16+'. In P. Broadfoot (Ed.).

Selection, Certification & Control: Social Issues in Educational Assessment, 179–97. Sussex: The Falmer Press.

Bramley, T., Dawson, A. & Newton, P. (2014). 'On the limits of linking: Experiences from England'. Paper presented at the 76th annual meeting of the National Council on Measurement in Education (NCME), Philadelphia, PA, 2–6 April.

Clark, L. (2012). 'Fiddling of GCSE grades "is common" and extends beyond English, watchdog reveals'. *The Daily Mail.* 2 November. (Available from: https://www.dailymail.co.uk/news/article-2226600/Grading-fiasco-scandal-hit-English-GCSEs-blamed-cheating-teachers.html#ixzz2B4rK6N2I)

Colwill, I. (2007). 'Improving GCSE: Internal and controlled assessment'. QCA/07/3207. London: Qualifications and Curriculum Authority.

Crisp, V. (2008). 'A review of literature regarding the validity of coursework and the rationale for its inclusion in the GCSE'. *Research Matters: A Cambridge Assessment publication,* 5: 20–4.

Cuff, B. M. P., Zanini, N. & Black, B. (2018). *An Exploration of Grade Inflation in 'Older Style' Level 3 BTEC Nationals 2006 to 2016.* Ofqual/18/6459/2. Coventry: Office of Qualifications and Examinations Regulation.

Daley, K. (Akala) (2018). *Natives: Race & Class in the Ruins of Empire.* London: Two Roads.

Daugherty, R. (1995). *National Curriculum Assessment: A Review of Policy 1987–1994.* London: The Falmer Press.

Daugherty, R. (1997). 'Consistency in Teachers' Assessments: Defining the Problem, Finding the Answers'. *British Journal of Curriculum and Assessment,* 8(1): 32–8.

Dearing, R. (1994). *The National Curriculum and Its Assessment: Final Report.* London: School Curriculum and Assessment Authority.

Department for Education (2011). *Qualifications for 14–16 Year Olds and Performance Tables.* London: Department for Education.

Department for Education (2020). Department for Education Blog: 'Exams are the best and fairest way for young people to show what they know and can do' – The Education Secretary on the importance of exams. 29 November. (Available from: https://educationhub.blog.gov.uk/2020/11/29/exams-are-the-best-and-fairest-way-for-young-people-to-show-what-they-know-and-can-do-the-education-secretary-on-the-importance-of-exams/)

Department for Education and Skills (2005). *14–19 Education and Skills* (Cm 6476). Norwich: HMSO.

Garner, R. (2012). 'Damning report reveals GCSE marking scandal: Pressure on teachers blamed for rash of cheating'. *The Independent.* 2 November. (Available from: https://www.independent.co.uk/news/education/education-news/damning-report-reveals-gcse-marking-scandal-8274749.html)

Grove, J. (2015). 'Proportion of top BTEC students doubles: Hefce report'. *Times Higher Education.* 26 February. (Available from: https://www.timeshighereducation.com/news/proportion-of-top-btec-students-doubles-hefce-report/2018796.article)

Hardman, I. (2012). 'How teachers felt forced to "cheat" on GCSE English marking'. *The Spectator*. 2 November. (Available from: https://www.spectator.co.uk/article/how-teachers-felt-forced-to-cheat-on-gcse-english-marking)

Ingram, J., Elliott, V., Morin, C., Randhawa, A. & Brown, C. (2018). 'Playing the system: Incentives to "game" and educational ethics in school examination entry policies in England'. *Oxford Review of Education*, 44(5): 545–62.

Ipsos MORI (2011). *Evaluation of the Introduction of Controlled Assessment: Report on Qualitative and Quantitative Research*. Ofqual/11/5049. Coventry: Office of Qualifications and Examinations Regulation.

Isaacs, T. (2014). 'Curriculum and assessment reform gone wrong: The perfect storm of GCSE English'. *The Curriculum Journal*, 25(1): 130–47.

Jessup, G. (1991). *Outcomes: NVQs and the Emerging Model of Education and Training*. London: The Falmer Press.

Kingdon, M. & Stobart, G. (1988). *GCSE Examined*. Lewes: The Falmer Press.

Latham, H. (1886). *On the Action of Examinations Considered as a Means of Selection*. Boston, MA: Willard Small.

Lee, M. W. & Newton, P. E. (2021). *Systematic Divergence between Teacher and Test-Based Assessment: Literature Review*. Ofqual/21/6781. Coventry: Office of Qualifications and Examinations Regulation.

MailOnline (2005). 'Cheating claims prompt GCSEs review'. 22 November. (Available from: https://www.dailymail.co.uk/news/article-369366/Cheating-claims-prompt-GCSEs-review.html)

Mansell, W. (2007). *Education by Numbers: The Tyranny of Testing*. London: Politico's Publishing.

Meadows, M. (2015). 'Teacher ethics in summative assessment. Presentation to Oxford University Centre for Educational Assessment invited symposium', St Anne's College, Oxford, 26 March. (Available from: http://oucea.education.ox.ac.uk/about-us/news/events/past-events/invited-symposium-teacher-ethics-in-assessment/)

Meadows, M. & Black, B. (2018). 'Teachers' experience of and attitudes toward activities to maximise qualification results in England'. *Oxford Review of Education*, 44(5): 563–80.

Millar, F. (2013). 'Radical action is needed now to stop schools cheating at GCSEs'. *The Guardian*. 9 September. (Available from: https://www.theguardian.com/education/2013/sep/09/schools-gcse-exam-cheats)

Newton, P. E. (2003). 'The defensibility of national curriculum assessment in England'. *Research Papers in Education*, 18(2): 101–27.

Newton, P. E. (2005). 'The public understanding of measurement inaccuracy'. *British Educational Research Journal*, 31(4): 419–42.

Newton, P.E. (2007). 'Clarifying the purposes of educational assessment. Assessment in education: Principles', *Policy & Practice*, 14(2): 149–70.

Newton, P. E. (2015). 'Ripping off the cloak of secrecy'. In L. Gray, C. Jackson, and L. Simmonds (Eds.). *Examining Assessment*, 70–8. Guildford, UK: Centre for Education Research and Practice, Assessment and Qualifications Alliance.

Newton, P. E. (2017a). 'Assessment dilemmas'. *Research Intelligence*, 133, 18–20.

Newton, P. E. (2017b). 'There is more to educational measurement than measuring: The importance of embracing purpose pluralism'. *Educational Measurement: Issues and Practice*, 36(2): 5–15.

Newton, P. E. (2021). 'Demythologising A level exam standards'. Research papers in education, DOI: 10.1080/02671522.2020.1870543

Ofqual (2012). GCSE English 2012. Ofqual/12/5225. Coventry: Office of Qualifications and Examinations Regulation.

Ofqual (2013a). 'Review of controlled assessment in GCSEs'. Ofqual/13/5291. Coventry: Office of Qualifications and Examinations Regulation.

Ofqual (2013b). Reforms to GCSEs in England from 2015. Summary. Ofqual/13/5338. Coventry: Office of Qualifications and Examinations Regulation.

Ofqual (2020). 'Consultation Decisions: Regulating performance table qualifications'. Ofqual/20/6589/1. Coventry: Office of Qualifications and Examinations Regulation.

Opposs (2016). 'Whatever happened to school-based assessment in England's GCSEs and A levels?' *Perspectives in Education*, 34(4): 52–61.

Paton, G. (2007). 'GSCE coursework scrapped to stop cheating'. *The Telegraph*. 13 June. (Available from: https://www.telegraph.co.uk/news/uknews/1554362/GSCE-coursework-scrapped-to-stop-cheating.html)

QCA (2005). *A Review of GCE and GCSE Coursework Arrangements*. London: Qualifications and Curriculum Authority.

QCA (2006). *A Review of GCSE Coursework*. London: Qualifications and Curriculum Authority.

QCA (2007). *Controlled Assessments*. London: Qualifications and Curriculum Authority.

Scott, D. (1991). 'Issues and themes: Coursework and coursework assessment in the GCSE'. *Research Papers in Education*, 6(1): 3–19.

Shorrocks-Taylor, D. (1999). *National Testing: Past, Present and Future*. Leicester: BPS Books.

Syal, R. (2013). Rise in number of teachers claiming they are under pressure to inflate grades. *The Guardian*. 11 August. (Available from: https://www.theguardian.com/education/2013/aug/11/academy-schools-teachers-grade-inflation)

Task Group on Assessment and Testing (1988). *National Curriculum Task Group on Assessment and Testing: A Report*. London: Department of Education and Science and the Welsh Office.

Torrance, H. (2018). 'The return to final paper examining in English national curriculum assessment and school examinations: Issues of validity, accountability and politics'. *British Journal of Educational Studies*, 66(1): 3–27.

Torrance, H., Colley, H., Garratt, D., Jarvis, J., Piper, H., Ecclestone, K. & James, D. (2005). *The Impact of Different Modes of Assessment on Achievement and Progress in the Learning and Skills Sector*. London: Learning and Skills Development Agency.

15

Braiding Research, Practice, Policy and Dissemination

Bronwen Cowie

Introduction

This chapter explores two lines of research on classroom assessment – one in the UK by Paul Black and colleagues and the other in Aotearoa New Zealand that I, the author of this chapter, have been part of. There are important similarities that can be drawn from the storylines of research development in the two countries, as well as distinguishable differences relating to how research ideas were adopted, adapted and pursued into practice. Both of these aspects offer significant insights into the domain of long-term research-informed practice and the realities of close-to-practice research. Within the chapter I acknowledge and expand on Paul Black's contribution to how we might as researchers address the complexities of working closely with classroom teachers to anticipate and respond to their needs and interests. It is not my intention to provide an overview of Paul's contribution to our specific understanding of formative assessment rather my aim is to foreground the way Paul and his colleagues interleaved an evolving research project agenda with dissemination activities aimed at ensuring research possibilities could become classroom realities. As part of this selective overview of Paul and his colleagues' research trajectory I direct attention to the role and importance of researcher and researcher-teacher relationships in enabling the research team to develop an ever more sophisticated understanding of the dynamics of classroom assessment.

The inception, implementation and dissemination of research ideas are influenced by the contexts that teachers and researchers work in. Having identified the trajectory of the interplay of research project foci, dissemination and relationships in the UK context I critically interrogate to what extent and whether these aspects formed part of research programmes I have been associated with in Aotearoa New Zealand. My aim here was to test out and illustrate the potential transferability of these aspects in the design, conduct and dissemination of research about pedagogy. That is, how research-informed ideas about pedagogy can evolve, develop and come to be implemented into practice by teachers within the particular cultures and contexts they find themselves in.

Based on my analysis of the UK and NZ research trajectories I propose that these programmes were sustained over time because of the way the three aspects of research, implementation and dissemination came together and interacted as a cohesive and cumulative whole. I employ the metaphor of a braid and braiding to conceptualize how the three aspects working together contributed to the sustained nature and influence of research programme findings on teacher classroom practices; the braiding of the three aspects affected how the research trajectories progressed and what was produced. I conclude by speculating on ways forward for each of these aspects.

A selective overview of a UK trajectory anchored on Paul's research involvements

Paul Black had been actively involved in curriculum and assessment research prior to 1998 but it was his review paper on formative assessment with Dylan Wiliam that brought him to international attention. *Assessment and Classroom Learning* (Black & Wiliam, 1998a) provides a sophisticated analysis of the literature related to formative assessment evidencing its value and emphasizing the role of feedback and of active student participation. The paper was published as a special journal issue accompanied by commentary by high-profile assessment scholars, thereby capturing the attention of the research community. The actions Paul and Dylan took next distinguish their approach to bridging the divide between research and practice to inform and stimulate change in classroom practice.

Paul and Dylan recognized that it was not possible to meet the needs of researchers, teachers and policymakers in the same document (Black & Wiliam, 2003) and they published *Inside the Black Box: Raising Standards through Classroom Assessment* (Black & Wiliam, 1998b) to make the review findings accessible to teachers and policymakers. *Inside the Black Box* was the first of a cluster of dissemination activities they employed to inform and instigate change. The black box metaphor was a deliberate choice intended to highlight that what happens in the classroom between teacher and students is largely ignored by policymakers (Black & Wiliam, 2003): what happens inside the box (the classroom) is neither known nor speculated about; inputs and outputs only are visible. *Inside the Black Box* sets out a range of reasons and suggestions for how teachers might enact formative assessment but emphasizes that every teacher needs to develop their own ways of including the ideas into their classroom practice (p. 15). To ensure the widest possible impact, Paul and Dylan launched the booklet via a conference and a series of events for journalists and the specialist educational press. Their research findings were reported nationally in daily newspapers. They followed up by presenting findings in a large number of forums including school, regional and national meetings throughout the UK. By 2020, over 100,000 copies of *Inside the Black Box* had been sold and the booklet has been translated into Welsh and Polish and adapted for a US audience.

Within the review Paul and Dylan assert that teachers need 'living examples of implementation' (1998a:10) to help them to translate research evidence into something that can be used in their classrooms. In *Inside the Black Box*, they make the following recommendations to policymakers with respect to this support for teachers: (i) teachers need access to a variety of examples from teachers with whom they can identify and from whom they can derive conviction and confidence that they can enhance their practice and how they might do this, and (ii) research to develop these examples should involve close collaboration between researchers, teachers and schools and be followed by pro-active dissemination of resources. Importantly, these recommendations position teachers as knowledgeable, critical, reflective and agentic; they construe teaching as a complex situated activity with affective, knowledge and practical aspects. This orientation is a significant and ongoing feature of Paul's research programme.

The collaborative King's-Medway-Oxfordshire Formative Assessment Project (KMOFAP), initiated in 1999, was designed to provide 'living examples' of classroom practice. In this project, Paul and his colleagues worked closely with a group of teachers (n = 36) in a process of 'supported development' (Black & Wiliam 2003: 629). Teachers were involved in teacher meetings and regular classroom observations over 18 months – a 6-month exploratory/experimental phase and a school year of each teacher piloting the formative ideas they believed would work. The KMOFAP project provided teachers with time, scope and support from colleagues and researchers to develop and reflect on their practice (Harrison et al., 2006). Through this approach the KMOFAP project generated examples of formative assessment practice in everyday secondary science, mathematics and

English classrooms. The multi-subject focus illuminated differences in practice that could be attributed to the nature of disciplinary knowledge and to the way curricula were interpreted in the various schools and between different teachers. Paul and colleagues assert these differences are consequential for teacher identity and for teacher formative actions and interactions. The KMOFAP project alerted the King's team to the value of professional discussions among teachers about how and why new practices might work and how and why they might recognize and explore these in their own classrooms (Harrison, 2013; Serret et al., 2017).

Following the success of *Inside the Black Box* the research team disseminated KMOFAP project findings via a second booklet W*orking inside the Black Box: Assessment for Learning in the Classroom* (Black et al., 2002). Congruent with KMOFAP findings that assessment for learning is more than a generic practice the team went on to edit a series of eight subject-specific black box booklets. Follow-up projects with schools in Wales led to a booklet for primary schools (Harrison & Howard, 2009). Their book *Assessment for Learning: Putting It into Practice* (Black et al., 2003) targeted a general educational audience. Findings were shared via international journals (Black et al., 2004). Researchers and teachers collaborated to disseminate findings through teacher conferences (e.g. Association of Science Education). Looking across these research and dissemination activities we can appreciate that the team paid careful attention to classrooms and the different disciplines as offering particular contexts for teacher formative assessment thereby maintaining a practice of responsive and respectful ways of working together for and with teachers.

The King's Researching Expertise in Science Teaching (KREST) project that followed was a direct response to evidence from teachers in some of the Kings pre-service partnership schools that they were finding the practice of formative assessment challenging (Harrison, 2005). This collaborative action research project sought to understand how and why teachers could be assisted to change their practice. It began with the premise that effective professional development requires attention to how new practices can be evolved or shaped from existing classroom practice (Harrison, 2005; Harrison et al., 2006). Teachers worked with the research team to collect, analyse, reflect and act on evidence from their classrooms. This process led to a nuanced appreciation of how and why teachers select and use particular approaches in their classrooms. A key insight arising from this project was that anticipated gains were not achieved when teachers implemented strategies without consideration of how these were intended to strengthen feedback and develop student capacity for self- and peer assessment (Harrison, 2013, 2017) (see also Marshall & Drummond, 2006). Harrison and

Howard (2009) explain this in terms of the need for consistency of principle rather than uniformity of practice. Here again, in my view, there is clear evidence that the research team recognized and respected teacher expertise and agency and appreciated the situated and dynamic complexity of classroom assessment processes. In terms of dissemination, apart from publications, workshops and conference presentations, Christine Harrison and Dylan Wiliam have run a number of MOOCS to share findings and support teachers to develop and hence their formative practices. These have attracted teachers from around the world with up to seventeen thousand teachers signing up for these online courses each time they were aired.

Other team-based projects have continued the ideas seeded in the initial review and *Inside the Black Box*. These include the King's Oxfordshire Summative Assessment Project (KOSAP) project that explored teacher summative classroom assessment and teacher judgement in assigning quality criteria to tasks (Black et al. 2011). This project took up the challenge of understanding the breadth of teacher classroom assessment responsibilities and practice. It reiterated that classroom assessment is shaped by disciplinary practices and teacher agency (Black et al., 2011). The team has also been involved in a number of international research and development projects focused on the assessment of inquiry in STEM (SAILS and ASSISTME). At one and the same time these projects have narrowed (to inquiry) and expanded (to STEM) the legitimate and required focus of teacher assessment. Interestingly, many teachers were only prepared to consider new approaches to inquiry and its assessment when inquiry was not part of their national assessment system. They then thought they had the space they needed to be able to explore the synergies between inquiry and formative assessment. In SAILS, in particular, this led to teachers developing greater student participation and agency through a stronger focus on peer and then self-assessment thereby creating more opportunities for shared feedback sessions within lesson time. SAILS and ASSISTME included outreach seminars with policymakers where teachers presented their work both at national level and across the EU. Websites were established to host publications and resources for teachers (e.g. www.kcl.ac.uk/sails).

As in earlier studies, a number of teachers who were involved in the SAILS project in 2013 were also involved in the follow on ASSISTME project from 2014 to 2018, with this continuity of participation deepening teachers' own knowledge and fast-forwarding the ASSISTME research. The King's researchers' ways of working together and working with teachers over time can be seen to be anchored in and sustained by a commitment to enhancing teaching and learning, with this focus supported by relationships of mutual trust and respect. These enabled and encouraged researchers and teachers to take risks and explore new ideas and practices. They supported teacher agency in classroom practice and their longer-term collaborative involvement in research-supported teachers to deepen and enhance their practice.

To this point I have provided a selected overview of UK research projects, instigated or informed by Paul and his colleagues, to highlight how a research trajectory can evolve and be sustained through a series of projects which pursue possibilities and follow up on teacher concerns, thereby increasing the utility of findings for teachers. I have also sought to highlight the team's sustained focus on the dissemination of findings and explicate the nature and role of researcher and researcher-teacher relationships.

A selective overview of an Aotearoa New Zealand research trajectory

In Aotearoa New Zealand work on formative assessment can be traced to a literature review by Terry Crooks (1988): 'The impact of classroom evaluation practices on students'. Crooks' paper was summarized in Black and Wiliam (1998a). His review explored the link between assessment and learning and foregrounded the direct and indirect, intended and unintended impacts of everyday classroom assessment on students' approaches to learning; this included how students construct a sense of themselves as learners and what they understand and value as important to learn and know. In the review, Crooks emphasizes the need to assess what is important, not just what is easy to generate data on. His review was highly influential in shaping the *New Zealand Curriculum Framework*, the National Education Monitoring Project (which Crooks co-led), and two national professional development programmes (Crooks, 2011).

Interest in and research on formative assessment in Aotearoa New Zealand can also be seen to have developed out of the Learning in Science Project (LISP) series of studies (Bell, 2013). LISP researchers in the first two studies employed an action research approach to working with teachers to identify student alternative conceptions of natural phenomena (e.g. energy, plants, mixtures), which the LISP researchers labelled 'children's science'. They developed and tested a range of teaching approaches aimed at working with these (Osborne & Freyberg, 1985) and prepared a series of teachers guides to illustrate these approaches; see for example Biddulph and Osborne (1984). Findings were shared through weekly seminars to which local teachers were invited. These provided opportunities for researchers and practitioners to discuss how classroom activities and approaches might be altered to introduce more constructivist approaches to learning. Sharing and discussing research ideas within this mix of stakeholders provided teachers with an entry point into the LISP project, while at the same time providing researchers with a means to test out the applicability of the approaches they had designed.

Constructivist understandings of learning linked to the early LISP studies informed the 1995 science curriculum: *Science in the New Zealand* curriculum (Bell & Baker, 1997). This raised the challenge for NZ teachers of how to identify and respond to student ideas (Bell, 1993), given these were likely to be different from those of scientists and resistant to change. LISP (Assessment) sought to address this challenge (Bell & Cowie, 2001). Twelve teachers and two researchers collaborated over 1995 and 1996 with the goal of understanding teacher formative assessment practices. Through classroom case studies and reflective meetings the group identified that teacher formative assessment practices involved the dynamic interplay of planned assessment tasks and in-the-moment interactions with students (Cowie & Bell 1999). The researchers and teachers developed, tested out and agreed that teachers and students noticing, recognizing and responding to student learning during the learning were central to formative assessment. For the LISP teachers, recognition of the formative intent and value of their informal interactions was important because it acknowledged both the dynamics of classroom relations (interpersonal and with science as a subject) and their professional expertise. This acknowledgement was central to validating the changes in assessment practices that teachers pursued as they deliberately implemented a more formative approach in their classrooms.

A similar approach of researchers working closely with teachers (n = 15) was employed with the Learning in Technology Education (LITE) project. The role of teacher pedagogical content knowledge in focusing and informing their formative assessment practices was highlighted by the LITE project largely due to technology being a new curriculum for teachers (Jones & Moreland 2004). The Classroom InSiTE project brought together technology and science education researchers and twelve primary school teachers (students aged 5 to 12 years), some of whom had been in the LITE project (Cowie et al., 2008). The InSiTE study was founded on the argument by Paul Black and Mike Atkin that what really counts in education is what happens when teachers and students meet. The wisdom of any decision about education is best judged on the basis of whether or not it raises the quality of these interactions. (Atkin & Black, 2003, p. ix). The InSiTE findings echoed the KMOFAP findings in identifying that formative assessment has discipline-specific aspects and a generic aspect, this time in primary school settings. Subsequently, the project team added the need to consider and be responsive to the epistemological aspects of a discipline as part of noticing and responding, specifically the need to consider how a discipline generates, legitimizes and communicates meaning. (Cowie et al., 2013; Cowie & Moreland, 2015). The InSiTE project reiterated that assessment for learning relies on teachers' pedagogical content knowledge where this includes conceptual, procedural and epistemic aspects (see also Cowie et al., 2018). Researchers from the InSiTE project co-wrote *Design and Technology inside the Black Box: Technology Education* (Moreland et al., 2008); the entire *Black Box* series is currently listed on a New Zealand government-supported website that provides resources for teachers.

The InSiTE researchers and teachers shared a desire to disseminate findings more broadly with other teachers and they worked together to identify which ideas and practices they would share, preparing booklets. The booklet *Teachers Talking to Teachers, a Story of Practice* was developed through a collaboration between researchers and teachers to illustrate aspects of classroom practice that were relevant to formative assessment. Teachers valued the process of collaborative writing; they considered articulating and sharing how and why their formative actions enhanced student learning deepened their understanding of formative assessment processes and validated the changes they made to their classroom practice. The InSiTE project established a pattern of co-authoring with teachers to disseminate findings, a practice which shifted researcher-teacher relationships and roles in this, and subsequent projects towards more of partnership model. While there are some similarities between the ways in which classroom assessment research changed in Aotearoa New Zealand and in the UK, in the 1990s and early part of the millennium, that indicated that the role of the teacher and the discipline were important in fostering changes in practice, there was one distinct area that was key in the Aotearoa New Zealand context. Beginning with the LISP projects in Aotearoa New Zealand researchers have paid attention to the diversity of student views and experiences. LISP (Assessment) included a direct focus on student experiences of classroom assessment. It identified that students experienced classroom assessment as a situated and social practice that had consequences for their relationships and their sense of identity as learners and knowers (Cowie 2005). Student comments positioned them as active and intentional participants in classroom assessment processes indicating their ideas and viewpoints were well worth research and teacher attention: student views and experiences have been a feature of other NZ scholars notably Graham Nuthall (Nuthall & Alton-Lee 1993; Nuthall, 2007). Direct policy recognition of the need to attend to the diversity of student backgrounds and experiences can be found in the Aotearoa New Zealand Ministry of Education's commissioning of the *Quality Teaching for Diverse Students in Schooling* best evidence synthesis report (Alton-Lee, 2003). This synthesis positions diversity and difference as central to classroom practice and fundamental to honouring *Te Tiriti o Waitangi* (the Treaty Waitangi). *Te Tiriti* is the foundation document of Aotearoa as a bicultural nation and requires the government, and hence teachers and schools, to give due consideration to the knowledges, interests and needs of Māori as the indigenous people of the land.

A number of scholars have explored culturally responsive pedagogy within the Aotearoa NZ context (e.g. Bishop & Glynn, 1999). The Waikato team partnered with ten primary teachers over the course of a year and supported them in action research that explored how they might serve as 'cultural brokers' (Aitkenhead, 1996) who incorporated aspects of students' cultural worlds into their science teaching. The Ministry funded this project as part of the Quality Teaching Research and Development (QTR&D) programme that was designed to generate examples of 'quality teaching' for and with Māori and Pasifika students. The QTR&D teachers found that when they did this their students took collaborative responsibility for seeking out information on science topics from both Western and Māori world views and for asking and answering learning questions (Glynn et al., 2010). The research team and three of the teachers then chose to continue their exploration of how student funds of knowledge (Moll et al., 1992) might be made visible and valued through the Culturally Responsive Pedagogy and Assessment in Primary Science Classrooms: Whakamana Tamariki project (Cowie et al., 2011). Findings from this study affirmed the value of inviting student and community funds of knowledge into the classroom and curriculum for discussion alongside science ideas as a means of engaging students *and* fostering student critical engagement with when, where and why different ways of thinking are valuable (Cowie & Trevethan, 2021).

The QTR&D and Culturally Responsive projects represent a shift in my Aotearoa New Zealand research trajectory for the way they expanded the unit of analysis for what counted as valued learning to encompass student and community funds of knowledge alongside science conceptual, procedural and epistemological understandings. These two projects also expanded the unit of intervention and analysis for teaching and learning and hence for how assessment for learning was understood by teachers and researchers and a broader range of stakeholders. Family members, and occasionally community members, were positioned as contributors to classroom curricula and as potential partners with teachers in the provision of feedback. This expansion was consistent with New Zealand interpretations of culturally responsive pedagogy (Bishop & Glynn, 1999), with assessment policy (Ministry of Education, 2011) and with Māori cultural values. For these studies researchers and teachers together reported findings to children's parents and whanau, at school staff meetings and at whole school assemblies attended by the school community (e.g. Cowie et al., 2012). Beyond local dissemination, teachers are named as 'research partners' on the project webpage and report (Cowie et al., 2011) and are authors on some papers (e.g. Parkinson et al., 2011).

The final Aotearoa NZ project we discuss is more recent, the Enhancing Boys' Writing project (Cowie & Khoo, 2018). The project was initiated and led by a principal who was an ex-masters student from the University of Waikato. The project goal was to enhance the writing achievement of year 1–8 boys in the school through peer feedback. The principal involved all the teachers in her school in three cycles of collaborative action research over two years. The two researchers acted as critical friends who contributed ideas and support for the research process and for self- and peer assessment. Findings indicated that influences on transforming practice came from both within and beyond the classroom. While much of our earlier work focused on the teacher and students with a recognition of and for the communities they originated from, this study indicated the need for a systems approach to understanding the research process and teacher pedagogical practice outcomes. At the classroom level, our ecosystems analysis highlighted a productive synergy between commonplace writing pedagogy strategies and assessment for learning practices. At the school level, the teachers considered it was significant that peer assessment practices were made explicit and taken up across the whole school and shared with the parent community. The national policy context, which provided funding, also allowed for teacher and school development of assessment and reporting practices and hence a warrant for teacher inquiry. In this study teachers initiated reporting via school newsletters and the local press as well as a cross school meeting of teachers. Teachers co-authored articles and took the lead in presenting at academic conferences. Hence, for this project the orientation was much more towards developing practice-based evidence (Bryk, 2015) than an exploration of possible instantiations of evidence-based practice.

Conceptualizing long-term research programmes as a braid of focus, relationships and dissemination

The invitation to contribute a chapter on Paul's contributions prompted me to revisit Paul's writing on formative assessment/assessment for learning. Within and across the published material it was the interplay of research and dissemination – evidence of a cumulative and evolving research focus in conjunction with ongoing attention to dissemination to teachers and policymakers along with the continuity of relationships within the research team that attracted my attention. These aspects provided the impetus for and are the focus of this chapter. To reiterate, my intention in this chapter was not to scope Paul's contributions to our understanding of the formative assessment but to prompt colleagues to consider his contribution to our understanding of what might be the elements of an evolving, influential and sustained research programme.

In 2003, writing about the KMOFAP project, Paul and Dylan draw on Pickering's notion of a mangle of practice to describe the series of activities they had designed and implemented as 'a trajectory buffeted by combinations of factors. … [where] what it is possible to research, and what it is good to research keeps changing' (p. 635). Seen this way, they propose their 1998 review, their work with teachers, the strategies they employed to convince policymakers and teachers of the value of formative assessment including broader publicity campaigns make 'a kind of sense' (p. 635). With the benefit of being able to look back over 30 years I propose that the metaphor of a braid and the notion of braiding offer a more generative way of conceptualizing the nature and impact of Paul's work. This metaphor worked for me when I analysed my research trajectory, and it resonates with the thinking of other Aotearoa New Zealand scholars (e.g. Macfarlane et al., 2015).

The metaphor of a braid and braiding offered me a way to conceptualize the interleaving, interconnectedness and co-influence of research project foci, dissemination activities and researchers' ongoing relationships with each other and with teachers. In practice, braids reflect and embody a process for exploring activity over time. Braids are the outcome of deliberate design and effort over time by weavers and they are informed and influenced by wider community preferences and contexts. This was certainly the case of the two programmes as the researchers working together over time and contexts crafted a research agenda based on close relationships with teachers and their classroom realities. The metaphor of a braid brings to mind threads of different kinds and colours that have been woven into a whole in which each thread is distinct but some are sometimes hidden; the threads are separate but also clearly interlaced (Casanave, 2003). It is the interlacing or weaving of the threads that provide strength and elegance beyond that of the individual threads. In the programmes outlined here research and dissemination were foregrounded and backgrounded at different times as the nature of both aspects evolved towards closer attention to disciplinary influence on teacher practice and greater teacher agency in all aspects of the research process. This said, context did matter. The UK programme tended to foreground teacher concerns and practices whereas the NZ programme gave more consideration to student and community views and experiences.

We propose that it was the weaving of a responsive-to-practice research agenda with proactive dissemination, with both achieved through relationships that were also sustained over time, into a cohesive whole that led to the programmes being robust, responsive and influential. The combination of these three aspects is more likely to influence policy and practice because together they are more likely to contribute insights into the how and why of classroom teaching, learning and assessment that impact teacher and student lives day to day. Braided together these aspects are more likely to lead to research that builds on what teachers know and can do, to accommodate teachers' current concerns and to anticipate those still on the horizon and hence to generate insights into what teachers might do and where they might go next.

Expanding the braid idea

Classroom-based studies have extended our understanding of the demands on teachers but they have been less successful in understanding how to foster student engagement and capability as discerning and agentic learners (Black, 2018). This makes student experiences an obvious focus for further research, with the possibility of engaging students in shaping the scope and direction of research. Increasingly, policymakers, researchers and communities are also acknowledging that the responsibility for supporting student learning cannot be located solely within the classroom nor met by the teacher alone. Paul and Dylan acknowledge this in *Inside the Black Box* when they state inputs extend beyond students and teachers and include resources, school organization and culture; parents and the school community, and formal external assessment regimes. This focus has emerged more explicitly as part of the New Zealand trajectory driven in part by our political and cultural context and in part by concerns around equity of participation and achievement. However there is an international trend towards viewing education as an ecosystem that encompasses students, their family/whānau, school communities, professional development providers, business organizations, prospective employers and so on, with this view extending to considering assessment as a system process (Stiggins, 2008). The argument is that understanding the various layers and levels of the system matters for how equity and equality are understood and how equity of participation and achievement might be accomplished. The realization of this understanding poses a compelling challenge to the classroom-based research agenda.

Thinking about dissemination, the sustained and trans-national reach of the signature *Black Box* series clearly illustrates the impact of careful and strategic crafting of research findings in a way that speaks to teacher wisdom and realities. At the same time in both country contexts researchers have employed a process of 'layering' (Anderson & McLachlan 2016) whereby different forms and formats are used to communicate ideas to different audiences. Important in this, the focus is on how to support knowledge use via the 'cross-linking' of what Anderson and McLachlan refer to as 'high-impact pieces with the long-form and technical versions' (p.307). This focus allows stakeholder groups 'to move back and forth among these layers to access a wider diversity of information as needed' (p.307). Anderson and McLachlan also point to the need to build bridges to encourage communication across different knowledge communities which resonates with the current rhetoric around knowledge brokers, knowledge mobilization and impact.

Knowledge mobilization aims to make research findings accessible to non-academic audiences such as school leaders and teachers and as such it can be seen to provide a pathway to impact or uptake of findings (Phipps et al., 2016). Knowledge mobilization and impact have emerged as a consequence of the introduction and developments in the REF in the UK and the PBRF in New Zealand. The scope of valued impact is as yet unclear with questions as to relative importance attributed to impact on participating teachers and schools and other 'local' groups compared with national reach and uptake in policy open to discussion. Current wisdom is that knowledge mobilization and impact should be planned for as part of project inception and design so that knowledge mobilization becomes a process of knowledge exchange accomplished through the co-production of research that has both academic value and relevance for community action (Phipps & Shapson, 2009).

The third aspect of the braid is that of relationships – those among researchers and those between researchers-teachers. Across the two trajectories outlined there have been clear shifts in researcher-teacher roles with these able to be conceptualized as consistent with a shift from evidence-based practice to practice-based evidence (Bryk, 2015). A number of research programme designs have emerged which rely on active and collaborative teacher and/or community participation (Bang et al., 2015; Penuel & Gallagher, 2017). These approaches challenge traditional expectations about the power dynamics between researchers and 'the researched' leading to new roles and relationships in all elements of research processes oriented towards pedagogical change and equity. They emphasize the agency of participants; researchers collaborate with participants as partners who are involved in the scoping of a project, who take an active part in all aspects of the project conduct, and whose contributions are publicly acknowledged. These approaches recognize the role of context, the need for practice value and the need to produce outputs that meet the needs of a range of stakeholders (Penuel et al., 2020). They acknowledge that teachers are important knowledge brokers through their relationships and reputations with colleagues in their own school and across their professional networks.

Conclusion

The opportunity to contribute this chapter has alerted me to the importance of the temporal and wider contextual aspects of classrooms and schools and to how our research foci and agendas are shaped by these factors and by our own beliefs and commitments. To conclude I cite a whakataukī or proverb that came to my attention through discussions with my Maori colleagues: Kia whakatōmuri te haere whakamua: I walk backwards into the future with my eyes fixed on my past.

Paul Black's work has illustrated what a commitment to honouring teacher views and voices propelled by a commitment to enhance classroom assessment, teaching and learning can achieve. Our challenge is to understand how to work in partnership with teachers, students, communities and policymakers to progress equity of engagement, participation and achievement for all teachers and students, and for other groups with an interest in and potential to benefit from education.

References

Aikenhead, G. (1996). 'Science education: Border crossing into the subculture of science'. *Studies in Science Education*, 27: 1–52.

Alton-Lee, A. (2003). *Quality Teaching for Diverse Students in Schooling: Best Evidence. Synthesis*. Wellington: Ministry of Education.

Anderson, C. & McLachlan, S. (2016). 'Transformative research as knowledge mobilization: Transmedia, bridges, and layers'. *Action Research*, 14(3): 295–317.

Atkin, M. & Black, P. (2003). *Inside Science Education Reforms: A History of Curricular Change*. New York: Teachers College Press.

Bang, M., Faber, L., Gurneau, J., Marin, A. & Soto, C. (2015). 'Community-based design research: Learning across generations and strategic transformations of institutional relations toward axiological innovations', *Mind, Culture, and Activity*, 23(1): 28–41.

Bell, B. (1993). *Taking into Account Students' Thinking: A Teacher Development Guide*. Centre for Science and Mathematics Education Research, University of Waikato.

Bell, B. & Baker, R. (1997). 'Curriculum development in science: Policy-to-practice and practice-to-policy', in Bell, Beverley & R. Baker (Eds.), *Developing the Science Curriculum in Aotearoa New Zealand*, 1–17. Auckland: Addison Wesley Longman.

Bell, B. & Cowie, B. (2001). *Formative Assessment in Science Education*. Dordrecht: Kluwer.

Bell, B. (2013). *Learning in Science: The Waikato Research*. London: Routledge.

Biddulph, F. & Osborne, R. (1984). *Making Sense of Our World: An Interactive Approach*. SERU, University of Waikato.

Bishop, R. & Glynn, T. (1999). *Culture Counts: Changing Power Relations in Education*. Palmerston North, New Zealand: Dunmore Press.

Black, P. & Wiliam, D. (1998a). 'Assessment and Classroom Learning'. *Assessment in Education: Principles, Policy and Practice*, 5(1): 7–74.

Black, P. & Wiliam, D. (1998b). *Inside the Black Box: Raising Standards through Classroom Assessment*. London: King's College London School of Education.

Black, P. & Wiliam, D. (2003). 'In praise of educational research': Formative assessment'. *British Educational Research Journal*, 29(5): 623–37.

Black, P., Harrison, C., Lee, C., Marshall, B. & Wiliam, D. (2002). *Working inside the Black Box: Assessment for Learning in the Classroom*. GL Assessment.

Black, P., Harrison, C., Lee, C., Marshall, B. & Wiliam, D. (2003). *Assessment for Learning: Putting It into Practice*. Buckingham: Open University Press.

Black, P., Harrison, C., Lee, C., Marshall, B. & Wiliam, D. (2004). 'Working inside the black box: Assessment for learning in the classroom'. *Phi Delta Kappan*, 86(1): 8–21.

Black, P., Harrison, C., Hodgen, J., Marshall, B. & Serret, N. (2011). 'Can teachers' summative assessments produce dependable results and also enhance classroom learning?' *Assessment in Education*, 18(4): 451–69.

Black, P. (2018). 'Helping students to become capable learners'. *European Journal of Education*, 53(2): 144–59.

Bryk, A. (2015). 'Accelerating how we learn to improve'. *Educational Researcher*, 44(9): 467–77.

Casanave, C. (2003). 'Narrative braiding: Constructing a multi strand portrayal of self as writer'. In C. P. Casanave & S. Vandrick (Eds.), *Writing for Scholarly Publication: Behind the Scenes in Language Education*. New York: Lawrence Erlbaum.

Crooks, T. J. (2011). 'Assessment for learning in the accountability era: New Zealand'. *Studies In Educational Evaluation*, 37(1): 71–7.

Crooks, T. J. (1988). 'The impact of classroom evaluation practices on students'. *Review of Educational Research*, 58: 438–81.

Cowie, B. (2003). Learning perspectives: Implications for pedagogy in science education Waikato Journal of Education, 9, 65–75.

Cowie, B. (2005), Pupil commentary on assessment for learning. The Curriculum Journal, 16: 137–151.

Cowie, B., & Bell, B. (1999). A Model of Formative Assessment in Science Education. Assessment in Education, 6, 101–16.

Cowie, B., Moreland, J., Jones, A. & Otrel-Cass, K. (2008). *Classroom InSiTE Project: Understanding Interactions to Enhance Technology and Learning in Science and Technology in Years 1–8*. Wellington, New Zealand: Teaching and Learning Research Initiative.

Cowie, B., Otrel-Cass, K., Glynn, T. & Kara, H., et al. (2011). *Culturally Responsive Pedagogy and Assessment in Primary Science Classrooms: Whakamana Tamariki*. Wellington, New Zealand: Teaching and Learning Research Initiative.

Cowie, B., Otrel-Cass, K. & Moreland, J. (2012). 'Finding out about fossils in an early years classroom: A context for developing a 'practical explanatory theory'. In B. Kaur (Ed.), *Understanding Teaching and Learning: Classroom Research Revised*, 159–69. Rotterdam, The Netherlands: Sense.

Cowie, B., Moreland, J. & Otrel-Cass, K. (2013). *Expanding Notions of Assessment for Learning*. Rotterdam, The Netherlands: Sense.

Cowie, B. & Moreland, J. (2015). 'Leveraging disciplinary practices to support students' active participation in formative assessment'. *Assessment in Education*, 22(2): 247–64.

Cowie, B. & Khoo, E. (2018). 'An ecological approach to understanding Assessment for Learning in support of student writing achievement'. *Frontiers in Education*, 3: 11.

Cowie, B., Harrison, C. & Willis, J. (2018). 'Supporting teacher responsiveness in assessment for learning through disciplined noticing'. *The Curriculum Journal*, 29: 464–78.

Cowie, B. & Trevethan, H. (2021). 'Funds of knowledge and relations as a curriculum and assessment resource in multicultural primary science classrooms: A case study from Aotearoa New Zealand'. In: Atwater M.M. (Eds) *International Handbook of Research on Multicultural Science Education*. Springer International Handbooks of Education. Cham: Springer. https://doi-org.ezproxy.waikato.ac.nz/10.1007/978-3-030-37743-4_59-1

Glynn, T., Cowie, B., Otrel-Cass, K. & Macfarlane, A. (2010). 'Culturally responsive pedagogy: Connecting New Zealand teachers of science with their Māori Students'. *Australian Journal of Indigenous Education*, 39(1): 118–27.

Harrison, C. (2005). 'Teachers developing assessment for learning: Mapping teacher change'. *International Journal of Teacher Development*, 9(2): 255–63.

Harrison, C., Hofstein, A., Eylon, B. & Simon, S. (2006). 'Evidence-based professional development of science teachers in two countries'. *International Journal of Science Education*, 30(5): 577–91.

Harrison, C. & Howard, S. (2009). *Inside the Primary Black Box*. London: GL Assessment.

Harrison, C. (2013). 'Collaborative action research as a tool for generating formative feedback on teachers' classroom assessment practice: The KREST project'. *Teachers and Teaching*, 19(2): 202–13.

Harrison, C. (2017). 'Adapting pedagogy for formative assessment'. *Encyclopaedia of Educational Philosophy and Theory*. London: Routledge.

Harrison, C., Nieminen, P., Correia, C., Serret. N., Papadouris, N., Tiberghien, A., Grangeat, M. & Rached, E. (2017). 'Assessment-on-the-fly: Promoting and collecting evidence of learning through dialogue'. In J. Dolin & R. Evans (Eds.), *Transforming Classroom Assessment in STEM*. London: Routledge.

Jones, A., Moreland, J. 'Enhancing Practicing Primary School Teachers' Pedagogical Content Knowledge in Technology'. *International Journal of Technology and Design Education*, 14: 121–140.

Macfarlane, S., Macfarlane, A. & Gillon, G. (2015). 'Sharing the food baskets of knowledge: Creating space for a blending of streams'. In A. Macfarlane, S. Macfarlane, & M. Webber (Eds.), *Sociocultural Realities: Exploring New Horizons*. Christchurch: Canterbury University Press.

Marshall, B. & Drummond, M. (2006). 'How teachers engage with Assessment for Learning: lessons from the classroom'. *Research Papers in Education*, 21(2): 133–49.

Ministry of Education. (2011). *Ministry of Education Position Paper: Assessment (Schooling Sector)*. Wellington, New Zealand: Ministry of Education.

Moll, L., Amanti, C., Neff, D. & Gonzalez, N. (1992). 'Funds of knowledge for teaching: Using a qualitative approach to connect homes and classrooms'. *Theory into Practice*, 31: 132–41.

Moreland, J., Jones, A. & Barlex, D. (2008). *Design and Technology inside the Black Box*. London: GL Assessment.

Nuthall, G., & Alton-Lee, A. (1993). Predicting learning from student experience of teaching: A theory of student knowledge construction in classrooms. American Educational Research Journal, 30(4), 799–840.

Nuthall, G. & Alton-Lee, A. (1995). 'Predicting learning from student experience: A theory of student knowledge construction in classrooms'. *American Educational Research Journal*, 30: 799–840.

Nuthall, G. (2007). *Hidden Lives of Learners*. Wellington, New Zealand: NZCER Press.

Osborne, R. & Freyberg, P. (1985). *Learning in Science: Implications of Children's Science*. Heinemann: Pearson Education New Zealand Limited.

Parkinson, A., Doyle, J., Cowie, B., Otrel-Cass, K. & Glynn, T. (2011). 'Engaging whānau with children's science learning'. *Set: Research Information for Educational Research,* 1: 3–9.

Penuel, W. & Gallagher, D. (2017). *Creating Research-Practice Partnerships in Education*. Harvard Education Press.

Penuel, W., Riedy, R., Barber, M., Peurach, D., LeBouef, W. & Clark, T. (2020). 'Principles of collaborative education research with stakeholders: Toward requirements for a new research and development infrastructure'. *Review of Educational Research*, 90(5): 627–74.

Philippou, S. & Priestley, M. (2019). 'Beyond binaries in curricular discussions: what does it mean to argue for curriculum as at the heart of educational practice?' *The Curriculum Journal*, 30: 217–22.

Phipps, D. & Shapson, S. (2009). 'Knowledge mobilisation builds local research collaborations for social innovation'. *Evidence & Policy: A Journal of Research, Debate and Practice*, 5(3): 211–27.

Phipps, D., Cummings, J., Pepler, D., Craig, W. & Cardinal, S. (2016). 'The co-produced pathway to impact describes knowledge mobilization processes'. *Journal of Community Engagement and Scholarship*, 9(1): 31–40.

Serret, N., Harrison, C., Correia, C. & Harding, J. (2017). 'Transforming assessment and teaching practices in science inquiry'. *Journal of Emergent Science*, 12: 48–55.

Stiggins, R. (2008). *Assessment Manifesto: A Call for the Development of Balanced Assessment Systems*. A position paper. Portland, OR: ETS Assessment Training Institute.

16

Research Design Principles for Dynamic Teacher-Researcher Collaboration: Two Stars and a Wish

Natasha Serret and Catarina F. Correia

Introduction

Assessment for learning (AfL) has been conceptualized through different perspectives in the literature (Wiliam, 2011a). For the purposes of this chapter, we define AfL as a pedagogical approach to teaching and learning which aims to promote learning by supporting the development of autonomous and self-regulated learners (Heritage & Harrison, 2019). Among the core tenets of AfL is teacher and student responsiveness to learning as it is taking place (Cowie and Bell, 1999), and the recognition that teaching and learning are situated practices (Pryor and Crossouard, 2008).

Responsive teaching requires teachers and learners to take action on evidence that arises and so relies on the formative use of assessment. Research on teachers' views, experiences and enactment of formative assessment has been shaped by action research principles (Torrance & Pryor, 2001; Black et al., 2003). For the purposes of this chapter there are two key principles of action research that should be highlighted. Firstly, action research generally seeks to promote transformation in practitioners' practices, as well as changes in their understanding of those practices (Kemmis, 2009). Secondly, action research is shaped by the agents involved and embodies 'a respect for people and for the knowledge and experience they bring to the research process' (Brydon-Miller, Greenwood, and Maguire, 2003:15).

A brief critical review of key publications in the field shows multiple examples of teacher-researcher collaborative practices (Torrance and Pryor, 2001; Black et al., 2003; Cooper & Cowie, 2010; Harrison, 2013; Willis and Cowie, 2014).

However, most of these studies tend to focus on teachers experiences in the classroom and the supports that they need to develop their practice. What is less often brought to the fore are the interactions that occur between teachers and researchers when they meet to plan possible changes in classroom practice or when they reflect on how such changes have affected the routines, rituals and outcomes of teaching and learning from the different agent perspectives. While the rationales and processes regarding the ways of working together in collaborative approaches are briefly discussed in these publications, there seems to be a lack of theoretical principles that can describe and explain teacher-researcher collaborative practice.

The importance of making principles of collaboration explicit can be explained through an analogy between research in AfL and theatre production. The front stage of research in AfL is often dominated by theory and practice in teaching and learning and by recommended ways to support teachers' professional development (e.g. see Black et al., 2003; Wiliam, 2011b; Heritage, 2013; and Heritage & Harrison, 2019). As we engage with the literature, it is front stage that is visible. The back stage of the research, which is far less visible, is driven by the multiple ways in which teachers, teacher educators and researchers work together to 'produce' what is presented in the front stage. We claim here that developing a theoretical understanding of the backstage activities is very important to support the outcomes in the front stage because this 'tacit knowledge' which is often carried within the community of research groups can be made explicit and used to design, project and potentiality create opportunities for more equitable teacher-researcher collaborations (Penuel et al., 2020).

In view of the above, we aim to document and discuss Paul Black's contribution to the development of collaborative teacher-researcher practices. The work that is reviewed here which was instigated by Paul Black was done in close collaboration with Christine Harrison and Dylan Wiliam at King's College London. It covers nearly two decades of practice from 1999 to 2018. In this chapter, we revisit some of their key AfL research projects through a lens of teacher-researcher collaboration to identify some of the principles, approaches and outcomes that enabled and strengthened the collaboration between the participating teachers and the research team involved in a range of projects. As researchers who worked directly on some of the projects, this chapter has given us the opportunity to pause and reflect on how and why collaboration between researchers and teachers has been such an instrumental driver across AfL projects (our stars). We conclude by looking ahead to highlight our research aspirations for future teacher-researcher collaborations (our wishes).

At the heart of AfL is feedback that allows assessment conversations which provides guidance and instigates formative action. Some teachers who have developed their AfL pedagogy communicate their response to and regulation of progress in learning through a strategy known as 'two stars and a wish'. The two stars capture areas of strength in learning and the wish captures the next steps. This strategy allows teachers to recognize success and be proactive in setting the next targets for learners When used effectively, this allows teachers and learners to articulate their regulation of the learning in a succinct and purposeful way. This strategy has also been used by teachers to evaluate and make sense of the progress they have made as they have sought to change their classroom practice. It provides a means of mapping progress in an ipsative way and this is especially useful when meetings and interactions between teachers and researchers are intermittent, in that it allows teachers to focus on current practice by noting what has improved since previous meetings, while looking forward to where they hope their practice will develop in the future.

The importance of collaborative teacher-researcher interactions

The dynamics of interaction between teachers and researchers in educational research falls into a spectrum of practices that range from cooperative to more collaborative and participatory models of interaction (Impedovo, 2021).

Traditionally, much of educational research that involved teachers and researchers working together relied on models of cooperation. In cooperative interactions, the researchers and the teachers are assigned to different roles which are guided by clear expectations of participation (Penuel et al., 2020). Cooperative models of interaction are visible in both small- and large-scale studies. For example, in small-scale qualitative empirical research projects in assessment for learning, researchers often conduct case studies in schools observing and interviewing teachers and pupils. In cooperative models, researchers are expected to identify a gap or problem in practice. They will then use theory to inform and develop potential solutions and design interventions, or simply observe classroom practices as a 'non-interfering' observer. Where interventions are designed, teachers are expected to implement these which will then enable researchers to evaluate the impact that those interventions have in addressing the problems or gaps identified (Bryk, 2015).

These models of cooperation are driven by a paradigm of educational research that seeks to address an identified deficit in learning and/or practice (Bryk, 2015), For example, a cooperative teacher-researcher project focusing on science inquiry might wish to explore challenges with capturing evidence of learning in science inquiry, identify gaps in progress in student understanding of inquiry or uncover scientific literacy failings. Each intervention has the purpose of correcting practice or bridging gaps in learning and the rhetoric within the intervention implies that these new ways of working can fix teachers and replace weaker practices.

According to Penuel et al. (2020) the valuing of traditional models of cooperation is underpinned by a paradigm that research is trustworthy if it is not biased. Behind this is a further assumption that closeness and negotiation between researchers and practitioners can lead to bias in how one or both groups interpret evidence of change. However, the problem that arises from this distancing between researchers and practitioners can then lead to all sort of perverse effects. For instance, maintaining an objective, non-participant distance between the research team and practitioners could foster a relationship of distrust where practitioners regard researchers as being 'outsiders' and prevent researchers from capturing the lived experience and perspectives of practitioners. Practitioner insights often reveal some of the deeper challenges associated with implementation of new approaches and can inform theory, shape practice and drive key policy changes. As such, it is essential that teachers' views are sought and considered as important evidence in judging the success of innovative practices. Recent 'close to practice' models of research (Wyse et al., 2020) strive for a more empathetic and collaborative researcher-practitioner dynamic.

Collaborative models of interaction challenge the assumption that close interaction between researchers and practitioners is an inescapable source of bias which constitutes a threat to the validity and trustworthiness of the research (Bryk, 2015). In fact, these collaborative models emphasize the importance of genuine collaboration, which involves closeness to provide a deeper understanding of a problem and greater insights into potential solutions (Bryk et al., 2011). Provided that these partnerships contain protocols that enable scrutiny and accountability, in relation to the processes and the ways in which the knowledge that was co-constructed, many would argue that this is a hallmark of credibility strengthening the trustworthiness of the research (Cohen, Manion & Morrison 2018).

In recent years, evidence-based education has driven policy agendas dictating 'what works' and teachers are left with the groundwork of implementing 'what works' into actual practice. In a climate where there is a tendency to cherry-pick and interpret educational research to fit with particular paradigms and how learning can be best promoted (Oancea & Pring 2008), examination of the ways teachers and researchers interact during periods of change provides evidence of the processes involved. In the current political climate in England, building collaborative ways of teachers and researchers working together that recognize, respect and value the different skills and expertise of teachers and researchers is so important.

Illustrations of teacher-researcher dynamic collaborative research

As stated in the introduction, we will now revisit some key projects of Paul Black and the King's College team as we seek to distil the key principles that inform our proposed dynamic model for teacher-researcher collaboration. Our intention is to build an argument as to why these principles of interaction are important in producing meaningful change in teaching practices.

In this section, we review key AfL projects from the King's College London team as a historical sequence to highlight how the each project built on the collaborative lessons learnt from the previous one. Through this discussion, we identify some emerging principles which indicate that collaboration lies at the heart of the research design, professional development approach and key findings that emerge from the research:

Dynamic collaborative research

- recognizes and values the expertise of both teachers and researchers
- works through a process of research as an iterative cycle
- allows for a personalized and responsive approach to the research and flexibility in professional development design
- models the theoretical and pedagogical principles that underpin the project.

We do not claim that any of these principles are novel or innovative. The first and third principles are closely related to those that guide most participatory action research, while the second is a principle of design-based research (Cohen, Manion & Morrison 2018). Our aim is rather to make them explicit, especially because some of these principles can be obscured or overlooked within a field that is required to pay close attention to design and outcomes. Our review demonstrates how these often hidden principles enabled a transformation of practice in the context of the projects reviewed here.

As discussed earlier in this chapter, some research models work from a premise of 'them and us'. Researcher expertise is seen as authoritative, evidence-informed and, for some in the teaching community, this is regarded as theoretical. Teacher expertise is seen as practical, purposeful and, for some in the research community, this is regarded as contextual (e.g. see Bryk, 2015). A challenge prevails surrounding how to bridge this teacher-researcher divide so that classroom practice is research-informed (Harrison, 2013) and research has clear implications for classroom practice.

Paul Black's work starts with the premise of bringing together teacher and researcher expertise. This collaborative expertise is shared and interdependent.

King's-Medway-Oxfordshire Formative Assessment Project (KMOFAP)

One of the key findings of the Black and Wiliam (1998) seminal review was that while there was significant research evidence that formative assessment practices could lead to significant improvements in students' learning, the research lacked the fine-grain detail that could guide and support teachers in implementing effective formative assessment in their classrooms. KMOFAP aimed at addressing this gap by studying how teachers developed and implemented the findings from research in authentic contexts under the pressures imposed by curriculum and external assessment (Black et al., 2003). However, as the project unfolded it became clear that the project would not simply be about translating and adapting research evidence into classroom practice, but in fact that classroom practice would also inform research and generate new knowledge both in the areas of formative assessment and teacher education.

The collaborative teacher-researcher part of the project ran from January 1999 to July 2001, and it was funded by Nuffield Foundation and US National Science Foundation. Thirty-six secondary mathematics, science and English teachers from six schools and two local education authority (LEA) advisors participated in the project. The project established a steering committee with advisors from the LEA involved, the King's team and representatives from the Department For Education and Skills (DFES), Qualifications and Curriculum Authority (QCA), and the teacher training agency. The steering committee's role was to support and evaluate the development of the project. The way in which this collaboration unfolded is well documented (see chapter 3 in Black et al., 2003). There were eleven full-day teacher-researcher meetings intercalated with frequent classroom observations and teacher interviews. A mixed-methods approach was used to collect and analyse multiple sources of data such as interview transcripts, field notes from classroom observations and teacher-researcher group meetings. The findings of the project have been reported elsewhere (Black et al., 2003; 2004).

KMOPAP was designed as a collaborative endeavour that respected and valued distributed expertise, where researchers and teachers had different roles that were mutually dependent. The teachers were asked to plan and implement individualized innovations to their practice and reflect and evaluate these (Black et al., 2003). The researchers presented ideas for innovation and supported teachers in the process of planning, implementing and reflecting on the changes made (Black et al., 2003). In the KMOPAF authors' words, 'the plan was to work in a genuine collaborative way ... suggesting directions that might be fruitful to explore and supporting them (teachers) ... but avoiding the trap of dispensing "tips for teachers"' (Black et al., 2003, pp. 21 - text in parenthesis added here).

The researchers' expertise in science and mathematics education acted as double-edged source for the collaboration. On the one hand, there is evidence from research that effective formative assessment requires subject expertise both in terms of content and pedagogical content knowledge (Coffey et al., 2011; Bennet, 2011). In relation to this, researchers' expertise can provide a good support for teachers while developing and making sense of their practice. On the other hand, teachers perceived researchers' expertise as an authoritative source of what Black et al., (2003) called a 'prescriptive model of effective classroom action'. This was problematic as it not only rendered collaborative work difficult, but it also created a barrier for teachers to take ownership of those ideas and adapt them in response to their own classroom contexts. As Biesta (2007) points out, research can support intelligent decision-making that can inform but not prescribe practice. So a considerable effort was then put, both during the teacher-researcher meetings and school visits, into changing teachers' mindset towards a more genuine collaborative way of working of distributed expertise, where teachers took ownership of not only adapting ideas from research into their practice but generating new ideas as well. The cycles of teacher-researcher meetings and classroom implementation coupled with sustained dialogue between teachers and researchers meant that over time the agenda of the teacher-researcher meetings became more driven by the teachers' agenda, responding in real time to what was emerging from the teachers' experiences in classroom (Black et al., 2003). This is very much aligned with Clandinin and Connelly (2000) view on the importance of explicit negotiation and redefinition of shared values in teacher-researcher collaborations.

KMOFAP was planned as three six-month phases. In the first phase of the project, the focus was on encouraging teachers to experiment with ideas from research and to develop an individualized action plan where they identified areas in their formative assessment practice that they wanted to develop. The second phase was focused on teachers implementing and reflecting on their action plans and making changes accordingly. In the third phase, teachers who had already developed some expertise through their own practice supported their new colleagues in engaging in a similar process (Black et al., 2003).

In this collaboration model, researchers used their expertise to respond to the needs of teachers and capture the new ideas that emerged rather than directing the process of change. The teachers engaged in a somewhat informal individual 'action research' approach where they explored new ways of working, making decisions about the efficacy of the changes both for their students and for themselves. KMOFAP created a community of practice that could inform, support and sustain this action research.

Two important lessons emerged from the KMOFAP project, which in our opinion, have shaped the work that came afterwards. The first lesson is that distributed expertise between teachers and researchers is fundamental for developing sustainable changes in teachers' formative assessment practices and for developing a theoretical understanding of formative practices that are grounded and situated in authentic contexts. The second lesson is that teachers' practice develops at an idiosyncratic pace and teachers need both time and a safe environment for gaining confidence in themselves to develop and try out ideas (Harrison, 2013).

Within AfL collaborative research projects, an iterative cycle emerges of research, pedagogy and thinking about assessment which is shared and evolves continuously within teacher and researcher interactions. Consequently, for many of the KCL assessment research projects, opportunities were consciously built into these projects so that the professional development secured a safe space for teachers to develop, test and implement thinking. In this model, researchers have the privilege of observing and documenting this participatory knowledge construction in action. This is complimented by ensuring sufficient time is dedicated for teachers and researchers to come together to share, reflect and redevelop their ideas alongside those of others in the community.

The King's Oxfordshire Summative Assessment Project (KOSAP)

The KOSAP project (Black et al., 2011) took place between 2005 and 2007 and involved eighteen teachers working in the English and mathematics departments, from three participating schools. The project's aim was to work with teachers to identify, explore and develop opportunities in English and maths secondary classrooms that generate evidence of learning that can inform teachers' summative assessments of students in Year 8 (12–13 years old) in England. Over the duration of the project, a range of data sources were employed and these included classroom observations, audio-recorded observations of within school and inter-school moderation meetings and transcribed focus groups. We also carried out individual teacher interviews and collected evidence of the summative assessments they designed and the teachers wrote reflective diaries that captured their responses to changing assessment practices during the project. This enabled them to illustrate the change processes they noticed to the research team (Black et al., 2011).

From the onset, the teachers involved in this 18-month study were regarded as collaborators in research and not merely participants. Gardner, Harlen, Hayward and Stobart (2011) in Analysis and Review of Innovations in Assessment study (ARIA) cited this project to highlight how success in research requires an empowerment of teachers. For KOSAP, the professional knowledge, experiences and perspectives of these teachers were fundamental to the design and evolution of this project. In the first phase, an initial audit captured the teacher classroom experiences and their critical evaluations of current summative assessment practices in their schools and within their own classrooms. This evidence helped to reveal particular, often unintended, consequences of a dominating national testing culture and how, for instance, this has discouraged and disempowered teachers from relying on their professional capabilities in creating test questions or assessment tasks. The main phase of the project married the assessment knowledge of the research team and the collaborating teachers in the design and development of new classroom assessment tasks that more closely matched the aims and skill development the teachers valued as important for lower secondary pupils within their subject areas. These tasks were implemented, trialled and improved through iterative cycles. Powerful findings drew attention to how these teachers noticed, through this task co-construction, and how 'quality' and 'fairness' are articulated in the design, facilitation, assessment and moderation of the tasks. In other words, these teachers were reflecting on how they can build 'validity' and 'reliability' into their own summative assessments. Through collaboration and co-construction of the assessment tasks, the research team were able to identify how an understanding of 'quality' permeates through decisions regarding what teachers decide to assess and how they set about assessing these aspects. What became evident and a point of investigation is the extent to which notions about quality within a particular subject area (in this case maths and English) can differ between teachers, even within one school subject department. A naive assumption might be to start from the premise that all teachers and researchers share a common understanding of what 'quality' looks like. In some respects, Paul Black and the KOSAP team were seeking to counter professional disempowerment, experienced by teachers as a result of national testing (Pollard et al., 2000) and investigate how teacher summative assessment and moderation can become foci for professional learning that can and rebuild confidence in teacher assessment into the profession.

One of the findings that emerged from KMOFAP and KOSAP was the need to tailor the research and professional development design to respond to the diversity of professional starting points in teachers' classroom assessment practices. The diversity of existing practices within one cohort of participants created an imperative to avoid a 'one-size fits all' approach. If the collaborations are to create opportunities for meaningful reflection and transformation in practice then it is necessary co-identify (teachers and researchers together) where the practitioner is in their practice, where they want to go and how to get there. These are the core principles of AfL to support learning (ARG, 2002).

Assess Inquiry in Science, Technology, and Mathematics Education (ASSISTME)

ASSISTME, a more recent project, continued to draw upon dynamic collaborative research model principles while also recognizing and responding to what has been learnt from the application of these features within previous projects. This learning is especially reflected in the bespoke professional development approach that this project employed in order to promote and assess inquiry in primary and secondary STEM classrooms. Working in collaboration with eleven partners from nine different countries in Europe, ASSISTME employed a three-phase (2013–2017) design to capture how teachers create opportunities for formative feedback during inquiry-based lessons. Four distinct classroom assessment strategies were identified to support inquiry-based pedagogy. These were 'On-the-fly' informal assessment conversations, structured assessment dialogue (SAD), written feedback and peer feedback (Grangeat, Harrison and Dolin, 2021). These strategies were implemented and investigated in science, technology and mathematics (STEM) classrooms in both the primary and secondary education. Working alongside international partners, the King's College team focused on 'On-the-fly' informal assessment conversations in science secondary and primary classrooms and secondary mathematics lessons.

Data sources drew from written teacher reflections, audio-recordings of lessons and teacher professional development meetings combined with field notes, and teacher interviews (Harrison et al., 2018).

What was quickly established, at the onset for the UK group, was how the professional development programme, designed to support this research, needed to be adapted to respond to the different professional starting points of the participating secondary and primary teachers. A key illustration of this personalized approach to the professional development design is how inquiry activities were introduced to the primary and secondary teachers.

For the primary teachers, the local authority advisors, who had worked closed with these teachers and schools, identified that while these teachers had a good grasp of assessment for learning pedagogy, their confidence with science subject knowledge and understanding of the nature of science needed to be further developed for them to provide productive inquiry learning activities. The areas that the primary teachers needed support related to the science subject knowledge and how to transform science learning into inquiry activities.

The participating science secondary teachers were more confident in their science subject knowledge and had already some experience with inquiry-based pedagogy and assessment of inquiry competencies. The secondary teachers had been part of a previous project the Strategies for Assessment of Inquiry Learning in Science Project (SAILS) where teachers had built up teacher expertise in inquiry and how to assess this (Harrison 2014). While on the SAILS project the teachers had been provided with inquiry activities, the professional learning for the ASSISTME secondary teachers focused more on how they could design and construct assessment tasks. This influenced the design of the professional development for the participating secondary teachers as they were in a position to consider how to develop and incorporate inquiries within this existing professional repertoire. As a consequence, teachers co-developed and implemented new inquiry activities with their classes, focusing on informal assessment conversations as means to gather evidence of learning and support students in deciding where to go next and how to get there (see example vignette in Harrison et al. 2018, pp. 88–92).

Throughout the year-long ASSISTME professional development programmes, understanding was a symbiotic process. The project did not aim for a prescriptive approach, where teachers are provided with a 'polished product' to implement in their classrooms. Instead, the project provided a 'protected professional space', where key ideas from research were shared and teachers become the collaborators and instigators of assessment research and practice. The professional development designed to support this project for both the primary and secondary teachers brought the research and theory around inquiry-based learning and formative assessment into the consciousness of teachers. The research team listened, observed and reflected on how teachers took this learning and translated this into their classroom practice. Teachers shared through dialogue and written reflections, how this experience had shifted and influenced their perspectives and approaches to learning and teaching (Serret et al., 2017; Correia & Harrison, 2020). Teacher engagement with practical hands-on bounded (teacher-directed) and open (student-led) inquiries during professional development drew their attention to the significance of conceptual understanding. Primary teachers were able to identify their own limitations (evidenced in written accounts from the day) and this prompted teachers to seek and build confidence in the conceptual subject knowledge underpinning the inquiries (Serret et al., 2017; Harrison et al., 2018). Secondary teachers were able to develop their confidence in designing and facilitating student-led inquiries and in assessing inquiry skills, in real time, through teacher-student and student group informal conversations (Harrison et al., 2018; Correia & Harrison, 2020).

The theoretical and pedagogical principles of dynamic collaborative research models

AfL principles and practices emphasize learner autonomy and self-regulated learning (Heritage & Harrison 2019). Having had the privilege of working with Paul Black, we recall his analogy of how assessment, pedagogy and curriculum can support and inhibit classroom learning. Paul Black would describe a ship with the teacher and class of learners on board. An inhibitive learning environment is akin to a ship sailing in a fog, where the teacher and the learners are not clear, collectively, about where they are going and certainly how to get there, especially as their vision is obscured. A supportive learning environment is where, regardless of fog, both the teacher and the learners are clear about where they are heading. There are some agreed sign-posts along the way and everyone on board is seeking and sharing when they can spot these indicators, to help them all move forward and reach their destination.

Ultimately, within a classroom that places AfL at the heart of teaching and learning, the learner owns and drives their progress (Dann, 2014). This requires a learning environment where the teacher and the learners have a clear and shared understanding of the learning outcomes (where they are heading) (Wiliam &

Thompson, 2007). Furthermore, there is a shared grasp of the specific classroom activities; these might be bespoke and adapted to meet a range of needs and capabilities, be shaped by previous evidence to inform next steps (sometimes referred to as success criteria) with differentiated support that each and every learner may need to achieve the outcomes (how they will get there) (Wiliam & Thompson, 2007; Dann, 2017). This principle of 'starting from the position of the learner' has been translated into many of the AfL research projects as 'working with the expertise/experiences/understanding of the teacher'. Teachers are empowered to draw on assessment theory as well as their lived experiences and translate to implement meaningful classroom practice. This requires teachers to be confident in their assessment focus, evidence collection and decisions. Teacher agency steers this approach.

Next steps for research

In this chapter, we have drawn attention to features of some of the research projects that Paul Black has influenced that help to articulate some principles for dynamic researcher-teacher collaborations. In addition, this chapter begins to highlight some implications and questions that arise when research acknowledges the role of the teacher and researcher as having shared responsibilities within a project. While many classroom educational projects are instigated by researchers, it is through the interactions and actions of both teachers and researchers that new ideas can be explored and challenged, resulting in new ways of working that legitimizes and develops both research and practice possibilities. Consequently, this chapter argues for a reconsideration of a dynamic design of educational research projects where principles for collaboration are recognized as a driving force that provides the potential for context to ground and inform the direction of the dynamic research process.

Conclusion

We conclude with some possibilities for future and further research developments into collaboration. Research findings in several of the project examples in this chapter indicate that collaboration implies a degree of teacher autonomy and confidence as central aspects of the research project. A redefined model of teacher-researcher partnerships needs to be prepared to adapt its aims and outcomes in instances where teacher autonomy and confidence might need to be supported initially and be more sensitive to teachers' funds of knowledge and shaped by cultural expectations. Highlighting and valuing teacher-researcher interactions and requiring both teachers and researchers to share and negotiate their interpretations of research ideas and classroom events across a range of scenarios build the trust that allows uncertainty and mistrust to be tolerated and mitigated, leading to more productive learning.

Expectations about roles and outcomes of collaborative research will need to be communicated and discussed from the onset, so that those teachers expecting to be dispensed with 'tips for teachers' understand the purpose and their role as being more active and creative within a collaborative research project.

We conclude this chapter with an ambitious research wish. Ultimately, if the goal of educational research is to improve learner progress, research projects need to be redefined so that research listens to and responds to the learner. This requires scope and space for learner input and reflection as part of the collaborative endeavour that both teachers and researchers engage in as well as outcomes that are valued by all concerned.

References

Assessment Reform Group, (2002). *Assessment for Learning: 10 Principles: Research-Based Principles to Guide Classroom Practice*. University of Cambridge, School of Education.

Bennett, R. E., (2011). 'Formative assessment: A critical review. Assessment in education: Principles, policy & practice', 18(1): 5–25.

Biesta, G., (2007). 'Why "what works" won't work: Evidence-based practice and the democratic deficit in educational research'. *Educational Theory*, 57(1): 1–22.

Black, P. & Wiliam, D., (1998). 'Assessment and classroom learning'. *Assessment in Education: Principles, Policy & Practice*, 5(1): 7–74.

Black, P., Harrison, C. & Lee, C., (2003). *Assessment for Learning: Putting It into Practice*. McGraw-Hill Education (UK).

Black, P., Harrison, C., Lee, C., Marshall, B. & Wiliam, D., (2004). 'Working inside the Black Box: Assessment for Learning in the Classroom'. *Phi Delta Kappan*, 86(1): 8–21.

Black, P., Harrison, C., Hodgen, J., Marshall, B. & Serret, N., (2011). 'Can teachers' summative assessments produce dependable results and also enhance classroom learning?'. *Assessment in Education: Principles, Policy & Practice*, 18(4), pp. 451–469.

Brydon-Miller, M., Greenwood, D. & Maguire, P., (2003). Why action research? *Action Research*, 1(1), pp. 9–28.

Bryk, A. S., (2015). '2014 AERA distinguished lecture: Accelerating how we learn to improve'. *Educational Researcher*, 44(9), pp. 467–77.

Bryk, A.S., Gomez, L.M. & Grunow, A., (2011). 'Getting ideas into action: Building networked improvement communities in education'. In *Frontiers in Sociology of Education*: 127–62. Dordrecht: Springer.

Coffey, J.E., Hammer, D., Levin, D.M. & Grant, T., (2011). 'The missing disciplinary substance of formative assessment'. *Journal of Research in Science Teaching*, 48(10): 1109–36.

Cohen, L., Manion, L. & Morrison, K., (2018). *Research Methods in Education* (eight edition). Abingdon, Oxon.

Connelly, F.M. & Clandinin, D.J., (2000). 'Narrative understandings of teacher knowledge'. *Journal of Curriculum and Supervision*, 15(4): 315–31.

Cooper, B. & Cowie, B., (2010). 'Collaborative research for assessment for learning'. *Teaching and Teacher Education*, 26(4): 979–86.

Correia, C.F. & Harrison, C., (2020). 'Teachers' beliefs about inquiry-based learning and its impact on formative assessment practice'. *Research in Science & Technological Education*, 38(3): 355–76.

Cowie, B. & Bell, B., (1999). 'A model of formative assessment in science education'. *Assessment in Education: Principles, Policy & Practice*, 6(1): 101–16.

Dann, R., (2014). 'Assessment as learning: Blurring the boundaries of assessment and learning for theory, policy and practice'. *Assessment in Education: Principles, Policy & Practice*, 21(2): 149–166.

Dann, R., (2017). *Developing Feedback for Pupil Learning: Teaching, Learning and Assessment in Schools.* London: Routledge.

DfE (Department for Education) (2013). *Teachers' Standards.* (rev. Jun). London: Department for Education.

Donovan, M. S. & Snow, C., (2017). 'Sustaining research–practice partnerships: Benefits and challenges of a long-term research and development agenda'. In *Connecting Research and Practice for Educational Improvement*, 33–50. London: Routledge.

Gardner, J., Harlen, W., Hayward, L. & Stobart, G. (2011). 'Engaging and empowering teachers in innovative assessment practice'. In *Assessment Reform in Education*, 105–19. Dordrecht: Springer.

Grangeat, M., Harrison, C. & Dolin, J. (2021). 'Exploring assessment in STEM inquiry learning classrooms'. *International Journal of Science Education*, 43(3): 345–61.

Harrison, C. (2013). 'Collaborative action research as a tool for generating formative feedback on teachers' classroom assessment practice: The KREST project'. *Teachers and Teaching*, 19(2), pp. 202–13.

Harrison, C., (2014). 'Assessment of inquiry skills in the SAILS project'. *Science Education International*, 25(1): 112–22.

Harrison, C., Constantinou, C. P., Correia, C.F., Grangeat, M., Hähkiöniemi, M., Livitzis, M., Nieminen, P., Papadouris, N., Rached, E., Serret, N. & Tiberghien, A., (2018). 'Assessment on-the-fly: Promoting and collecting evidence of learning through dialogue'. In *Transforming Assessment*, 83–107. Cham, Switzerland: Springer.

Heritage, M., (2013). *Formative Assessment in Practice: A Process of Inquiry and Action*. Cambridge, Massachusetts: Harvard Education Press.

Heritage, M. & Harrison, C., (2019). *The Power of Assessment for Learning: Twenty Years of Research and Practice in UK and US Classrooms*. Thousand Oaks, CA: Corwin.

Impedovo, M.A., (2021). 'Teacher-researcher collaborations: Negotiations of research practices in school'. *Transformative Dialogues: Teaching and Learning Journal*, 14(2): 102–14.

James, M. & McCormick, R., (2009). 'Teachers learning how to learn'. *Teaching and Teacher Education*, 25(7): 973–82.

Kemmis, S., (2009). 'Action research as a practice-based practice'. *Educational Action Research*, 17(3): 463–74.

Marshall, B. & Jane Drummond, M., (2006). 'How teachers engage with assessment for learning: Lessons from the classroom'. *Research Papers in Education*, 21(02): 133–49.

Oancea, A. & Pring, R., (2008). 'The importance of being thorough: On systematic accumulations of "what works" in education research'. *Journal of Philosophy of Education*, 42: 15–39.

Penuel, W. R., Riedy, R., Barber, M. S., Peurach, D. J., LeBouef, W. A. & Clark, T., (2020). 'Principles of collaborative education research with stakeholders: Toward requirements for a new research and development infrastructure'. *Review of Educational Research*, 90(5): 627–74.

Pollard, A., Triggs P., Broadfoot, P., Mcness E. & Osborn, M. (2000). *What Pupils Say: Changing Policy and Practice in Primary Education*. London: Continuum.

Pryor, J. & Crossouard, B., (2008). 'A socio-cultural theorisation of formative assessment'. *Oxford review of Education*, 34(1), pp. 1–20.

Serret, N., Harrison, C., Correia, C. & Harding, J., (2017). 'Transforming assessment and teaching practices in science inquiry'. *The Journal of Emergent Science: Special Edition*, 12: 48–54.

Torrance, H. & Pryor, J., (2001). 'Developing formative assessment in the classroom: Using action research to explore and modify theory'. *British Educational Research Journal*, 27(5): 615–31.

Wiliam, D. & Thompson, M. (2007). 'Integrating assessment with instruction: What will it take to make it work?' In C. A. Dwyer (Ed.), *The Future of Assessment: Shaping Teaching and Learning*, 53–82. Mahwah, NJ: Erlbaum.

Wiliam, D., (2011a). 'What is assessment for learning?'. *Studies in Educational Evaluation*, 37(1), pp. 3–14.

Wiliam, D., (2011b). *Embedded Formative Assessment*. Solution Tree Press.

Willis, J. & Cowie, B., (2014). 'Assessment as a generative dance'. In Designing Assessment for Quality Learning, 23–37. Dordrecht: Springer.

Wyse, D., Brown, C., Oliver, S. & Poblete, X., (2020). 'Education research and educational practice: The qualities of a close relationship'. *British Educational Research Journal*. 10.1002/berj.3626

Chronological List of Paul Black's Key Publications

Black, P. J. (1993). 'Formative and summative assessment by teachers'. *Studies in Science Education*, 21(1): 49–97.

Black, P. (1997). 'Testing: Friend or foe? In *Theory and Practice of Assessment and Testing*. London: Routledge.

Black, P. & D. Wiliam (1998). 'Inside the black box: Raising standards through classroom assessment'. *Phi Delta Kappan*, 80(2): 139–48.

Black, P. (1999). 'Assessment, learning theories and testing systems'. In P. Murphy (Ed.), *Learners, Learning and Assessment*, 118–34. London: Paul Chapman, in association with Open University.

Black, P. (2000). 'Research and the development of educational assessment'. *Oxford Review of Education*, 26(3–4): 407–19.

Black, P. & D. Wiliam (2003). 'In praise of educational research: Formative assessment'. *British Educational Research Journal*, 29(5): 623–37.

Black,P., Harrison, C., Hodgen, J., Marshall, B. & Serret, N. (2011): Can teachers' summative assessments produce dependable results and also enhance classroom learning?, Assessment in Education: Principles, Policy & Practice, 18:4, 451–469.

Broadfoot, P. & P. Black (2004). 'Redefining assessment? The first ten years of Assessment in Education'. *Assessment in Education*, 11(1): 7–27.

Black, P. & D. Wiliam (2005). 'Changing teaching through formative assessment: Research and practice: The King's-Medway-Oxfordshire formative assessment project'. In Centre for Educational Research and Innovation (CERI) (Ed.), *Formative Assessment: Improving Learning in Secondary Classrooms*, 223–40. Paris: OECD.

Black, P. & D. Wiliam (2005). 'Developing a theory of formative assessment'. In J. Gardner (Ed.), *Assessment and Learning*, 81–100. London: Sage.

Black, P. & D. Wiliam (2005). 'Lessons from around the world: How policies, politics and cultures constrain and afford assessment practices'. *The Curriculum Journal*, 16(2): 249–61.

Black, P., M. Wilson & S. Y. Yao (2011). 'Road maps for learning: A guide to the navigation of learning progressions'. *Measurement: Interdisciplinary Research and Perspectives*, 9(2–3): 71–123.

Black, P. (2013). 'Formative and summative aspects of assessment: Theoretical and research foundations in the context of pedagogy'. In J. H. McMillan (Ed.), *SAGE Handbook of Research on Classroom Assessment*, 167–78. London: Sage.

Black, P. & D. Wiliam (2018). 'Classroom assessment and pedagogy'. *Assessment in Education: Principles, Policy & Practice*, 25(6): 551–75.

Dolin, J., P. Black, W. Harlen & A. Tiberghien (2018). 'Exploring relations between formative and summative assessment. Cham, Switzerland: Springer'. In J. Dolin & R. Evans (Eds.), *Transforming Assessment,* 53–80. Cham, Switzerland: Springer International.

Index

accountability 95, 136–7, 235–6
action research 55, 183, 244, 246, 249–50, 259, 263, 266
activity theory 69
assessment error 221–2, 224, 229, 232, 234
assessment for learning (AfL) 3, 36, 47–8, 56, 65–6, 82, 84, 86–7, 133–5, 137, 165–6, 184–5, 197, 244, 248, 250
assessment in Australia 114–8
Assessment is for Learning (AifL) 53
assessment literacy 80, 90, 133–4
Assessment of Performance Unit (APU) 20, 45
Assessment Policy Task Group 32–7
Assessment Reform Group 36, 46, 128
Assessment Training Institute (ATI) 80
ASSISTME 245, 268–70

BEAR assessment system (BAS) 212
benchmarks 31
bias 232–5, 262
black box 110–11, 113, 115, 117–18, 186, 242
British Educational Research Association (BERA) 32

CCSSO formative assessment group 97–8, 104
certification 75, 97, 115, 221, 232
Chappuis, Jan 83
cheating schools 225–7
cheating students 224–5
Chelsea Centre for Science and Mathematics Education 16, 20
classroom assessment 2–7, 45, 80, 96, 114–8, 129, 133–5, 137, 241, 245–6, 248, 268
classroom discussion 186–7, 190, 210–11
close-to-practice research 183, 241, 252
cognitive commentary 119
Collaborative Action Research 7, 244, 250

Common Core State Standards (CCSS) 96–7, 99, 102, 104
connected learning goals 103
constructivism 71, 247
construct map 6, 198–200, 202–3, 210–11
contractual perspective 231–36
co-regulation 4, 127, 132–9
coursework 59, 222–8
crystal physicist 12–14, 16
culturally responsive pedagogy 249–50
curriculum, pedagogy and assessment (CPA) 195–7

data analytics 118–21
diagnostic assessment 148, 168–71
dialogue 51, 58–9, 69, 71, 99–100, 210–11
digital 118, 120–2, 136–9
Dweck, Carol 4, 30, 163–4

Educational Testing Service (ETS) 38
Education Endowment Foundation 39
Education Reform Act 1988 31–2
Embedding Formative Assessment programme 39
emotional dynamics of assessment 82
engagement perspective 229–30, 232
Enhancing Boys' Writing project 250
equity 4, 132–4, 137, 139, 143–4, 146–9, 151, 156–8
evaluative expertise 4, 110, 113, 116
Every Students Succeeds Act (ESSA) 95
Examination Board 20
expertise perspective 229–30, 232–3, 235
external assessment/exam 94–5, 97, 118, 222–3, 228–9, 232–4

fairness 59, 118, 127, 132–3, 139, 146–8, 267
feedback 5, 36, 48–51, 53, 58–9, 68–71, 73, 83, 104, 114–15, 129–30, 137–8, 144–5, 148, 156, 168–9, 172, 188–89, 196, 200, 212, 250, 261, 268

formative assessment 3–5, 7–8, 33–4, 36–40, 47, 50–1, 56, 58–9, 64–6, 70–4, 82–3, 93–105, 115, 129–30, 133, 143–5, 182, 184–6, 195–7, 242–8, 251, 264–5
formative-summative relationship 95
formative-summative spectrum 211–12
formative use of tests 64, 185–6

General Certificate of Education (GCE) 21–2
General Certificate of Secondary Education (GCSE) 22
goals, learning goals 64, 67–8, 70, 73–5, 101, 103
Graded Assessment in Mathematics (GAIM) 22, 25, 29
Graded Assessment in Science Project (GASP) 21–2
Graded Assessment Projects 21–2
grade inflation 224, 227–8, 234–5
grain-size (re construct) 197, 199
group work and collaborative learning 210
Growth Mindset 163–4, 177
growth portfolio 82, 86–7, 89

improvement-oriented feedback 104
information perspective 229–30, 232
Inner London Education Authority 21–2, 30
inquiry in STEM 245
Inside the Black Box 35–8, 49, 51, 53, 57, 242–4
InSiTE 247–8
ipsative approach 128, 261
item bank 211

King's-Medway-Oxfordshire Formative Assessment Project (KMOFAP) 37, 52, 182–6, 190, 192, 243–4, 251, 264–6
King's Oxfordshire Summative Assessment Project (KOSAP) 112, 245, 266–8
King's Researching Expertise in Science Teaching (KREST) 244
Knight of Saint Gregory 14

language of learning 188
Lawrence Bragg Medal 15
learning hierarchies 30

Learning How to Learn Project 38
Learning in Science Project (LISP) 7, 246–8
living examples of implementation 182, 243

malpractice 227, 231, 233–6
mastery learning 29, 47, 70
Medway 37–8, 52, 54, 182
middle years moderation 119–20
mindset intervention 164
moderation 75, 96–7, 113–21

National Curriculum 22–4, 30–2, 65, 94, 131, 222–3
National Curriculum Assessment 30–2, 46
Next Generation Science Standards 96–7, 99, 102, 104
No Child Left Behind Act (NCLB) 95

Ofqual 224, 226–8, 235
online moderation 119–21
Oxfordshire 37–8, 52, 54, 182

pairwise comparison 119
partiality 231, 233–6
participatory action research 183, 263
peer assessment 101–2, 135, 148, 151, 187–8, 250
performance assessment, Graduate Teacher Performance Assessment (GTPA) 120–1
plagiarism 224–5
practice-based evidence 250, 254
prejudice 231, 233–6
professional learning 7, 54, 90, 97, 104–5, 112, 118, 132, 136–8, 181–3, 190, 192–3, 268–9
Programme for International Student Assessment (PISA) 147
progressions 4, 99, 102–4, 195
public confidence 96, 118, 224, 229, 234–5

Qualifications and Curriculum Authority 223, 264
questioning 58, 184, 186–8, 193

reporting 64, 73–5, 113, 119, 121, 136, 250
researcher-teacher relationships 241, 246, 248, 259
research-informed practice 181, 241

responsive teaching 259
roadmap 102–4, 196–7, 199, 203–8
role of students in formative assessment 99–102
rubrics 96, 151, 165, 168, 170

scaffolding 69
Secondary Mathematics Individualised Learning Experiment (SMILE) 29, 33
self-assessment 70, 86, 95, 101, 128, 153, 156, 168–9
self-regulated learning processes 95
social contract 231, 233, 235
social moderation 96, 113, 117
Specialist Schools and Academies Trust (SSAT) 39
standards 3, 68, 81, 86, 93, 95–7, 99–100, 103–4, 109, 111–20, 132, 135–6, 227–8
student agency 133
student role in assessment 80, 83–4
student thinking 100, 102, 104, 176
summative assessment 19, 57–8, 64–5, 73–6, 93–8, 101, 120, 128, 144, 189, 197, 209, 267
surveys 76

Task Group on Assessment and Testing (TGAT) 23–7, 31–2, 45, 65, 93
teacher agency 245–6, 252, 271
teacher assessment 6–7, 22, 25, 59, 63, 94, 134, 221–9, 232–5
teacher education 38, 104, 120–1, 129, 137, 192
teacher judgement-making 4, 53–4, 109–10, 113–19, 121
teacher learning communities 39
teacher moderation 25, 96–7
technology 127, 136–8
Te Tiriti 249
the Strategies for Assessment of Inquiry Learning in Science Project (SAILS) 245, 269
toxic narrative 221–9, 233–6

upper anchor 198

validity 6, 20, 25, 59, 74, 95–6, 133, 209, 212–3, 225, 227
values 2, 70, 229, 231–2, 250

www.ingramcontent.com/pod-product-compliance
Lightning Source LLC
Chambersburg PA
CBHW071808300426
44116CB00009B/1245